200 KITCHEN-TESTED, SALT-FREE RECIPES THAT PROVE YOU CAN CUT DOWN ON MEAT WITHOUT SACRIFICING FLAVOR OR NUTRITION

A Little Meat Goes a Long Way...

by Nancy Albright

author of *The Rodale Cookbook*

Editor: **Charles Gerras**

Assistant Editor: **Carol Munson**

Recipe Testing and Consultation: **Anita Hirsch, JoAnn Benedick, and Karen Haas, Janice Kay, Irene Nicholson**

Editorial Assistant: **Camille Bucci**

Book Design: **Merole Berger**

Illustrations: **Susan Rosenberger**

 Rodale Press, Emmaus, Pennsylvania

Printed in the United States of America on recycled paper, containing a high percentage of de-inked fiber.

Library of Congress Cataloging in Publication Data

Albright, Nancy.
    A little meat goes a long way.

    Includes index.
    1. Cookery (Meat) I. Title.
TX749.A433   641.6′6   81–19163
ISBN 0-87857-376-3   hardcover   AACR2
ISBN 0-87857-355-0   paperback
2   4   6   8   10   9   7   5   3   1   hardcover
2 . 4   6   8   10   9   7   5   3   1   paperback

Contents

A Little Meat . . . Makes Some Great Dishes

In the process of making a little meat go a long way, the resourceful cooks of the world have created dishes so memorable that they often symbolize an entire culture. The Italians make meatballs of ground meat stretched with bread crumbs, grated hard cheeses, and eggs, and surround them with pasta; the Mexicans fill flat corn bread (tortillas) with rice, mashed beans, and sometimes a little meat. In the Middle East, people blend bits of lamb with spices and rice or bulgur to make the traditional highly seasoned entree called kibbi. Latin Americans savor chili—a thick, spicy stew of simmered tomatoes, beans, and, when it's available, meat. From the Scottish cuisine comes a famous hearty soup made of several vegetables and braised chunks of beef or lamb, thickened with barley and appropriately called Scotch Broth.

Obviously, meat-stretching is a style of cooking that is almost universal. More than that, it is a healthful way of cooking that intrigues me. I like the idea of teaming up vegetables, sauces, dairy foods, grains, nuts, and herbs to enhance the flavor and expand the "presence" of even small amounts of meat. The recipes I've created for this book do just that, and from all reports they taste great, too!

Serving less meat per person is certainly one way to continue putting meat on the table without breaking the bank. Another way is to make sure you get the most—and the best—meat for the money you do spend. Therefore, you will find a wealth of suggestions for selecting meat on sale, for buying large quantities of meat when the price is right, and for cutting and grinding meat at home. I also describe methods of cooking the less tender cuts of meat and provide important storage information to help avoid waste from spoilage.

When you glance through the recipes, you'll notice I use herbs and spices generously and don't use salt at all. I am convinced that we should all eat less of it due to its damaging effect on the circulatory system. Also, I believe that many of us use salt as a habit or as an excuse to avoid thinking of a more imaginative seasoning.

Occasionally, you'll come across a recipe that requires several pounds of meat, but that usually includes large quantities of bone. Mostly, you'll see that I like to combine small servings of meat with substantial portions of freshly prepared grains, legumes, vegetables, or pasta to make the meat go further.

Some Nutritional Properties of Meat

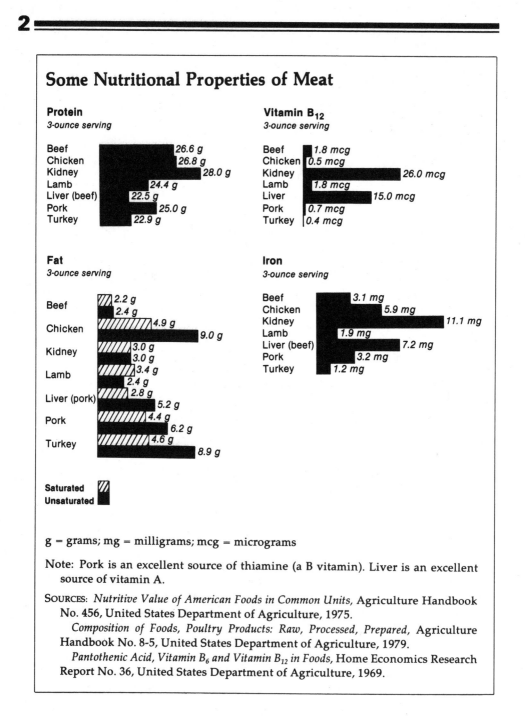

Protein
3-ounce serving

Beef	26.6 g
Chicken	26.8 g
Kidney	28.0 g
Lamb	24.4 g
Liver (beef)	22.5 g
Pork	25.0 g
Turkey	22.9 g

Vitamin B₁₂
3-ounce serving

Beef	1.8 mcg
Chicken	0.5 mcg
Kidney	26.0 mcg
Lamb	1.8 mcg
Liver	15.0 mcg
Pork	0.7 mcg
Turkey	0.4 mcg

Fat
3-ounce serving

Beef	2.2 g	2.4 g
Chicken	4.9 g	9.0 g
Kidney	3.0 g	3.0 g
Lamb	3.4 g	2.4 g
Liver (pork)	2.8 g	5.2 g
Pork	4.4 g	6.2 g
Turkey	4.6 g	8.9 g

Iron
3-ounce serving

Beef	3.1 mg
Chicken	5.9 mg
Kidney	11.1 mg
Lamb	1.9 mg
Liver (beef)	7.2 mg
Pork	3.2 mg
Turkey	1.2 mg

Saturated ▨
Unsaturated ■

g = grams; mg = milligrams; mcg = micrograms

Note: Pork is an excellent source of thiamine (a B vitamin). Liver is an excellent source of vitamin A.

SOURCES: *Nutritive Value of American Foods in Common Units,* Agriculture Handbook No. 456, United States Department of Agriculture, 1975.

Composition of Foods, Poultry Products: Raw, Processed, Prepared, Agriculture Handbook No. 8-5, United States Department of Agriculture, 1979.

Pantothenic Acid, Vitamin B₆ and Vitamin B₁₂ in Foods, Home Economics Research Report No. 36, United States Department of Agriculture, 1969.

Essential Equipment

I consider the following utensils essential to simplifying the preparation of meat dishes at home.

A slow cooker is ideal for braising the less tender cuts of meat since it's designed to cook foods for long periods (three to four times the normal cooking time) at low temperatures with very little or no added moisture. Good slow cookers have thermostats (cookers operate on electricity) and snug-fitting lids; they come in 4- and 6-quart sizes. The best ones have heat control switches. You can use a slow cooker in many of the recipes where I give a conventional cooking method.

A pressure cooker is the pot for the cook who is in a hurry yet wants to maximize nutrients. This handy utensil steams food at 10 to 15 pounds of pressure, so meats are done in about one-third the normal cooking time. Soybeans and most beans that require lengthy cooking do not need prior soaking and will become tender in 30 to 45 minutes in a pressure cooker. To use a pressure cooker, follow the manufacturer's directions closely. You can use one in any recipe that says to simmer meat.

A boning knife greatly simplifies the task of removing bone from meat and poultry. It has a slender blade especially designed for getting in close to bones. You can buy boning knives with 5-, 6-, 7-, or 8-inch blades. The 6-inch blade is the most versatile. Select one with a light, flexible blade for boning poultry and a heavy, stiff one for tackling cuts of meat with large bones. (I also use this knife for cutting a chicken into parts.)

French chef's knives are available in several blade lengths. Though some cooks like the 8-inch blade, I recommend the 10- or 12-inch one. The tapered shape of the blade on this knife allows you to work quickly, without lifting the knife completely off the cutting surface. Most people use this knife for slicing and chopping vegetables, but I like to slice meat with it, too.

Wooden cutting boards are much easier to clean than your counter top and they save the counter from becoming crisscrossed with scars. Cutting boards come in numerous shapes and sizes. Select one that has few or no seams and that is big enough to accommodate the cutting of a large turkey or piece of meat.

Since a cutting board is an excellent breeding place for harmful bacteria, wash it thoroughly with hot soapy water after each use and either scrub it with scouring powder or wipe it with chlorine bleach. Then, rinse it completely with plain water and let it air-dry.

A meat thermometer can make the difference between a perfectly done roast and a culinary disaster. The thermometer preferred by chefs is the small

"Bi-Therm." When inserted into the meat, it gives an instant, precise reading. The Bi-Therm is more expensive than the meat thermometers found in supermarkets, but it's much more convenient to use. Restaurant and hotel supply stores usually carry them.

A meat rack permits heat to circulate evenly around a roast while it's cooking and it keeps the meat above the greasy drippings. Look for an adjustable rack that can be used with any size roast.

A meat grinder makes it possible for you to blend your own sausage as well as to grind raw or cooked meat. If you have an old-fashioned grinder which screws onto the counter or table top, you are lucky indeed. If not, an inexpensive plastic one which attaches to the counter surface with a suction base will work fine. A food processor is nice to have, but in my opinion the ordinary meat grinder does a superior job and is easier to clean.

A blender is considered a must-have item by many cooks who like to make a little meat go a long way. I know I use mine regularly for grinding the nuts, blending the sauces and the dressings, and making the purees that bring up the flavor of meat and poultry. A blender with a glass jar, a close-fitting lid, and a strong motor is best. One with 12 different motor speeds is the most versatile but one with only two speeds is satisfactory for just about any job that comes along.

Getting and Keeping the Best in Knives

A top quality knife is made of either carbon steel, stainless steel, or high-carbon stainless. A carbon steel knife retains a fine edge better than the others do, but carbon steel tends to rust and discolor fruits and vegetables. The edge on a good cutting knive is straight, not serrated, and it's flat ground, not machine hollow ground. There should be two or three rivets attaching the blade to the full length of the handle.

High quality knives are expensive but they will last a lifetime if they are properly cared for.

- Store knives in a rack where they will retain their edge yet be accessible.
- Wash and dry knives immediately after use. Dishwashers and soaking are out for knives. Too much water and harsh detergents dull and distort both handles and blades.
- Always cut on a wooden board. Plastic boards may seem more sanitary, but they ruin a fine edge—as will using the knife to cut string, paper, or cartons.
- Own a sharpening steel and use it often to hone (renew) the edge of the blade.
- Sharpen knives with a whetstone. (If you prefer, you can have them sharpened by a professional.) Don't use other sharpeners because they merely wear down the blade.

Poultry

CHICKEN

One of the most satisfying ways to cut down on your food bill is to bring home—not the bacon—but the chickens. Yes, I said the chicken*s*. Watch for those "specials" when chickens are sold for that low, low price. And buy four or maybe five at a time.

Broiler-fryers are probably the best buy. They weigh 2 to 2½ pounds and are young (only 9 to 12 weeks old) and tender. They are great for broiling, frying, and baking.

Roasters, too, are a good buy and have tender meat that browns nicely when roasted. They are older than broiler-fryers (3 to 5 months) and weigh slightly more (3 to 5 pounds).

Stewing hens on sale are a wise choice if you are planning to make chicken soup, chicken fricassee, or any other dish such as my favorite, Chicken Pot Pie (see Index), where you want full, rich flavor. Because stewing hens are at least 10 months old, they are less tender. But with proper cooking, a hen is as tender as a bird less than half its age. (To cook a 6-pound hen, put it in a large saucepan and just barely cover it with water. Put a lid on the pan and bring the water to a boil. Lower the heat and simmer for about 2½ hours.)

Capons (castrated males) are generally a better buy than stewing hens. Weighing between 4 and 8 pounds, they provide exceptionally tender meat and a lot of it.

Cornish hens, immature birds that weigh less than 2 pounds, are seldom on sale, but they are a special treat. Like the broiler-fryers, Cornish hens have tender, juicy meat and are outstanding candidates for sauteing or roasting.

When buying fresh poultry, look for short, plump legs and fleshy breasts. The skin should have a whitish or yellowish cast with no discolorations, and it should feel moist and smooth. If you want a tender, young bird, check the breastbone. It's fairly flexible in young birds but rigid in older ones. When purchasing a frozen chicken (or turkey) also examine the wrapping. There should be no tears in it and no pink ice.

"Naturally Raised" Chickens

There is a lot more fat in chickens these days because of the breeding techniques used by poultry producers, techniques which have kept the price of chicken amazingly low over the last two decades. It is worth noting that today's chicken is still lower in saturated fat than are beef, lamb, and pork. To get really lean chickens (and chickens not treated with antibiotics or hormones), you will have to search out a local grower who raises them as they were raised 20 years ago, letting them run and scratch for some of their food. You will probably have to pay a higher price for these "old-fashioned" chickens—still another reason for learning to make your purchase "go a long way." If you do buy a naturally raised chicken, be sure to wait 24 hours after it has been killed before you cook it. It takes that long for nature to tenderize the meat.

You may have to pluck and draw the bird yourself if the grower doesn't provide that service. This is the way to do it:

For easiest plucking and drawing, chill the bird thoroughly. Pluck the large feathers first, then use a pair of tweezers to pull out the pin feathers. You can easily remove the remaining fine hairs by quickly singeing (burning) them over a low flame, then brushing them away. (If you plan to freeze the bird, wait to singe until you are ready to cook. Heat from the flame breaks down the fat just under the skin and hastens rancidity.)

To draw the bird, make a shallow incision at the vent; it should be just large enough for your hand. Reach in and loosen the intestines. Carefully pull out the intestines, the giblets (heart, liver, and gizzard), the lungs, the kidneys, and any surplus fat. Go slowly and take care not to break the gall bladder which is attached to the liver. Discard the inedible viscera but clean and save the heart, liver, and gizzards for adding flavor and nutrients to stuffings, sauces, and other dishes. Next, cut the skin at the back of the neck and remove the crop, windpipe, and neck bone. Cut out the oil sac at the base of the tail. Finally, cut off the feet. Rinse the bird thoroughly inside and out. Pat dry.

When preparing and storing chicken, be cautious. After drawing, cutting up, or packaging raw chicken, always scrub the cutting area and utensils thoroughly to eliminate the chance of future contamination.

As soon as possible after purchasing any raw chicken, refrigerate it. First, remove the giblets and wash them. Pat dry and store them in a covered container in either the refrigerator or the freezer. Wash the chicken, pat it dry, and cover it loosely. Refrigerate. You can keep it this way for up to 2 days, but after that it must be cooked. Never stuff a chicken and put it aside for later baking; a stuffed chicken should be cooked immediately.

Thaw frozen chicken only before you are ready to use it. The best but slowest way to thaw it is in the refrigerator. For a bird weighing less than 4 pounds, allow 12 to 16 hours to thaw; allow 1 to 1½ days for a heavier one. However, if you are in a hurry, you can thaw chicken in 1 to 2 hours in cold water. Be sure it is in the original wrap or some other watertight plastic bag.

Make Your Own Chicken Parts

"Whole" is the only sensible way to buy chickens these days, as you know if you have priced the packages of chicken parts. Sometimes you can buy backs and necks cheaply, but these come "free" if you buy whole chickens.

We have to pay for convenience. It costs money to have someone do a job we choose not to do. But if we do the work ourselves we reap the reward of a lower price. And cutting those chickens up to get the most from them can be fun, really it can!

With freezer paper and tape ready, remove the giblets and extra lumps of fat from inside the chickens. Wash the birds well, inside and out, with cool, running water, then pile them on a tray by the sink. Rinse the gizzards, necks, livers, and fat. If the livers look healthy (firm, with a good pink color), wrap and freeze them right away for a future meal. Frozen at 0°F, they will retain a high degree of their original quality for up to 1 month.

Store the fat in the refrigerator in a covered container for rendering the next time you use the oven. (Put the chicken fat in a small Pyrex dish in the oven and let it reduce to a liquid.) Store the rendered fat in the refrigerator for a week or two, or freeze it for up to 6 months. Use it in sauces or for sauteing. It will add greatly to the flavor of any chicken or turkey dishes. Chicken fat is a better cooking fat than butter for those concerned about cholesterol.

Set the gizzards and hearts aside with the necks, for making stock later. Use within 2 days or freeze for up to 3 months.

Now you are ready to cut the chickens. Use a sharp chef's knife and a board you have reserved especially for cutting raw meat.

Lay the first chicken on your cutting board, breast-side up. Stretch each leg away from the body and cut through the skin between, without cutting into the leg flesh. Flatten the leg against the board, cutting through the skin where the leg is joined at the back, and you will see the joint attaching the leg to the

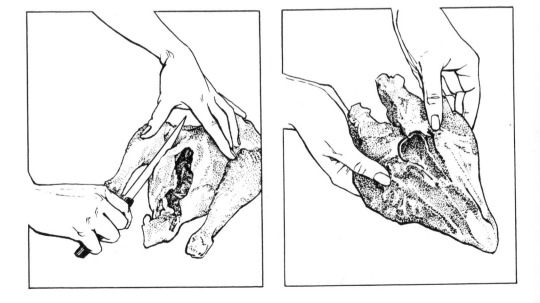

body. Cut right through it. Do the same with the other leg. Next, take hold of each wing and cut through the joint where it is attached to the body, without cutting into the flesh of the breast.

Now lay the body on its side and, with the point of your knife, cut through the cartilage part of the ribs which holds the breast and back together, starting at the place where the wing was removed. After this is done, it should be easy to separate front from back at the neck or shoulder. You can almost pull it apart without using the knife.

From here on you can either leave the back and breast whole, or divide them. You can cut the back in two, across the middle, again using your hands or the knife to break it. The breast can be split in two across the middle or lengthwise, by cutting along the breastbone. Start at the neck and cut along the "wishbone," continuing to the open cavity of the bird.

If you do decide to do this, it would be easier to simply bone the breast. Just run the knife along the rib cage, loosening the flesh in one piece. That will give you two long, slim pieces rather like cutlets, ready to be skinned and sauteed with mushrooms or cut into thin slivers, Chinese style, for a stir-fry. Save the bones for stock. Of course if the breast halves are too large, cut them in two across the middle. Depending on the size of the chicken, because you will sometimes want to cut up roasting chickens as well as fryers, you will end up with either two or four portions of breast from one chicken.

The legs are easily divided into thigh and drumstick by cutting across the "knee," which will be apparent by the white of the cartilage showing through the flesh. Cut the tips off the wings (put them aside for the stock), and package the wings with the thighs and drumsticks or with the wings from the other chickens. Similarly, you can make packages of just thighs, legs, or breasts, if you prefer. Make up appropriate-size packages for your family and the type of chicken entrees you plan.

Backs will take up too much space in the freezer so I suggest that you cook them right away, for stock, along with the wing tips, necks, gizzards, hearts, and breastbones (if you boned the breasts). You may want to use the chicken backs along with other pieces of chicken for an upcoming meal. They have a surprising amount of meat on them and they are included in some of my recipes as chicken pieces.

Incidentally, you can feel free to substitute different cuts of chicken for those called for in the recipes, unless breasts or legs are mentioned specifically. Simply adjust the amounts accordingly.

Chicken Stock—A Simple Routine

Making chicken stock can become as routine as washing the dishes. After a meal of roast chicken or after you have cut up those five chickens, you are left with the inedible but still valuable parts—the bones, skin, and the like. Put them in a large pot, cover them with cold water, add a stalk of celery with top, an onion, a bay leaf, some parsley and, if you want to, a carrot. Cut the vegetables into chunks. Add any other herbs or spices you like, cover the pot, and bring it to a boil. Turn down the heat and simmer over very low heat for 3 hours. The stock should never boil, just barely simmer, and it doesn't require as much cooking as meat stocks do. Three hours is plenty. Strain the stock, discard bones and other expendables, and cool. Refrigerate the stock. When the fat has hardened, remove it and save it for cooking. It is a good idea to make extra stock and freeze the surplus, so as to have some on hand at all times. You can put it in small bread pans lined with foil to freeze; once it is set, turn it out of the pan and return the foil-wrapped block of stock to the freezer.

As I say, this process can become routine. I can't bear to throw out a chicken carcass before I've extracted every bit of goodness out of it. It seems such a waste. If your freezer space is limited or if you want a more concentrated stock, strain the stock and then let it boil, uncovered, for half an hour or so, until it has reduced as much as you want it to. Freeze the concentrated stock in an ice cube tray. Once the stock is frozen, you can pop the cubes into freezer bags and use the tray to freeze turkey or another concentrated stock.

When a recipe calls for cooked chicken and you don't have leftover chicken, cover several raw chicken parts with water or stock and simmer over low heat for 30 to 45 minutes or until tender. Let the chicken cool in the broth for 1 hour. Then both chicken and stock are ready for use. (If you used stock to cook the chicken, the new stock will be highly concentrated.)

Sometimes it is a pleasant change to roast one of those five chickens whole. You can still use the generous leftovers from a large bird in several of the delightful dishes that call for cooked chicken. If you favor stuffing the bird, allow about 1 cup dressing for each pound of ready-to-cook poultry. Truss the bird after stuffing it so that it roasts evenly.

Place the trussed bird with the breast-side up on a rack in an open roasting pan. During cooking, occasionally baste with a mild oil. If the bird browns shortly after roasting has begun, cover it lightly with foil. When you

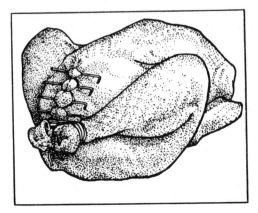

To truss a bird, skewer and lace the openings shut. Fold the wings back and under the body, and tie the drumsticks close to the body.

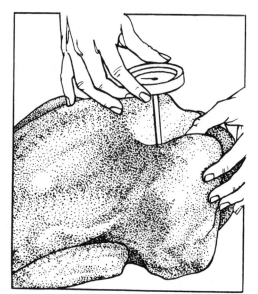

Insert the meat thermometer into the center of the inner thigh muscle. The thermometer should not touch any bone.

think the bird may be done, press the fleshy part of the thigh with your fingers. The meat is done if it feels soft, the leg wiggles easily, or the hip joint breaks.

A meat thermometer is an excellent guide to doneness. The temperature of the inner thigh should read 185°F and the stuffing 165°F or higher.

Careful with Cooked Chicken

Cooked chicken requires the same careful handling that raw chicken needs. Chill it quickly at the end of a meal, but first remove any stuffing from the inside of the bird. Cover and store separately the stuffing, the meat, and any gravy. Keep in the coldest part of the refrigerator and use the chicken within 4 days to make any tasty dish like Chicken Kasha Tabouli (see Index) which calls for cooked chicken. Use the stuffing and gravy within 2 days. If your plans include keeping leftover chicken longer than the 4 days, freeze it. Chicken slices frozen without broth or gravy will keep 1 month, but pieces covered with a sauce will keep for up to 4 months.

Chicken was once a symbol of prosperity. Here is a new slogan for people who want to have their chicken and to keep their money, too: "A chicken in every pot plus four more in the freezer!"

TURKEY

Benjamin Franklin was a great admirer of the turkey. In a letter to his daughter, he expressed his regret that the bald eagle had been chosen to

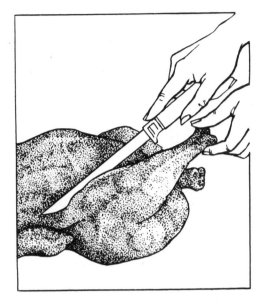

Pull the leg away from the body and cut it off. Trim the meat off the leg and the thigh.

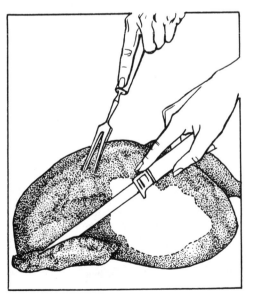

Remove the wing.

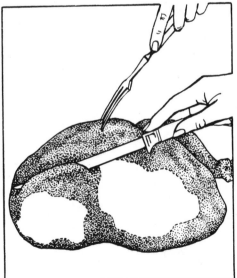

Slice the breast meat.

represent our country instead of the turkey. The turkey is "a much more respectable character" than the eagle, he said, and "a true original native of America." Well, I can't really share his negative attitude toward the eagle, but I do agree that a lot more should be made of the turkey.

Working on this cookbook has led me into some interesting new experiences, and the ones I am most enthusiastic about have to do with turkey. I feel as though I have discovered a new kind of meat! Raw turkey can be used in any way that veal is used. It can be ground and used for meat loaf and for meatballs; the turkey breast can be separated into cutlets and cooked as in Wiener Schnitzel or Veal Scallopini; it can even be chunked and cooked like a veal stew.

A Great Money-Saver

I began experimenting and had spectacular results. My Blanquette de Dinde (instead of de Veau) and Turkey Paprika proved that you don't need veal

Timetable for Roasting Poultry

Kind	Approximate weight[1] (pounds)	Hours[2,3] (325°F)
Chicken		
Whole		
Broiler-fryer	2¼ to 3¼	1¾ to 2½[4]
Capon	5 to 8½	3 to 4[4]
Roaster	3¼ to 4½	2 to 3[4]
Rock Cornish game hen	1 to 2	1½ to 2[4]
Pieces	¼ to ¾	1 to 2½
Turkey		
Whole	6 to 8	3 to 3½[4]
	8 to 12	3½ to 4½[4]
	12 to 16	4½ to 5½[4]
	16 to 20	5½ to 6½[4]
	20 to 24	6½ to 7[4]
Halves, whole breasts	5 to 11	3 to 5½
Quarters, thighs, drumsticks	1 to 3	2 to 3½
Boneless turkey roasts	3 to 10	3 to 4

[1]Weight of giblets and neck included for whole poultry.
[2]Poultry at refrigerator temperature at start of roasting.
[3]Cooking time is only approximate; a meat thermometer can be used to help determine doneness of whole turkeys, large turkey pieces, and boneless turkey roasts. The temperature in the inner thigh of whole turkeys and in the center of the thickest part of turkey pieces should reach 180°F to 185°F. Turkey roasts are done when the temperature reached 170°F to 175°F in the center. Stuffing temperature should reach at least 165°F.
[4]Cooking time suggested is for stuffed poultry; unstuffed poultry may take slightly less time to cook.

SOURCE: *Poultry in Family Means: A Guide for Consumers,* Home and Garden Bulletin No. 110 United States Department of Agriculture, 1979.

if you can get turkey! And think of the savings! Next time you are at the meat case, compare the prices of turkey and veal. There is one small catch, and I really mean *small*. You do have to cut and bone the turkey. I had never done that before. But it is no more difficult than cutting up a chicken—and you end up with so much more meat. From a 12¾-pound turkey, I got 6 pounds and 4 ounces of boneless raw meat. That's almost half of the original weight. Figuring 4 ounces of meat to a person, that one turkey provided enough meat to feed 24 people. Some of these recipes were among the least expensive of all the recipes I developed for this book. They were surely the lowest-cost *fancy* dishes. One recipe which especially amused me because of its economy was Curried Turkey Timbale, a "posh" entree. The minced turkey in it (3 cups) came from the neck.

But I have only begun! There is much that sets turkey apart from other meat. It is the leanest of all meats and therefore has the highest protein content per pound. And that protein is of a very high quality.

"Turkey apparently surpasses all other meat and poultry in its ability to complement plant protein," writes Frances Moore Lappe in *Diet for a Small Planet* (New York: Ballantine Books, 1971). "Experiments show that if you add only one-fifth as much turkey to a meal of wheat, peanuts, or black-eyed peas, the protein quality of the combination will be the same as if the entire meal had been beef!" Half a pound of turkey contains more grams of protein than half a pound of lean porterhouse steak. But while the turkey slices add about 300 calories to your diet, the porterhouse adds 500 calories. Now you understand why I am singing the praises of turkey. It definitely deserves to be liberated from typecasting as a holiday meal or the stand-by for church suppers.

The turkey industry is clearly determined to do more with turkey. Just consider all the new turkey products on the market these days that weren't there before—turkey ham, turkey hot dogs, turkey sausage, and turkey kabobs, to mention a few. In some areas, fresh ground turkey and turkey steaks are on sale, and many markets offer fresh turkey breasts and legs from time to time. In these forms, however, turkey is seldom a bargain.

Cost-conscious shoppers should know that there is no difference in tenderness between a hen or a tom turkey, but there is often a difference in price. Oddly, the hens are often sold at a higher price.

Incidentally, turkey and chicken are quite similar and can be handled in much the same way. In fact, the meats can be used interchangeably. So check the Chicken section for additional recipes and information.

Taking a Turkey Apart

To bone a turkey, begin just as you did with the chicken. Remove the giblets and neck. Wash them and the turkey in cool, running water. Freeze the liver for a future meal and put the neck and giblets in the stock pot. Cut off the legs and the wings. Refrigerate them until you are ready for them. Now separate the breast from the back in the same way you did with the chicken. It

Freezing Tips for Poultry

- Do not stuff poultry before freezing. It lengthens the freezing and thawing time and encourages undesirable bacterial growth to take place. Freeze stuffing separately.
- Pack giblets separately. Their storage life is shorter than the rest of the bird, so they must be used first. If you plan to use the bird within 3 months, which is the storage life for giblets, you may insert the giblets (separately wrapped) into the cavity of the bird. Livers should be packed separately, since storage life is only 1 month.
- Tie leg ends of bird together and press the wings close to the body. Pad the tips of the wings and the legs with extra freezer wrap to keep them from breaking through the package and getting freezer burn.
- Place the bird in a plastic bag or wrap it in freezer paper using the drugstore wrap method shown below.

will take a bit more strength, but if your knife is sharp you can do it.

Cut and break the back into small enough pieces to fit into your stock pot, but not before you have removed the "oysters" in those hollows near the tail and the small "tenderloins" which lie on either side of the backbone. These are too choice to be used for stock.

Now put the back in the pot and give your whole attention to the turkey breast. Remove the skin. Cut the breast in half, starting at the neck and cutting to the breastbone (the place where the wishbone breaks, if you are lucky). Continue to cut along the ridge of the breastbone to the cavity opening. Then

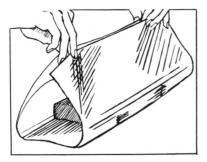

Place meat in the center of the wrapping paper.

Bring the long sides of the paper over the meat and fold together about 1 inch of the edges. Fold again to bring the sheet tight and flat on top of the meat.

run your knife along the rib cage to loosen each half of the breast in one whole piece. Put the rib cage halves in the stock pot, along with the skin from the breast. You will notice that a smaller muscle running lengthwise, somewhat like a "tenderloin," separates quite naturally from the rest of the breast half. Remove that and cut it through, lengthwise, to make a thin cutlet. Make similar-size cutlets out of the remaining meat of the breast, or, for turkey steaks, cut across the grain where the breast is at its thickest. If you wish to have meat loaf or meatballs, set aside some of the breast to be ground. Use either a food processor or an ordinary meat grinder; both work equally well.

Storing and Using the Parts

One thing I must emphasize. As soon as possible after cutting the turkey, wrap the part you have ready and get it into the freezer. You will probably have partially thawed the turkey in the first place, before starting to cut it. And I hope you thawed it in the refrigerator over a period of days and not at room temperature. (In the refrigerator, you'll need 1 to 2 days for completely thawing a 4- to 12-pound turkey, 2 to 3 days for a 12- to 20-pound one, and 3 to 4 days for a 20- to 24-pound one. Thawing in cold water takes much less time—about one-fourth of that for room temperature.) You can refreeze the turkey parts as long as the meat contains numerous ice crystals and has remained in the refrigerator. Frozen turkey parts will keep for up to 6 months, but the whole turkey will keep for a year.

Turkey is very perishable, like chicken, and I am sure you have heard the oft-repeated warning about never stuffing a turkey or chicken the night before you plan to roast it, as well as never refrigerating a cooked stuffed bird with the stuffing inside. The combination of warm stuffing and raw turkey—or even cooked, still-warm turkey—is too risky. It offers a good breeding ground for

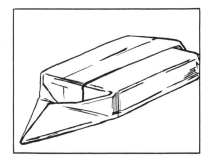

Press the wrapping close to the meat to force out the air.

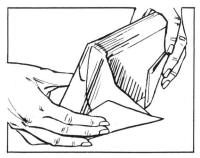

At each end, fold the corners of the paper toward each other. Pull tight. Seal.

dangerous bacteria. For this reason, too, never partially roast or cook turkey or chicken and then store it, with the idea of finishing it later. Use the same procedures for storing raw or cooked turkey and its fixings as for chicken.

If you plan to make your own turkey breast roll, leave the breast skin on. Take the two boned breast halves and lay them one on top of the other, skin-side out, with the large end of one over the small, pointed end of the other. Tie them with clean cotton string, from end to end, tightening to pull the roll into shape, then tie around the roll a number of times, with the string about two inches apart.

When you cook the turkey breast roll, cook it slowly at 325°F and cover the roasting pan with a lid or foil. If you like, you can put a little turkey stock in the pan, though the breast will make liquid of its own. Most of us have had the sad experience of overcooking turkey, either because the oven temperature was too high or because we cooked it too long in order to get the legs done. The way to avoid this when roasting a turkey whole is to cover the bird during most of the roasting, removing the cover at the end to brown the turkey. And remember the low oven temperature. Use a meat thermometer to check the internal temperature, which should register between 170°F and 175°F when the meat is done. Or, pierce the flesh at the thickest part with a long-pronged fork to see whether the juice runs pink (the turkey isn't done) or clear.

Now about those wings and legs you have set aside in the refrigerator. Separate each leg into thigh and drumstick, as you did with the chicken legs. The drumsticks and wings can be cooked with the bones and skin, to make stock right away, or they can be packaged raw to be cooked at another time. They'll keep in the refrigerator for a day or two, and much longer in the freezer.

If you do cook them now, as part of the stock-making process, be sure to keep track of them and remove them from the pot as soon as they are tender. (It takes about 1 hour to cook the legs.) Briefly cool them, then remove the meat and store it in freezer or refrigerator and return the skin and bones to the stock. Continue cooking the stock for another 2 hours. When it is done, strain and cool it. Save the fat that congeals on top of the cooked stock. Turkey fat is every bit as useful as chicken fat.

The thighs, which have a lot of meat in proportion to bone, can be easily boned. Remove the skin and cut around the bone, then lift it out. This dark meat makes lovely "veal" stew, "hamburgers," or kabobs.

Of course, the turkey meat—white or dark—in the following recipes is interchangeable. I have made a note of it when I thought one more suitable than the other, but that is not a hard and fast rule.

I hope you simply can't wait to take on the Big Bird.

CHICKEN

Chicken, Fruit, and Vegetable Curry

4	tablespoons oil	2½	pounds chicken (drumsticks and thighs)
3	medium-size onions, sliced		
3	garlic cloves, minced	2 to 3	cups Chicken Stock (see Index)
2	cinnamon sticks, broken in half	4	cups cut green beans (about 1½ pounds)
1	teaspoon whole cloves		
1	tablespoon ground ginger	2	cups sliced green peppers
½	teaspoon cumin seeds	3	cups sliced yellow summer squash
1	teaspoon ground cumin		
2	teaspoons turmeric	2	apples, peeled, cored, and finely chopped (about 2 cups)
4	teaspoons ground coriander		
¼	teaspoon cayenne pepper	2	bananas, sliced (about 2 cups)
¼	teaspoon oregano	¼	cup lemon juice
½	teaspoon ground cardamom		

1. In a 5-quart Dutch oven, heat oil and saute onions, garlic, and spices over low heat until onions are soft. Stir frequently.

2. Add the chicken pieces (cut thighs in half if they are large) and brown on all sides. Then add 2 cups of the stock, cover, and simmer over low heat until chicken is almost done (about 30 to 45 minutes).

3. Stir in the green beans and cook for 5 minutes. Then add the green peppers and squash and simmer another 5 minutes. Add more stock if needed.

4. About 5 minutes before serving, add apples, bananas, and lemon juice. Cook just until apples are soft.

Serves 6

Remarks This is an unusual, colorful, tasty combination, seasoned with spices used in India for curried dishes. Serve with cooked brown rice.

Chicken Drumsticks over Millet

- 1½ cups millet
- 3¼ cups water
- 3 to 4 tablespoons oil
- 12 chicken drumsticks
- 2 medium-size onions, sliced
- 2 teaspoons paprika
- ¼ teaspoon thyme
- ¼ teaspoon sage
- 4 to 5 cups Chicken Stock (see Index)
- 3 cups coarsely chopped cauliflower
- 3 cups coarsely chopped broccoli
- 3 cups sliced zucchini
- 3 to 4 tablespoons cornstarch
- ½ cup cold water

1. Combine millet and water in a 2-quart double-boiler and cook for 30 minutes or until millet is soft and water is absorbed. Remove from heat and keep warm.

2. In a 10-inch Dutch oven or 5-quart, heavy-bottom pot, heat oil and brown chicken, onions, and spices. Add chicken stock, cauliflower, and broccoli. Cover and cook over low heat until chicken and vegetables are almost tender.

3. Add zucchini and continue cooking until chicken is tender. Add more stock if desired. Thicken sauce with cornstarch dissolved in the cold water. Bring sauce to boil and serve over millet.

Serves 6

Chicken Kasha Tabouli

- ¾ cup buckwheat groats
- 1 egg
- 1½ cups boiling Chicken Stock or Beef Stock (see Index)
- ¼ cup unhulled sesame seeds
- 6 green onions, finely sliced
- ⅔ cup finely chopped green peppers
- 1⅓ cups finely chopped tomatoes
- 3 cups slivered cooked chicken breasts
- ¼ cup chopped parsley
- 4 teaspoons dried mint
- ¼ cup olive oil
- 6 tablespoons wine vinegar
- ¼ cup lemon juice
- romaine lettuce

1. To make kasha, place buckwheat groats in a 1½-quart, heavy-bottom saucepan. Add egg and stir over medium heat until egg is absorbed. Add boiling stock and stir until well blended. Cover pan and simmer over low heat for about 15 minutes or until the stock is absorbed. Turn kasha out into a 3-quart bowl and fluff with a fork. Set aside to cool.

2. Toast sesame seeds in a small-size dry skillet over medium heat for about 1 minute, stirring constantly. Add to kasha.

3. Add the remaining ingredients, except lettuce, and mix gently with a fork. Chill thoroughly and serve in a salad bowl lined with the lettuce.

Serves 6

Chicken Pot Pie

1	stewing chicken (4 to 6 pounds)	2	bay leaves
2	medium-size onions, cut into quarters	¼	cup butter
2	celery stalks with tops, coarsely chopped	¼	cup brown rice flour
		2	teaspoons basil
2	large carrots, coarsely chopped	1	teaspoon poultry seasoning
	several sprigs parsley	12	tiny white onions
		4	cups sliced potatoes (¼-inch thick)

Noodle Squares

⅔	cup whole wheat flour	2	tablespoons butter
½	cup oat flour (rolled oats ground in blender)	1	egg, beaten
1	teaspoon baking powder	¼	cup ice water
		¼	cup chopped parsley

1. In a 5-quart soup pot, combine chicken with onions, celery, carrots, parsley, and bay leaves. Add water to cover and cook until tender (about 2½ hours).

2. Remove chicken; strain stock and discard vegetables. Measure out 8 cups chicken stock for pot pie; reserve any remaining stock for another use. Remove chicken from bones as soon as it is cool enough to handle. Keep it in fairly large pieces. Set aside 3 cups chicken for pot pie and reserve any remainder for another use.

3. In the same pot, melt butter. Stir in flour and gradually add half the stock (4 cups). Continue stirring until thickened. Add remaining 4 cups stock.

4. Stir in chicken and seasoning. Add the onions, then the potatoes on top. Cover pot and cook for 15 minutes.

5. Meanwhile, make noodle dough. Combine both flours and baking powder in a small bowl. Cut in butter, as for pastry dough. Combine egg and ice water and add gradually to butter-flour mixture, tossing lightly with a fork. Knead dough briefly to work water in evenly. Roll out dough to a thickness of ⅛ inch and cut into 1½-inch squares.

6. Lay noodle squares on top of potatoes, sprinkle with parsley, cover pot, and simmer for 15 minutes longer. Serve immediately from the pot.

Serves 6

with Parsley Biscuit Topping

1	roasting chicken (about 3½ pounds)		1	tablespoon cornstarch
1	celery stalk with top, cut into chunks		1	cup milk
1	onion, cut into chunks		1	teaspoon basil
5 to 6	tablespoons butter		¼	teaspoon marjoram
¼	cup coarsely chopped onions		1	teaspoon tarragon
1½	cups coarsely chopped celery		¼	teaspoon thyme
2	cups sliced mushrooms		⅛	teaspoon sage
1½	cups sliced carrots		½	teaspoon nutmeg
¼	cup whole wheat pastry flour		½	teaspoon paprika
			1	tablespoon lemon juice

Parsley Biscuits

2¾	cups whole wheat pastry flour		9	tablespoons butter
1	tablespoon baking powder		½ to ¾	cup milk
½	teaspoon cream of tartar		1	egg, beaten
½	cup finely chopped parsley (well dried with paper towels)			

1. Cut wings and legs off chicken and separate back from breast. Place chicken pieces in a 4-quart pot and add cold water to cover. Add celery and onions and bring to a boil. Lower heat and simmer, covered, for 1 to 1¼ hours or until chicken is tender and comes away from the bones easily. Lift chicken out onto a tray to cool. Increase heat under chicken stock and boil, uncovered, for 10 to 15 minutes to reduce it. Remove chicken from bones. Return skin and bones to stock pot. Separate chicken into bite-size pieces and set aside in a 3-quart casserole.

2. In a large skillet, melt 2 tablespoons butter and saute onions, celery, and mushrooms over medium heat for about 1 minute. Add to chicken. In the same skillet, adding more butter if needed, saute carrots over medium heat for 1 minute.

3. Strain chicken stock into a 3-quart bowl. Discard bones, skin, and vegetables. Add 1 cup stock to carrots, cover, and cook 10 minutes or until they are tender. Add to chicken.

4. In the same skillet, melt 2 tablespoons butter over low heat. Stir in flour, then gradually add 2 cups stock, using a wire whisk to make a smooth sauce. (Reserve any remaining stock for another use.) Dissolve cornstarch in a little of the milk and add to the sauce, along with the remaining milk, stirring constantly until sauce is thickened. Add herbs, spices, and lemon juice. Pour sauce over chicken and vegetables, stirring to combine evenly. Set aside while you make the parsley biscuits.

5. Preheat oven to 400°F. In a 3-quart bowl, combine flour, baking powder, cream of tartar, and parsley. Cut butter into flour mixture.

6. In a 1-quart bowl, combine ½ cup milk and egg and lightly stir into butter-flour mixture with a fork. Toss gently to combine. Add more milk if necessary. Knead briefly and, using hands or a rolling pin, pat out or roll half of the dough on a lightly floured board until it is ¼-inch thick. Cut out 12 biscuits with a 2-inch cutter. Arrange them, slightly overlapping, around inside edges of casserole, over chicken and vegetables. Bake for 40 to 45 minutes or until casserole is bubbling and biscuits are baked. Pat or roll out remaining biscuit dough until it is ¾-inch thick. Cut out biscuits as before and arrange them on a buttered 14 x 9-inch cookie sheet. Bake along with casserole for 20 to 25 minutes or until done. Serve extra biscuits with casserole.

Serves 6

Chicken Zucchini Souffle

6	tablespoons butter	½	teaspoon nutmeg
1	medium-size onion, chopped	4	teaspoons lemon juice
2¼	cups sliced zucchini (about ¾ pound)	1	cup grated Muenster cheese
		2	tablespoons grated Parmesan cheese
1½	cups cubed cooked chicken breasts, skinned (½-inch cubes)		
		6	egg whites
½	cup brown rice flour	6	egg yolks
1½	cups Chicken Stock (see Index)		

1. In a large skillet, melt butter and saute onions and zucchini until lightly browned. Lift vegetables from skillet, combine with chicken in a 2-quart bowl, and set aside.

2. Stir flour into the juices left in the skillet. Gradually add stock, stirring over low heat to make a smooth sauce. Add nutmeg, lemon juice, and both types of cheese. Remove skillet from heat. Preheat oven to 350°F.

3. Beat egg whites until stiff and set aside. Then, with the same beaters, beat egg yolks until light. Add a little of the hot sauce to the yolks while beating, then add the yolk mixture to the sauce. Mix until smooth.

4. Pour sauce over vegetables and chicken and mix gently so as not to break the zucchini. Carefully fold beaten egg whites into vegetable-chicken mixture and pour immediately into an ungreased 2-quart casserole.

5. Bake souffle until it has risen and is golden brown on top (about 25 to 30 minutes). Serve immediately.

Serves 6

6	cups Chicken Stock (see Index)	¼	teaspoon thyme
4½	cups corn	¼	cup brown rice flour
1½	cups peeled and diced potatoes	3	cups milk
6	tablespoons finely chopped onions	3	cups shredded cooked chicken
1	cup finely chopped celery	1	tablespoon honey
6	tablespoons finely chopped green pepper	1	tablespoon tamari soy sauce
¾	teaspoon basil	3	tablespoons lemon juice
		¼	cup chopped parsley
			pinch of black pepper

1. Combine chicken stock, corn, potatoes, onions, celery, green pepper, basil, and thyme in a 4-quart soup pot. Bring to a boil, lower heat, and simmer for 30 minutes.

2. Dissolve flour in milk, then stir into soup and cook about 10 minutes.

3. Add chicken, honey, tamari, lemon juice, parsley, and pepper. Heat through but do not let soup boil. Keep hot over low heat until ready to serve.

Serves 6

═══ Fruity Chicken Salad ═══

3	cups cubed cooked chicken	½	cup raw cashew nuts
1	cup finely chopped celery	2	teaspoons ground coriander
1½	cups halved seedless grapes	1	teaspoon ground ginger
2	tart apples, cored and sliced (about 2 cups)	6	tablespoons Yogurt (see Index)
2½	cups sliced bananas	6	tablespoons Mayonnaise (see Index)
2	pears, cored and diced (about 1½ cups)	2	tablespoons lemon juice

Garnish

salad greens
dried mint

1. Combine chicken, celery, fruit, nuts, and spices, reserving some grapes and apple slices for garnish.

2. Combine yogurt, mayonnaise, and lemon juice. Pour over chicken and fruit mixture. Toss lightly. Serve on a bed of salad greens. Garnish with mint and reserved fruit.

Serves 6

Country Captain Chicken 23

6	tablespoons oat flour (rolled oats ground in blender)	1	cup coarsely chopped green peppers
4	tablespoons soy flour	2	cups sliced mushrooms
4	teaspoons curry powder	2	cups cooked tomatoes
4 to 5	tablespoons oil	2½	cups tomato juice
1	chicken (about 3 pounds), cut into 10 pieces—2 wings, 2 thighs, 2 drumsticks, breast and back cut into halves	¾	teaspoon thyme
		2	cups frozen peas
		¼	cup raisins
		¼	cup slivered almonds
1	cup coarsely chopped onions	¼	cup tomato sauce
2	garlic cloves, minced		

1. Combine both flours in a 2-quart bowl. Mix in 1 teaspoon curry powder. Roll chicken pieces in flour mixture.

2. In a large skillet, heat 2 to 3 tablespoons oil and brown chicken over medium heat. Remove from skillet and set aside. Then saute onions, garlic, green peppers, and mushrooms over medium heat for about 2 minutes, adding more oil if necessary.

3. Return chicken to skillet. Add tomatoes, tomato juice, thyme, and remaining curry powder. Reduce heat to low, cover skillet, and cook for 25 minutes.

4. Add peas, raisins, and almonds and cook another 5 minutes or until peas are soft. Stir in tomato sauce and serve.

Serves 6

Remarks   Serve over cooked brown rice.

Curried Chicken Soybean Salad

3	cups cubed cooked chicken	1	cup diced tomatoes
3	cups cooked soybeans	½	cup lemon juice
1	cup finely chopped green peppers	½	cup oil
		1	tablespoon honey
1	cup finely chopped celery	1	tablespoon basil
1	cup diced cucumbers	2	tablespoons curry powder
1	cup diced yellow summer squash	½	teaspoon ground ginger
		½	teaspoon ground cumin
4	green onions, finely sliced		Iceberg lettuce

1. In a 3-quart mixing bowl, combine chicken, soybeans, and vegetables.

2. Combine lemon juice, oil, honey, and seasonings in a small bowl and pour over chicken-soybean mixture. Toss gently to blend. Serve in a salad bowl lined with the lettuce.

Serves 6

Garlic Lemon Chicken with Millet Buckwheat Pilaf

12	garlic cloves	2	teaspoons savory
2½ to 3	pounds chicken legs, severed at the joints	½	cup lemon juice
		½	cup millet
3 to 4	tablespoons oil	⅔	cup buckwheat groats
1	cup sliced carrots	3	cups Chicken Stock (see Index)
2	cups sliced mushrooms	½	cup finely sliced green onions
2	teaspoons basil		

1. Crush garlic cloves and rub on the chicken. In a large, heavy-bottom skillet or 10-inch Dutch oven, heat oil and brown chicken. Add carrots, mushrooms, and herbs. Spoon lemon juice over chicken.

2. Add millet and buckwheat, stirring thoroughly so that the grains are evenly coated with the pan juices. Stir in the stock, reduce heat, cover, and simmer for 20 to 25 minutes. Watch carefully to be sure there is enough liquid, adding more stock if needed. Pilaf is done when chicken is cooked, grains are soft, and liquid is absorbed. Just before serving, add green onions to the pilaf.

Serves 6

Mulligatawny Stew

4 to 6	tablespoons oil	2½	cups Chicken Stock (see Index)
2	cups coarsely chopped onions	2	cups coarsely chopped turnips
2	garlic cloves, minced	2	cups coarsely chopped cauliflower
1	teaspoon turmeric		
1	teaspoon ground coriander	1	cup sliced green peppers
1	teaspoon ground cardamom	2	cups peas
1	teaspoon ground cumin	4	cups cooked tomatoes
½	teaspoon chili powder	2	tablespoons molasses
2½ to 3	pounds chicken (thighs, drumsticks, and wings)		

1. Heat oil in a 5-quart, heavy-bottom pot. Add onions, garlic, and spices and saute until onions are soft. Stir frequently.

2. Add chicken pieces and cook until browned.

3. Add 1 cup stock, stirring to loosen any bits on bottom of pot. Then stir in each vegetable as it is prepared.

4. Add remaining stock, tomatoes, and molasses. Turn heat to very low and simmer, covered, for at least 1 hour or until chicken is very tender. Bones may be removed before serving, but in India the stew would be served as is.

Serves 6

Hawaiian Chicken ══ 25

1	roasting chicken (about 3½ pounds), cut into 12 pieces—2 wings, 2 thighs, 2 drumsticks, breast cut into quarters, back cut in half	¾	cup unsweetened pineapple juice
1	tablespoon butter	1½	cups Chicken Stock (see Index)
1	tablespoon oil	2	tablespoons cornstarch
1	garlic clove, minced	¼	cup cold water
1	cup sliced celery	2	teaspoons wine vinegar
1	cup sliced carrots	1	teaspoon tamari soy sauce
2	cups coarsely chopped green peppers	¼	teaspoon ground ginger
2	cups unsweetened pineapple chunks	½	teaspoon ground coriander
		2	large bananas, cut in half lengthwise and then into 2-inch pieces

1. Remove most of skin from chicken parts. In a large skillet, heat butter and oil and saute chicken over medium heat until lightly browned. Remove from skillet and place in a 14 x 10 x 2-inch baking pan. Preheat oven to 350°F.

2. Saute garlic, celery, carrots, and green peppers in skillet over medium heat, adding more oil if needed, for about 1 minute. Add to chicken, along with pineapple chunks.

3. Heat pineapple juice and stock in skillet over medium heat and loosen brown bits in pan with a spoon. Dissolve cornstarch in the water and add to mixture, stirring until sauce is thickened. Add vinegar, tamari, ginger, and coriander. Pour sauce over chicken, pineapple, and vegetables. Cover with foil and bake for 1 hour or until chicken is done.

4. Remove cover, add bananas, baste with sauce, and brown for another 15 to 20 minutes.

Serves 6

Remarks   Serve over cooked brown rice.

3	tablespoons unflavored gelatin	2	tablespoons lemon juice
2	cups grapefruit juice	½	teaspoon ground ginger
¼	cup honey	1	cup orange segments
2	cups orange juice	3	cups diced cooked chicken
2	teaspoons grated onion	1½	cups avocado slices

1. In a small saucepan, soften gelatin in ½ cup grapefruit juice. Add honey and stir over low heat until gelatin is melted and honey is thinned.

2. In a 2-quart mixing bowl, combine gelatin mixture with remaining grapefruit juice and orange juice. Add onion, lemon juice, and ginger, then the orange segments, chicken, and avocado.

3. Pour into an 8-cup ring mold or a shallow 9 x 9 x 2-inch container which has been rinsed out with cold water. Refrigerate until set.

Serves 6

Remarks   If avocado is unavailable, banana slices may be substituted. Grapefruit segments may be used instead of orange segments, if desired.

If using a ring mold, turn salad out onto a round plate lined with lettuce. Set a bowl of Mayonnaise (see Index) in the center of the ring.

If using a shallow container, cut salad into six squares and serve on individual salad plates lined with lettuce. Top each serving with a dollop of the mayonnaise.

═══════════ Peanut Chicken Soup ═══════════

2	tablespoons butter	1	tablespoon tamari soy sauce
¾	cup finely chopped onions	1	teaspoon ground coriander
¾	cup finely chopped celery	¼	teaspoon cayenne pepper
¼	cup brown rice flour	2	cups shredded cooked chicken
4¾	cups Chicken Stock (see Index)	⅓	cup heavy cream
¾	cup unsalted peanut butter		finely chopped parsley
3	tablespoons lemon juice		

1. In a 3-quart, heavy-bottom saucepan, melt butter and saute onions and celery until soft. Stir in flour, then add 2 cups stock, and cook, while stirring, until thick.

2. Stir in peanut butter. Blend well. Add remaining stock, lemon juice, tamari, and spices.

3. Add chicken and cream. Heat through but do not let soup boil. Keep soup hot over very low heat until ready to serve. Garnish with chopped parsley.

Serves 6

Orange Chicken and Millet Pilaf 27

2¼	cups orange juice		1	chicken (about 3 pounds), cut into 10 pieces—2 wings, 2 thighs, 2 drumsticks, breast and back cut into halves
1	cup sliced onions			
¾	teaspoon ground cumin			
1	teaspoon tamari soy sauce		1	cup millet
4 to 5	tablespoons oil		¾	cup Chicken Stock (see Index)

1. Combine orange juice, onions, cumin, and tamari in a 4-quart bowl. Place chicken pieces in the mixture and marinate for 2 hours. If chicken pieces are not totally immersed, turn them over after the first hour.

2. In a large skillet, heat 2 to 3 tablespoons oil and brown chicken over medium heat. Remove from skillet and set aside.

3. Heat remaining oil in skillet. Add the onions from the marinade and the millet and saute over medium-low heat, stirring constantly, for about 1 minute. Add the marinade and stock, stirring to distribute millet evenly. Return chicken to skillet, cover, and simmer over low heat for 30 minutes or until millet is soft and liquid is absorbed. Do not stir millet during cooking.

4. Serve millet pilaf on a platter topped with chicken pieces.

Serves 6

Plantation Pudding

1	cup coarsely chopped onions		3	cups diced cooked chicken (preferably chicken breasts)
2	garlic cloves, minced			
1	cup sliced carrots		4	hard-cooked eggs, peeled and sliced crosswise
⅔	cup coarsely chopped green peppers			
			¼	cup chopped parsley
2	cups sliced mushrooms		4	eggs
4	cups Chicken Stock (see Index)		½	teaspoon mace
2	cups whole grain bread cubes (¼ inch)		1	teaspoon paprika
			½	teaspoon black pepper

1. Preheat oven to 350°F. In a 2-quart saucepan, simmer onions, garlic, carrots, green peppers, and mushrooms in 3 cups chicken stock, covered, for 10 minutes. Remove from heat.

2. Add bread. Then turn mixture into a 2-quart casserole.

3. Stir in chicken, hard-cooked eggs, and parsley.

4. Beat the raw eggs. Slowly add 1 cup heated stock to the eggs while continuing to beat. Stir in seasonings. Pour over mixture in casserole. Cover casserole and bake for 45 to 50 minutes or until set.

Serves 6

Remarks This is an unusual and delicious old Southern recipe.

Plantains, Black Beans, ==================
and Chicken Legs

2½	cups black beans	3	pounds chicken drumsticks
16	cups water	3	large garlic cloves, minced
2	tablespoons ground cumin	3	plantains
2	tablespoons chili powder	¼	cup lemon juice
¼	teaspoon cayenne pepper		chopped parsley
6	tablespoons oil		

1. Soak beans in water to cover for at least 8 hours. Drain and discard soaking water. Place beans in a 5-quart, heavy-bottom pot. Add 8 cups water and bring to a boil. Reduce heat and simmer, covered, for 30 minutes. Discard cooking liquid. Add another 8 cups water and bring to a boil again. Stir in half the amount of each spice, reduce heat, and simmer, covered, for another 30 minutes.

2. While beans are cooking, heat 2 tablespoons oil in a large skillet and brown chicken and garlic. Season with the remainder of the spices.

3. Add browned chicken and garlic to beans. Use some of the bean liquid to loosen the brown bits from skillet after pouring off excess fat, then add liquid back into the pot.

4. Cook chicken and beans for 30 to 45 minutes or until beans are tender but not mushy and chicken falls away from bones easily. If there is an excess of liquid, reduce it by simmering, uncovered, over low heat.

5. While beans and chicken are cooking, prepare plantains. Peel and cut crosswise into 1-inch slices. In the same skillet used for chicken, heat 4 tablespoons oil and saute slices until lightly browned and tender. Drain slices on paper towels and flatten them with the heel of your hand or with a flat-bottom glass, making them as thin as possible. Return slices to skillet and saute them until crisp. Drain on paper towels and keep warm.

6. Serve beans and chicken surrounded with plantain chips. Sprinkle lemon juice over beans and plantains. Garnish with chopped parsley.

Pressure Cooker Method

1. Using a 6-quart pressure cooker, cook 2½ cups unsoaked beans in 10 cups water for 15 minutes at 15 pounds pressure. Drain off cooking water and discard.

2. Follow steps 2 and 3 of the conventional method described above, seasoning chicken with half the amount of each spice.

3. Add 8 cups water to beans and chicken along with remainder of the spices and cook for an additional 15 minutes at 15 pounds pressure. Then, if there is an excess of liquid, reduce it by simmering in cooker, uncovered, over low heat.

4. Follow steps 5 and 6 of the conventional method.

Serves 6

Remarks Discarding the soaking water and the cooking water after the beans have cooked for 30 minutes rids the beans of carbohydrates that can cause intestinal gas.

══ Sesame-Glazed Chicken with Bulgur ══ 29

¼	cup unhulled sesame seeds	2½ to 3	pounds chicken pieces (thighs, drumsticks, and wings)
¼	cup oil		
¼	cup honey	2	cups bulgur
2	teaspoons grated orange rind	⅓	cup finely sliced green onions
¼	cup lemon juice	4	cups heated Chicken Stock (see Index)
½	cup orange juice		
4	teaspoons wine vinegar	1	tablespoon chopped mint or ½ teaspoon dried mint
4	teaspoons tamari soy sauce		
2	garlic cloves, minced		

1. Preheat oven to 350°F. Roast sesame seeds in a dry, heavy-bottom skillet over medium-high heat until you can smell their rich aroma. Stir them or shake the pan frequently to prevent burning.

2. Place seeds in a 1-pint mixing bowl and add oil, honey, orange rind, lemon juice, orange juice, vinegar, tamari, and garlic.

3. Lay chicken pieces in a 13 x 9 x 2-inch roasting pan, pour sesame seed mixture over them, and bake for 45 minutes. Baste once during cooking time.

4. Combine bulgur, green onions, and stock and pour into a shallow 3-quart casserole. Place chicken on top of bulgur in casserole and pour pan juices over the top.

5. Put casserole into hot oven and bake for 30 minutes until stock is absorbed and bulgur is soft. Before serving, garnish with mint.

Serves 6

══ Spanish Paella ══

1	cup black beans	1	cup sliced green peppers
6	cups water	1	cup brown rice
2	tablespoons oil	½	teaspoon turmeric
2½	pounds chicken legs, severed at the joints	½	teaspoon paprika
		⅛	teaspoon cayenne pepper
1	cup sliced onions	2	cups stewed tomatoes
2	teaspoons minced garlic	2	cups Chicken Stock (see Index)

1. Soak beans in enough water to cover for at least 8 hours. Drain and discard soaking water. Place beans in a 3-quart saucepan, add 6 cups water, and bring to a boil. Reduce heat and simmer 45 minutes. Drain beans and discard cooking water. Set aside.

2. In a 5-quart Dutch oven or heavy-bottom pot, heat oil and brown the chicken. Add onions, garlic, and green peppers. Then add rice. Stir thoroughly so that the rice is coated with the pan juices. Stir in the spices. Add the black beans, tomatoes, and the chicken stock. Blend well.

3. Cover pot, reduce heat, and simmer paella for 50 to 60 minutes, stirring every 15 minutes or so. Take care to prevent it from drying too soon—add more liquid if necessary. When liquid is absorbed and chicken and beans are cooked, the paella is ready to serve.

Serves 6

1½	cups Yogurt (see Index)	¾	teaspoon turmeric
1½	cups coarsely chopped onions	¼	teaspoon cayenne pepper
3	garlic cloves, minced	2½ to 3	pounds chicken legs, severed at
¾	teaspoon ground cumin		the joints
½	teaspoon black pepper	3	cups brown rice
½	teaspoon nutmeg	6	cups Chicken Stock (see Index)
½	teaspoon ground cloves	6	tablespoons raisins
¾	teaspoon ground coriander	¼	cup slivered almonds
¾	teaspoon ground ginger	6	tablespoons shredded coconut
½	teaspoon ground cardamom		

1. Combine yogurt, onions, garlic, and spices in a 4-quart bowl. Add chicken and mix thoroughly so that each piece is coated with the yogurt mixture. Cover and refrigerate for 24 hours.

2. Preheat oven to 500°F. Lay chicken skin-side up on a 13 x 9 x 2-inch roasting pan. Reserve the surplus yogurt mixture for cooking the pilaf. Brown chicken in oven for 20 minutes.

3. Reduce oven temperature to 350°F, baste chicken with pan juices, and continue to bake for 25 to 30 minutes or until chicken is tender.

4. In a 4-quart, heavy-bottom saucepan, combine rice, stock, raisins, almonds, and coconut. Stir in reserved yogurt mixture. Bring to a boil, reduce heat, and simmer for 30 to 35 minutes or until rice is soft and liquid is absorbed.

5. Place pilaf on a platter and top with chicken pieces. Serve hot.

Serves 6

TURKEY

Blanquette de Dinde ("White" Stew of Turkey)

1½	pounds boned, uncooked turkey leg	¾	teaspoon thyme
6	tablespoons butter	1	bay leaf
1½	cups onion chunks	¾	teaspoon marjoram
2	cups sliced mushrooms	6	tablespoons brown rice flour
1½	cups thickly sliced celery	3	egg yolks
1½	cups thickly sliced carrots	3	tablespoons Yogurt (see Index)
3	cups Turkey Stock (see Index)	3	tablespoons heavy cream
6	whole cloves	2	tablespoons lemon juice
		¼	cup chopped parsley

1. Cut turkey leg meat into 1-inch cubes.

2. In a 5-quart Dutch oven or heavy-bottom pot, melt 3 tablespoons butter and saute onions, mushrooms, celery, and carrots over medium-low heat for about 2 minutes. Do not let vegetables brown.

3. Add stock, cloves, and herbs. Simmer, covered, over very low heat for 10 to 15 minutes or until turkey is tender.

4. Melt 3 tablespoons butter in a 2-quart, heavy-bottom saucepan. Stir in flour, then gradually add the stock only from the simmering stew. There should be almost 3 cups. For a smooth sauce, stir with a wire whisk. Combine egg yolks with yogurt and heavy cream in a 1-pint bowl. Whisk a little hot sauce into the mixture, then gradually return this mixture to saucepan, while stirring. Remove from heat. Stir in lemon juice and pour sauce over meat and vegetables in the 5-quart pot. Warm over low heat for 1 to 2 minutes. Do not let boil or blanquette will curdle. Garnish with parsley before serving.

Serves 6

Remarks   Serve over cooked whole grain noodles.

1   pound fresh broccoli
2   cups cooked pieces of turkey
(or chicken)

Sauce
(2¼ cups hot leftover turkey gravy may be substituted for this section)

3   tablespoons butter
6   tablespoons rye flour or whole
wheat flour
2   cups Turkey Stock or Chicken
Stock (see Index)

¼   teaspoon thyme
¼   teaspoon sage
¼   teaspoon poultry seasoning

Stuffing
(3 cups leftover stuffing may be substituted for this section)

2   tablespoons oil
¾   cup chopped onions
⅔   cup chopped celery
4   cups cubed toasted whole grain
bread

½   teaspoon thyme
½   teaspoon sage
½   teaspoon poultry seasoning
1   cup Turkey Stock or Chicken
Stock (see Index)

1. Cut tough bottoms off broccoli stems. Trim and separate stalks into florets and stems and then slice stems. In a 2-quart saucepan, cook broccoli in as little water as possible until it is just tender but still firm. Drain.

2. Arrange broccoli on the bottom of a 3-quart casserole and place turkey over the broccoli.

3. In a 2-quart saucepan, melt butter over medium-low heat. Stir in flour until smooth. Then add stock, stirring with a wire wisk to avoid lumping. Simmer until sauce is thickened. Add thyme, sage, and poultry seasoning. Pour sauce over contents of casserole.

4. In a large skillet, heat oil and saute onions and celery over low heat for 4 to 5 minutes. Add bread, thyme, sage, and poultry seasoning and stir-fry for 3 to 5 minutes. Add stock, mixing it into bread evenly. Turn stuffing into casserole, spreading it evenly over the turkey and sauce.

5. Bake, uncovered, in a 350°F oven for 20 to 30 minutes or until casserole is bubbling. It is not necessary to preheat oven.

Serves 6

Remarks   This is a different way to use leftover turkey, gravy, and stuffing, but is also a lovely dish to make from "scratch!"

Breaded Turkey "Cutlets" 33

Cutlet Mixture

2	small potatoes (½ pound total weight), cut into chunks	1	teaspoon tamari soy sauce
1½	pounds boneless, uncooked turkey (dark or white meat)	1	teaspoon basil
		¼	teaspoon nutmeg
¼	cup heavy cream	½	teaspoon dry mustard
2	teaspoons lemon juice	½	teaspoon paprika

Breading

2¼	cups whole grain bread crumbs	½	cup whole wheat flour
3	eggs	½	teaspoon poultry seasoning
3	tablespoons water	¾	teaspoon paprika

1. In a 1-quart saucepan, cook potatoes in as little water as possible. Drain and mash them until smooth. There should be about 1 cup.

2. Put turkey through meat grinder using coarse, large-holed disc.

3. In a 2-quart bowl, combine turkey, potatoes, and remaining ingredients of cutlet mixture. Mix thoroughly.

4. Arrange 3 containers on counter top near the range. Place bread crumbs in one, beat eggs and water together in another, and mix flour with poultry seasoning and paprika in the third container.

5. Coat a rounded teaspoonful of turkey mixture with seasoned flour, gently patting it into a thin oblong cutlet shape, about 3 x 2 x ¼ inches. Next, coat both sides with egg mixture, then with bread crumbs, and place in a shallow 13 x 9 x 2-inch baking pan. Follow this procedure with each cutlet. Let the cutlets dry for 15 minutes before broiling them.

6. Preheat broiler. Set pan of cutlets about 6½ inches below broiler unit and broil 5 to 8 minutes on each side or until brown.

Serves 6

Remarks This dish, succulent and crunchy, is truly a unique turkey entree. Serve with Tomato Brown Sauce (see Index).

1½	cups frozen lima beans	¼	teaspoon cayenne pepper
3	tablespoons butter	1½	teaspoons chili powder
1	pound uncooked turkey, cut into 1½-inch cubes (about 2 cups)	1	tablespoon basil
		3	cups cooked tomatoes
		3	cups tomato juice
2	medium-size onions, coarsely chopped	1½	cups frozen corn
		3	cups sliced okra
5	cups Turkey Stock or Chicken Stock (see Index)		

1. In a 1-quart saucepan, cook lima beans, using as little water as possible, for 15 minutes.

2. In a 5-quart Dutch oven or heavy-bottom pot, melt butter and saute turkey and onions over medium-high heat until brown.

3. Add remaining ingredients along with lima beans and their liquid. Cover and simmer over low heat for 15 minutes.

Serves 6

California Salad

⅓	cup wine vinegar	2	cups cubed cooked turkey breast
⅓	cup oil		
2	teaspoons honey	1	cup sliced celery
1	teaspoon grated onion	1	cup coarsely chopped green peppers
½	teaspoon Mustard (see Index)		
½	teaspoon ground cumin	2	ripe avocados (about ¾ pound each)
¼	teaspoon paprika		
½	teaspoon dill weed	¼	cup lemon juice
⅛	teaspoon cayenne pepper		salad greens
3	cups cooked kidney beans		

1. Combine vinegar, oil, honey, grated onion, mustard, cumin, paprika, dill, and cayenne pepper in a 2-quart bowl.

2. Add kidney beans, turkey, celery, and green peppers. Mix gently with your hands to coat beans and turkey evenly with dressing, taking care to avoid breaking the beans. Marinate for at least 1 hour.

3. Peel avocados and cut each into 3 wedges of equal size. Coat avocado wedges with the lemon juice and arrange each wedge on a bed of salad greens. Add surplus lemon juice to bean and turkey mixture. Serve salad mounded on each of the avocado wedges.

Serves 6

Curried Turkey Soup

10	cups Turkey Stock (see Index)	2	tablespoons butter
½	cup brown rice	1	tablespoon curry powder
¼	cup finely chopped onions	6	tablespoons brown rice flour
½	cup finely chopped celery	1½	cups light cream
½	cup finely chopped green	2	cups cubed cooked turkey
	peppers	2	tablespoons tamari soy sauce
½	cup finely chopped tomatoes	2	tablespoons lemon juice

1. Place 8 cups of the stock and the rice in a 5-quart soup pot. Cover and simmer over low heat for 15 minutes.

2. Add onions, celery, green peppers, and tomatoes to stock and rice and simmer for another 10 minutes.

3. In a 3-quart, heavy-bottom saucepan, melt butter over low heat. Add curry powder and flour, and then the remaining 2 cups stock, stirring constantly. Gradually stir in cream.

4. Add a little liquid from the soup pot to the sauce, stirring constantly. Then stir sauce into soup pot. Blend well. Add turkey, tamari, and lemon juice. Heat soup through, but do not let boil.

Serves 6

Curried Turkey Timbale

3	cups cubed cooked turkey	1	tablespoon lemon juice
5	eggs, beaten	2	teaspoons curry powder
1¼	cups Turkey Stock (see Index)	½	teaspoon dry mustard
¾	cup Yogurt (see Index)	½	teaspoon paprika
½	cup finely chopped celery	½	teaspoon poultry seasoning
1	tablespoon grated onion	3	cups cooked peas
2	tablespoons chopped parsley		

1. Put turkey through meat grinder using coarse, large-holed disc.

2. In a 2-quart bowl, combine turkey with all remaining ingredients except peas. Mix well and turn out into 6 oiled, 8-ounce Pyrex cups or an oiled 1½-quart ring mold.

3. Set cups or mold in 1 inch of water in a 17¼ x 11½ x 2¼-inch pan. Bake in a preheated 325°F oven 1 hour for individual molds and up to 1¼ hours for the ring mold. Timbales are cooked when a knife inserted in the center comes out clean.

4. To serve, loosen edges of timbales with a knife and unmold on individual plates or a large round plate. Place heated peas either in the center of the ring mold or alongside the individual timbales.

Serves 6

2	cups coarsely chopped celery	½	cup chopped water chestnuts
8	green onions, finely sliced	½	cup sunflower seeds
1½	cups Turkey Stock (see Index)	3	cups cooked garbanzo beans
¼	cup brown rice flour	1⅓	cups Mayonnaise (see Index)
½	cup Yogurt (see Index)		romaine lettuce
4	cups cubed cooked turkey		
4	hard-cooked eggs, coarsely chopped		

1. Place celery, onions (white parts only—reserve green tops for garnish), and stock in a 1½-quart saucepan. Bring to a boil, reduce heat, and simmer, covered, for 2 to 3 minutes.

2. Strain stock, measuring out 1 cup and reserving any surplus for future use in soup. Turn celery and onions into a 3-quart bowl. Return cup of stock to saucepan, stir in flour, and cook over medium-low heat until thickened. Add yogurt, stirring until smooth. Remove sauce from heat.

3. Add turkey, eggs, water chestnuts, sunflower seeds, and garbanzo beans to celery and onions in bowl.

4. Stir mayonnaise into sauce and then pour over salad, tossing gently. Serve salad in a bowl lined with lettuce leaves and garnish with the reserved green onion tops.

Serves 6

══════════════ **Turkey Gumbo Soup** ══════════════

¾	cup coarsely chopped onions	3	cups sliced okra
8	cups Turkey Stock (see Index)	1½	cups cubed cooked turkey
¾	cup coarsely chopped green peppers	¾	teaspoon paprika
2	cups chopped cooked tomatoes with juice	¼	teaspoon cayenne pepper

1. In a 5-quart soup pot, bring onions and stock to a boil. Reduce heat and simmer, covered, for 15 minutes.

2. Add green peppers, tomatoes, and okra, and simmer another 10 minutes.

3. Add turkey and seasonings, bring to a boil, and serve.

Serves 6

2	cups black-eyed peas	6	whole cloves
6	cups water	½	pound Sausage, in casing (see Index)
4	cups Turkey Stock or Chicken Stock (see Index)	6	turkey or chicken livers
½	cup coarsely chopped onions	1	tablespoon oil
1	garlic clove, minced	2	tablespoons cornstarch
1	teaspoon tarragon	2	tablespoons cold water
1	teaspoon thyme	2	cups cubed cooked turkey
1	teaspoon basil	½	cup whole grain bread crumbs
1	teaspoon dry mustard	3	tablespoons melted butter

1. Place black-eyed peas and water in a 3-quart, heavy-bottom pot and bring to a boil. Cook at a rolling boil for 2 minutes, stirring occasionally. Remove pot from heat, cover, and set aside for at least 2 hours. Drain and discard water. Add stock, onions, garlic, herbs, and spices to the peas and bring to a boil. Reduce heat to very low, cover pot, and simmer for 20 minutes or until peas are tender.

2. Prick sausage with a sharp fork in several places to enable fat to escape during cooking. Place sausage in ½ inch of water in a large skillet, cover, and cook sausage on each side for 5 to 10 minutes over medium-high heat. Drain and discard most of liquid. Let sausage brown in its own juices over medium heat. Cut sausage into about 12 slices, remove from pan, and set aside.

3. Cut livers into halves or quarters, depending on their size. Heat oil in skillet and saute livers over medium-high heat until they are brown. Remove from pan and set aside.

4. Drain liquid from cooked peas into the skillet. There should be about 3½ cups. Bring liquid to a boil. Dissolve cornstarch in the water and add to boiling liquid, stirring until thickened. Return sauce to black-eyed peas.

5. In a 3-quart casserole, arrange a layer of half the peas, then a layer of the turkey, sausage, and livers, and then the remaining peas.

6. Combine bread crumbs with melted butter and sprinkle on top of casserole. Bake in a 300°F oven for 30 to 40 minutes or until surface is crusty and brown.

Serves 6

Creamed Turkey

1	tablespoon butter	2	cups chopped cooked turkey
2	tablespoons brown rice flour	1½	cups cooked peas
1½	cups Turkey Stock (see Index)	3	hard-cooked eggs, coarsely
½	cup Yogurt (see Index)		chopped

Pumpkin Pancakes

½	cup cornmeal	¼	teaspoon ground ginger
½	cup rye flour	2	eggs
¼	cup non-fat dry milk	½	cup drained cooked pumpkin
2	teaspoons baking powder	2 to 4	tablespoons oil
¼	teaspoon cinnamon	4	teaspoons honey
¼	teaspoon ground cloves	2	cups water

1. In a 2-quart, heavy-bottom saucepan, melt butter over low heat. Stir in brown rice flour, then gradually add stock and cook until thickened. Add yogurt and stir until well blended.

2. Add turkey, peas, and hard-cooked eggs. Set aside but keep warm.

3. Combine cornmeal, rye flour, non-fat dry milk, baking powder, and spices in a 2-quart mixing bowl. In another 1-quart bowl, combine eggs, pumpkin, 2 tablespoons oil, honey, and water. Stir into dry ingredients. Grease a large skillet with some of the remaining oil and heat it. Drop batter by the tablespoonful into skillet. Cook pancakes until bubbles form over the surface. Cook only a few seconds on the reverse side. Grease the skillet as needed by brushing it with an oiled brush or paper towel. There should not be any excess oil in skillet. Keep pancakes in a warm oven until ready to serve.

4. Arrange a ring of overlapping pancakes on individual plates. Place the creamed turkey in the center and serve.

Serves 6

Rice Ring with Creamed Turkey and Mushrooms === 39

Rice Ring

1	cup brown rice
2	cups water
4	tablespoons butter
½	cup finely chopped onions
¼	cup chopped parsley

¼	cup Turkey Stock or Chicken Stock (see Index)
½	teaspoon thyme
¼	teaspoon sage
⅛	teaspoon marjoram

Creamed Turkey and Mushrooms

3	tablespoons butter
1½	cups thickly sliced mushrooms
¼	cup rye flour or whole wheat flour
1	cup Turkey Stock or Chicken Stock (see Index)

¾	cup milk
1½	tablespoons cornstarch
3	tablespoons water
2	tablespoons lemon juice
½	teaspoon poultry seasoning
2½	cups cubed cooked turkey

1. Combine rice and water in a 1½-quart, heavy-bottom saucepan. Cover and bring to a boil, then reduce heat to medium and simmer for 30 minutes or until water is absorbed. Do not stir during cooking.

2. In a 2½-quart, heavy-bottom saucepan, melt 1 tablespoon butter and brush an 8¼-inch (1 quart) ring mold with it. Set aside. In the same saucepan, melt the remaining butter and saute onions over medium-high heat for 2 minutes. Remove from heat.

3. When rice is cooked, fluff with a fork and mix in sauteed onions, parsley, stock, and herbs. Pack into ring mold, pressing mixture in with the back of a spoon, and place in a warm oven.

4. To make the creamed turkey, melt butter in the same saucepan and saute mushrooms for 2 minutes over medium-low heat, stirring constantly.

5. Stir in flour and blend well. Gradually add stock and milk. Cook, while stirring, until sauce is smooth.

6. Dissolve cornstarch in the water and then add to sauce, stirring until thickened.

7. Add lemon juice and poultry seasoning, and then the turkey.

8. Loosen rice ring with a knife and unmold onto a round plate. Pour creamed turkey into center of ring and serve immediately.

Serves 6

Remarks   The rice ring may be made ahead and refrigerated for several days. To serve, heat it, covered, in a 350°F oven for 15 to 20 minutes.

1	pound broccoli	3	green onions, finely sliced
3	cups cubed cooked turkey	¾	cup Mayonnaise (see Index)
1½	cups chopped celery	¾	cup Yogurt (see Index)
6	tablespoons sunflower seeds	1	teaspoon ground ginger
3	oranges, peeled, with segments separated and cut into halves crosswise	¼	teaspoon black pepper

Garnish

salad greens
ground ginger

1. Separate broccoli florets from stems. Cut stems into slices about ¼ inch thick. Cook broccoli, in as little water as possible, for about 2 minutes or until tender. Drain and discard cooking water. Turn broccoli out into a 3-quart mixing bowl.

2. Add turkey, celery, sunflower seeds, orange segments, and onions (white parts only—reserve green tops for garnish).

3. In a 1-quart bowl, combine mayonnaise, yogurt, ginger, and black pepper. Pour dressing over salad and toss gently to combine. Serve in a salad bowl lined with salad greens. Garnish with the reserved green onion tops and a sprinkling of ground ginger.

Serves 6

===== Turkey Divan =====

4½	cups Turkey Stock (see Index)	1	cup grated Parmesan cheese
1	cup heavy cream	3	cups frozen corn
5	tablespoons brown rice flour	2	pounds fresh broccoli
5	teaspoons cornstarch	4	cups cubed cooked turkey (white meat only)
5	teaspoons cold water		
¼	teaspoon nutmeg		

1. Preheat oven to 350°F. Combine stock and cream in a 3-quart, heavy-bottom saucepan. Stir in flour. Dissolve cornstarch in the water and then stir into the stock mixture. Cook over medium-low heat, stirring constantly, until sauce has thickened. Add nutmeg and ¾ cup of the Parmesan cheese. Set aside.

2. In a 1½-quart saucepan, cook corn in as little water as possible. Lift out corn and place on the bottom of a 3-quart casserole. Reserve corn water.

3. Cut tough bottoms from broccoli stems and trim. Separate stalks into florets and stems, then slice stems. Cook broccoli in the corn water, just until tender. Drain.

4. Arrange a layer of the turkey on top of the corn, then a layer of broccoli stems, then the broccoli florets. Pour the sauce over the contents of the casserole, sprinkle the remaining ¼ cup of Parmesan cheese over the top, and bake for 30 minutes or until casserole is slightly browned on top.

Serves 6

Turkey Cacciatore (Italian Hunter's Turkey)

1½	pounds boneless, uncooked turkey breasts	2	garlic cloves, minced
3	tablespoons oat flour (rolled oats ground in blender)	3	cups thickly sliced mushrooms
		1½	cups Turkey Stock or Chicken Stock (see Index)
3	tablespoons rye flour	⅓	cup tomato paste
4 to 5	tablespoons olive oil	2	teaspoons basil
1½	medium-size onions, chopped	1	teaspoon oregano

1. Cut turkey breast into pieces about ¾-inch thick, 3½ inches long, and 2 inches wide (about the size of a chicken thigh).

2. Combine oat and rye flour and dredge turkey pieces in flour mixture.

3. In a large skillet, heat 2 to 3 tablespoons oil and saute turkey pieces over medium-high heat until browned. Remove turkey from skillet and place on a 14 x 10 x 2-inch oven-proof tray. Set in warm oven.

4. In the same skillet, heat 2 tablespoons oil and saute onions and garlic for 1 minute. Add mushrooms and saute, while stirring, for 2 minutes. Stir in stock, tomato paste, basil, and oregano.

5. Return turkey to skillet, cover, and simmer over low heat for 30 minutes or until turkey is tender.

Serves 6

Remarks   Serve with cooked whole grain noodles.

Turkey Scrapple

4	cups Turkey Stock (see Index)	¼	teaspoon ground coriander
2	cups cornmeal	½	teaspoon paprika
½	teaspoon thyme	2	tablespoons lemon juice
⅛	teaspoon marjoram	2	teaspoons grated onion
1	teaspoon basil	2	cups minced cooked turkey

1. Combine stock, cornmeal, herbs, and spices in a 4-quart, heavy-bottom sauce-pan. Bring to a boil, reduce heat, and simmer until mixture pulls away from the sides of the pan, stirring constantly.

2. Remove from heat. Add lemon juice, onion, and turkey.

3. Turn scrapple out into two 7½ x 3¾ x 2¼-inch loaf pans which have been rinsed with cold water. Refrigerate until firm.

Makes 2 loaves

Remarks   To serve, slice scrapple into ¼-inch slices, dip into rye flour or whole wheat flour, and saute in oil until brown on both sides. Serve with Mustard (see Index) or cranberry sauce.

Turkey-Cheese Balls with Yogurt Sauce

1	pound boneless, uncooked turkey breasts	1	teaspoon dill weed
1	cup dry cottage cheese	2 to 3	tablespoons butter
2	cups soft whole grain bread crumbs	2 to 3	tablespoons oil
1	tablespoon grated onion	4	cups Turkey Stock or Chicken Stock (see Index)
1	tablespoon lemon juice	4	teaspoons cornstarch
½	teaspoon celery seeds	3	tablespoons cold water
½	teaspoon tarragon	1	cup Yogurt (see Index)

1. Put turkey through food processor or meat grinder, using coarse, large-holed disc.

2. Combine ground turkey, cottage cheese, soft bread crumbs, onion, lemon juice, celery seeds, and herbs.

3. Form mixture into balls the size of walnuts. In a large skillet, heat butter and oil and saute turkey-cheese balls until lightly browned.

4. Add stock, cover skillet, and simmer over low heat for 5 to 10 minutes or until they are cooked through.

5. Dissolve cornstarch in the water and add to stock in skillet, stirring until thickened.

6. Place yogurt in a 1-quart bowl. Stir in some hot sauce from the skillet to thin it and then add the yogurt to the sauce. Blend well and serve.

Serves 6

Turkey Stuffing Soup

7½	cups Turkey Stock (see Index)	6	tablespoons chopped water chestnuts or almonds
3	cups stuffing	¾	cup chopped parsley
1½	cups frozen corn		
2	cups chopped cooked turkey		

1. Combine all ingredients in a 2-quart, heavy-bottom saucepan and simmer over low heat for 10 minutes.

2. Add chopped parsley and serve.

Serves 6

Turkey Cutlets with Winter Pears 43

1½	pounds boneless, uncooked turkey breasts	1	garlic clove, minced
1	tablespoon oil	½	teaspoon mace
½	cup coarsely chopped onions	½	teaspoon ground ginger
1	cup millet	6	tablespoons lemon juice
4	cups Turkey Stock (see Index)	6	tablespoons heavy cream
¼	cup butter	3	tablespoons chopped parsley
3	russet winter pears, cored and cut into eighths lengthwise		

1. Separate turkey breasts into 8 to 12 thin cutlets and flatten them with a meat cleaver or "dent" them across the grain of the meat with the edge of an ordinary saucer. Set aside.

2. In a 2-quart, heavy-bottom saucepan, heat oil and saute onions and millet until onions are soft. Add 3 cups stock, cover, and cook over very low heat for 30 to 40 minutes or until tender. Keep warm until ready to serve.

3. In a large skillet, melt butter and saute turkey cutlets, pear slices, garlic, and spices over medium-low heat until golden brown. Transfer cutlets and pears to a 13 x 9 x 2-inch baking pan and place in a warm oven.

4. Stir lemon juice, 1 cup stock, and cream into skillet, loosening brown bits in pan, and simmer over low heat 1 to 2 minutes.

5. Mound the millet in the center of a platter. Arrange cutlets on top and surround them with the pear slices. Pour sauce from skillet over the turkey and millet and garnish with chopped parsley.

Serves 6

¼	cup water	2	tablespoons chopped parsley
1	tablespoon unflavored gelatin	2	teaspoons grated onion
¾	cup Mayonnaise (see Index)	3	tablespoons lemon juice
1½	cups minced cooked turkey	½	teaspoon paprika
⅔	cup peeled, minced apples	½	teaspoon basil
¼	cup minced celery	½	teaspoon dry mustard
½	cup peeled, seeded, diced cucumbers	⅓	cup heavy cream

Garnish

watercress
small leaves of romaine lettuce

1. Place water in a 1-pint saucepan, sprinkle gelatin over water, and let soak for 5 minutes. Set pan over low heat and stir soaked gelatin until melted. Stir melted gelatin into mayonnaise and blend well.

2. Combine turkey, gelatin-mayonnaise mixture, and all remaining ingredients, except the cream, in a 3-quart bowl.

3. Place the cream in a 1-quart bowl and whip until stiff. Fold into turkey mixture, then turn mixture out into a 1½-quart ring mold or loaf pan which has been lightly oiled. Cover and refrigerate until set.

4. Unmold mousse onto a platter and garnish with watercress and lettuce leaves before serving.

Serves 6

Turkey Mushroom Watercress Soup

2	tablespoons oil	2	cups chopped cooked turkey
½	cup coarsely chopped onions	1	tablespoon tamari soy sauce
2	cups thickly sliced mushrooms	3	cups coarsely chopped watercress
½	cup buckwheat groats		
9	cups Turkey Stock or Chicken Stock (see Index)		

1. In a 3-quart saucepan, heat oil and saute onions and mushrooms over medium-low heat for 2 to 3 minutes.

2. Stir in buckwheat groats to coat them evenly with oil. Add stock, reduce heat, and simmer, covered, for 15 to 20 minutes or until buckwheat groats are soft.

3. Add turkey and tamari and continue simmering for 2 minutes. Add watercress and serve immediately.

Serves 6

Turkey Paprika === 45

1½	pounds boneless, uncooked turkey breasts	3	cups coarsely chopped mushroom caps and stems
½	cup milk	2	cups Turkey Stock (see Index)
½	cup whole wheat flour	½	cup heavy cream
2	teaspoons paprika	2	tablespoons cornstarch
1	teaspoon poultry seasoning	6	tablespoons Yogurt (see Index)
5	tablespoons butter	¼	cup chopped parsley
1	cup coarsely chopped onions		

1. Separate turkey breasts into 8 to 12 thin cutlets. Flatten them with a meat cleaver, or "dent" them across the grain of the meat with the edge of an ordinary saucer.

2. Place milk in a shallow dish. In another dish, mix together 6 tablespoons flour, paprika, and poultry seasoning.

3. Dip each cutlet into milk and then coat with seasoned flour. In a large skillet, melt 3 tablespoons butter and saute cutlets for 1 to 2 minutes or until golden brown. As cutlets are done, place them in a warm oven.

4. In the same skillet, melt 2 tablespoons butter and saute onions and mushrooms over medium heat for about 2 minutes. Stir in 2 tablespoons flour, then gradually add stock and cream, stirring until smooth.

5. Dissolve cornstarch in yogurt and stir into simmering sauce until thickened. Pour sauce over cutlets and garnish with chopped parsley.

Serves 6

Remarks   Serve with cooked whole grain noodles or brown rice.

5 to 8	tablespoons butter	¼	cup coarsely chopped onions
6	tablespoons brown rice flour	¼	cup chopped water chestnuts
3	cups Turkey Stock (see Index)	¼	teaspoon allspice
2¼	cups cubed cooked turkey	¼	teaspoon cinnamon
3	cups cubed cooked sweet	¼	teaspoon nutmeg
	potatoes	¼	teaspoon black pepper

1. In a 1½-quart saucepan, melt 2 tablespoons of the butter over medium heat. Stir in the flour, then gradually add the stock. Cook, while stirring, until sauce has thickened. Set aside but keep warm.

2. In a 3-quart bowl, combine turkey, sweet potatoes, onions, water chestnuts, and spices. Add ½ cup of the sauce. Mix lightly.

3. Melt 3 tablespoons of the butter in a large skillet and drop in turkey mixture with a large spoon. Flatten slightly with spoon to make patties about 2½ inches in diameter. Cook over medium-low heat until crispy. Turn patties and brown on reverse side, adding more butter if needed.

4. Serve hash patties with the remaining sauce over them.

Serves 6

Turkey Tetrazzini

3	quarts water	6	tablespoons cornstarch
1	tablespoon oil	¾	cup cold water
½	pound whole wheat spaghetti	3	cups Yogurt (see Index)
4	tablespoons butter	1½	cups grated Parmesan cheese
½	pound mushrooms, sliced	3	cups cubed cooked turkey
3	cups Turkey Stock (see Index)	½	cup slivered almonds

1. Bring water to boil in a 5-quart pot. Add oil, then drop in spaghetti, stirring to keep each strand separated. Boil, uncovered, for 10 to 12 minutes or until desired tenderness is reached. Drain and set aside.

2. Preheat over to 350°F. In a large skillet, melt butter and saute mushrooms over medium heat for 2 minutes. Add stock. Dissolve cornstarch in water and add to skillet, stirring constantly. Simmer until sauce is thickened.

3. Stir in yogurt, Parmesan cheese, and then add the turkey.

4. In a 3-quart casserole, layer spaghetti and sauce alternately, ending with sauce.

5. Sprinkle almonds over the surface and bake 15 to 20 minutes until the casserole is bubbling and top is browned.

Serves 6

Turkey Walnut Croquettes 47

2	tablespoons butter	½	teaspoon dry mustard
¼	cup rye flour	¾	teaspoon paprika
1	cup Turkey Stock or Chicken Stock (see Index)	2	tablespoons lemon juice
1	tablespoon cornstarch	1	tablespoon grated onion
2	tablespoons cold water	3	cups minced cooked turkey
2	egg yolks, beaten	1	cup minced walnuts
1	teaspoon basil	1	cup soft whole grain bread crumbs
1	teaspoon tarragon	⅔	cup dry whole grain bread crumbs
1½	teaspoons nutmeg		
¾	teaspoon ground coriander	½ to ¾	cup oil
⅛	teaspoon black pepper		

1. In a 3-quart, heavy-bottom saucepan, melt butter over medium heat and stir in flour. Gradually add stock, stirring to make a smooth sauce.

2. Dissolve cornstarch in water and add to sauce, stirring constantly. Cook over low heat until thickened.

3. In a 1-quart bowl, stir about ½ cup of the hot sauce into the beaten egg yolks, then return this mixture to saucepan and cook over low heat for about 1 minute, stirring constantly. Remove from heat and set aside.

4. Add herbs, spices, lemon juice, onion, turkey, walnuts, and soft bread crumbs. Mix well. Spread mixture in a 9 x 9 x 2-inch pan, cover, and refrigerate for at least 2 hours.

5. Score mixture into 12 oblong portions. Remove one portion at a time, shape into a rounded oblong croquette with your hands, and roll it in the dry bread crumbs.

6. In a large skillet, heat oil and saute croquettes over medium-low heat until golden brown. (Oil should be about ¼-inch deep in skillet.) Drain sauteed croquettes on paper towels and serve.

Serves 6

Remarks Croquettes may be served with Mushroom Sauce (see Index) or Tomato Brown Sauce (see Index).

and Turkey Casserole

3	cups apple juice	6	cups peeled and cubed
3	tablespoons cornstarch		butternut squash (or other
¾	cup raisins		winter squash)
¼	cup lemon juice	3	cups chopped cooked turkey
3	tablespoons honey	3	tablespoons sunflower seeds
½	teaspoon nutmeg	1	tablespoon butter
1½	teaspoons dry mustard		

1. In a 2-quart saucepan, combine apple juice, cornstarch, raisins, lemon juice, honey, nutmeg, and dry mustard and simmer over low heat for 5 to 10 minutes until sauce has thickened and raisins are plump. Set aside.

2. Preheat oven to 350°F. Cook squash in a 3-quart pot until tender, using as little water as possible.

3. Drain squash. Arrange half of the squash on the bottom of a 3-quart casserole. Then layer half the turkey on top of the squash. Pour half of the sauce over the turkey. Repeat process, layering remaining squash, turkey, and sauce.

4. Sprinkle sunflower seeds over surface of casserole and dot with butter. Bake for 20 minutes or until contents are hot and surface is slightly browned.

Serves 6

Zucchini Turkey Quiche 49

1	unbaked 9-inch Whole Wheat Pie Crust (see Index)
¼	cup butter
1	cup finely chopped onions
2	garlic cloves, minced
4	cups thinly sliced zucchini (about 1½ pounds)
3	eggs, beaten
1½	cups cooked turkey breast strips (about ¾ x ¼ x ⅛ inch)

1	cup grated Muenster cheese (about 4 ounces)
1	teaspoon basil
½	teaspoon oregano
⅛	teaspoon black pepper
¼	teaspoon paprika
2	teaspoons Mustard (see Index)

1. Make the pie crust.

2. Preheat oven to 400°F. In a large skillet, melt butter and saute onions, garlic, and zucchini over medium heat for about 10 minutes or until zucchini is tender but not too soft. Remove from heat and set aside.

3. In a 2-quart bowl, combine eggs, turkey, cheese, basil, oregano, black pepper, and paprika. Turn this mixture into skillet and gently combine it with the zucchini mixture, taking care to avoid breaking the zucchini.

4. Using your fingers, coat the unbaked pie shell evenly with the mustard. Then fill the shell evenly with zucchini mixture so that zucchini slices cover the whole surface. Bake for 10 minutes. Lower oven to 350°F and bake 25 minutes longer or until filling is set. Remove quiche from oven and cool on a rack at room temperature for 10 minutes before cutting and serving.

Serves 6

Beef

Beef is a royal meat. Someone put it that way and I must agree. There is no meat which can quite compare with roast beef au jus, or a perfectly cooked hamburger.

Beef is America's favorite meat. In fact, for many Americans, beef is their *only* meat. But too much of a good thing is never wise, so it is gratifying to see that in recent years we have reduced our intake of beef. After we reached the peak of beef consumption in 1974—116 pounds per capita, Americans began to cut down drastically. Per capita beef consumption dropped to 95.6 pounds in 1976, then to 79.6 pounds in 1980. No doubt costs had something to do with the reduction, but I think a growing awareness that we should cut back on animal fats for our health's sake was an equally strong factor in this change of habit.

Many health-conscious people also advocate eating organically grown beef so as to avoid meat from cattle that have been injected with hormones and antibiotics. Some farmers do allow their cattle to graze on pasture land and then feed them supplemental grains which are pesticide-free and have been fertilized naturally. It would be hard to argue that such animals, though leaner, are not healthier than the cramped, feedlot cattle; indeed, many gourmets insist that the flavor and texture of the meat is superior. You are fortunate if you are in a position to seek out these beef producers. Of course, you must be prepared to pay a premium for this kind of meat.

Lean Is In

Many of us can't find such a supplier, and couldn't afford the extra cost in any case. But we can make our wants known in the market place. In fact, this is just what has been happening. Shoppers have been passing up those marbled steaks in the meat case for the leaner ones. The message: fat is out, lean is in. The result is a whole new attitude in the beef business. Some ranchers are experimenting with crossbreeding heavy European strains of cattle with our Short-Horn, Angus, and Hereford types to produce animals that give beef which is tender and lean.

Beef industry leaders are asking the USDA to change the grade regulations to include leaner, less marbled beef in the Choice category. Furthermore, steers are being slaughtered well before they reach the traditional 1,000 pounds for Choice beef or 1,400 pounds for Prime. While this is primarily an economic measure in the beef industry, it is being encouraged by the consumer demand for leaner beef.

All Americans, consumers and producers alike, are being forced to adjust to the economic realities in the 1980s. No longer able to draw on unlimited resources, we find ourselves entering an age of limits. This is a good thing in many ways—not least of all, in the way it affects our diets.

Where the Cuts Come From

To make the most of the beef available to us we should learn to identify beef cuts by their appearance. It will take a little practice to recognize all of them because names differ in various parts of the country and may even vary from store to store within one town. The names range from the practical (like "pot roast") to the cutesy (like "his and hers steaks"). But, knowing where the cuts come from will help you determine a good buy. The chart "Beef Cuts" shows the major (primal) cuts.

Without becoming too involved with anatomy, we can understand that the most tender meat comes from that part of the animal which is the least active. It follows that the cuts near the middle of the back (sirloin, short loin, and rib) are the most tender since the muscles there are less exercised during the life of a steer. On the other hand, the round, flank, chuck, plate, brisket, and shank cuts (from the rump, flank, shoulder, neck, breast, and leg) come from areas that are strained quite a lot and are therefore less tender.

Freezing Basics for Beef, Lamb, and Pork
- Freeze only high quality, fresh beef, lamb, and pork.
- Package most meat in family-size portions. For company meals, make up a few large portions.
- Remove large bones, since they take up valuable storage space. Use the bones to make concentrated stock and freeze the stock in ice cube trays.
- Trim off excess fat which tends to become rancid during long storage.
- Slide extra freezer wrap between each chop or each ground meat patty so that you can easily separate the pieces of meat for thawing or for cooking.
- Wrap and seal meat in heavy paper or heavy plastic bags made especially for freezing.
- Label each package with the cut of meat, the date, and the weight or the number of servings or pieces.
- Limit storage to the recommended length of time (see chapters on Beef, Pork, and Lamb).

Beef Cuts

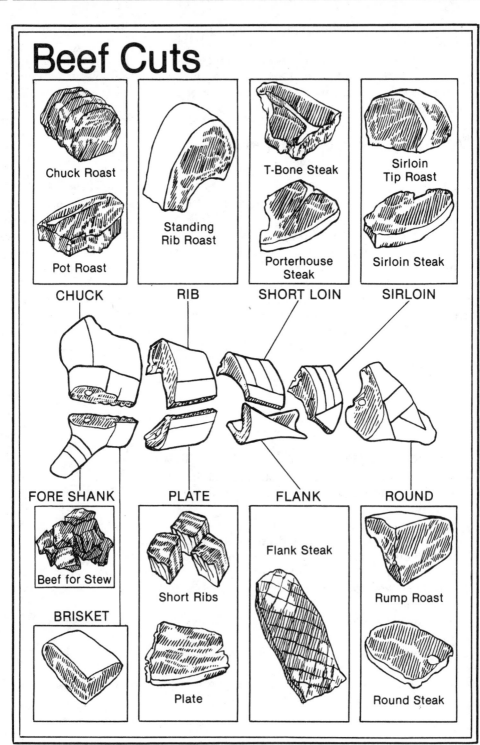

Chuck Roast

Pot Roast

CHUCK

Standing Rib Roast

RIB

T-Bone Steak

Porterhouse Steak

SHORT LOIN

Sirloin Tip Roast

Sirloin Steak

SIRLOIN

FORE SHANK

Beef for Stew

BRISKET

PLATE

Short Ribs

Plate

FLANK

Flank Steak

ROUND

Rump Roast

Round Steak

Generally speaking, the less tender cuts of beef are the least expensive. But it is possible that if a high-priced, tender roast is passed over in favor of the low-priced, less tender cuts, the high-priced roast will be marked down after a day or so, just to move it. This is the law of supply and demand working in an unusual way. If more people seek out the lower-priced cuts and the supply diminishes, the price for them may go up and the price of the other cuts come down. So check prices regularly and keep alert to surprises and bargains.

If you know what part of the animal the various cuts come from, you can do your own cutting and grinding, in case the large piece is cheaper. This is not always true. Stew and ground chuck are sometimes cheaper than the cut they were taken from. But you need to check to be sure.

Cook It Right

Another reason for knowing the anatomy of your cut of beef is to be able to cook it correctly. Butchers have a standard line: "There is no such thing as a tough piece of meat, if you cook it right." This is true. Less tender cuts require moist heat and longer cooking: simmering, boiling, braising. Tender cuts can be cooked for a shorter time with dry heat: roasting, broiling, frying.

Braising Tips

- Brown meat slowly on all sides. You may need to use a tiny bit of fat to keep the meat from sticking.
- Add ½ cup or less liquid to prevent overbrowning.
- Cover the pan tightly.
- Cook over low heat or in a 350°F oven. Add more liquid as needed.

Approximate Braising Times

Cut of meat	Approximate weight or thickness	Hours[1,2]
Flank steak	½ inch	1½ to 2
Pieces for stew	1½-inch cubes	1½ to 2½
Pot roast, such as chuck or round	3 to 5 pounds	3 to 4
Short ribs	2 x 2 x 4 inches	1½ to 2½
Steak, such as chuck or round	¾ to 1 inch	1 to 1½

[1]Meat at refrigerator temperature at start of braising.
[2]Cooking time is for meat braised at simmering temperature. Time needed for braising in a pressure cooker is considerably shorter; follow pressure cooker manufacturer's directions.

SOURCE: *Beef and Veal in Family Meals: A Guide for Consumers*, Home and Garden Bulletin No. 118, United States Department of Agriculture, 1978.

The round, almost any part of it, is usually a good buy. You will often find some part of it on "special." The top round roast is the most tender part because it comes from the inside of the animal's leg. London broil comes from this. The bottom round roast is on the outside of the leg and is less tender. Swiss steaks, beef birds, or paupiettes come from this cut. The eye of the round is the

Roasting Tips

- Use a 325°F oven.
- Place meat, fat-side up, on a rack. Using a rack will increase heat circulation and keep the meat raised above the drippings.
- Use a shallow pan because it allows heat to circulate around the roast.
- Fill boned roasts with a stuffing for variety.
- Allow roasts to stand 15 to 20 minutes after removing them from the oven. Carving will be easier.

Approximate Roasting Times

Cut of meat	Approximate weight (pounds)	Hours[1,2] (325°F)
Rolled rib		
Rare	5 to 7	2⅔ to 3¾
Medium	5 to 7	3¼ to 4½
Well done	5 to 7	4 to 5⅔
Rolled rump		
(Choice grade)	4 to 6	2 to 2½
Sirloin tip		
(Choice grade)	3½ to 4	2⅓
	6 to 8	3½ to 4
Standing ribs[3]		
Rare	4 to 6	2¼ to 2½
Medium	4 to 6	2½ to 3⅓
Well done	4 to 6	2¾ to 4
Rare	6 to 8	2½ to 3
Medium	6 to 8	3 to 3½
Well done	6 to 8	3½ to 4¼

[1]Meat at refrigerator temperature at start of roasting.
[2]Cooking time is only approximate; a meat thermometer can be used to determine doneness. For rare, the internal temperature should be 140°F; for medium, 160°F; for well done, 170°F.
[3]Eight-inch cut. For 10-inch ribs, allow about 30 minutes less time.

SOURCE: *Beef and Veal in Family Meals: A Guide for Consumers*, Home and Garden Bulletin No. 118, United States Department of Agriculture, 1978.

least tender part of the round and perceived by many experts as the most overrated and most over-priced cut of the round. I cut up my own slices off the bottom round for Beef Paupiettes—easy and economical.

The rump roast and sirloin tip roast come from the part of the round that is closest to the short loin; sometimes they are considered part of the sirloin primal cut, depending on which way the butcher cuts them. These can be cooked with dry heat as roasts. Minute or breakfast steaks can be sliced off them. The sirloin tip—sometimes called the knuckle, the veiny, the triangle, round tip, or crescent—is boneless and a most versatile cut. From it you can cut kabobs or strips for Stroganoff or Sukiyaki. If you ever see a "full cut round" on sale, buy it! It contains the top round, bottom round, and the eye of the round.

While the round constitutes nearly 25 percent of the animal, the chuck makes up over 26 percent. This means these cuts are more readily available, and that they will probably be cheaper as a result. Of all the nine primal cuts of beef, chuck offers the most money-saving possibilities. Pot roasts, cross rib pot roasts, boneless cross rib roasts, stew meat, Swiss steaks, ground chuck, probably most of the beef we eat comes from the chuck. With the exception of the boneless cross rib roast, which is sold in the western part of the United States and which can be roasted with dry heat, all the cuts from the chuck require moist, slow cooking.

This section includes recipes using short ribs, oxtail, beef neck bones, chuck and sirloin tip roasts, minute steaks, bottom round steaks, chuck stew, and, of course, ground chuck.

Simmering Tips

- Brown meat, if desired.
- Add water to cover meat.
- Cover pan with a tight-fitting lid.
- Cook over low heat.

Approximate Simmering Times

Cut of meat	Approximate weight (pounds)	Hours[1]
Beef brisket or plate (fresh)	8	4 to 5
Beef shanks	4	3 to 4
Pieces for stew (1- to 2-inch pieces)		2½ to 3

[1]Meat at refrigerator temperature at start of simmering.

SOURCE: *Beef and Veal in Family Meals: A Guide for Consumers,* Home and Garden Bulletin No. 118, United States Department of Agriculture, 1978.

Suggested Home Storage Periods to Maintain High Quality in Beef

	Refrigerator (days)	Freezer (months)
Fresh		
Ground	1 to 2	3 to 4
Roasts	3 to 5	6 to 12
Steaks	3 to 5	6 to 12
Stew meat	1 to 2	3 to 4
Variety meats	1 to 2	3 to 4
Cooked		
Cooked beef and beef dishes	3 to 4	2 to 3
Gravy and meat broth	1 to 2	2 to 3

SOURCE: *Beef and Veal in Family Meals: A Guide for Consumers,* Home and Garden Bulletin No. 118, United States Department of Agriculture, 1978.

In two recipes, I simmered the short ribs first and then browned them last. In another recipe, I browned them first and simmered them afterwards. Both methods were successful, as was the slow cooker method, for this kind of cut.

Although I did sometimes find beef neck bones and oxtail for soups, it was not always easy to find soup bones. Shank was seldom available at all, and when it was, it was expensive. It must be that law of supply and demand working again. A butcher informed me that his supermarket no longer sold soup bones or soup meat as such. He suggested that I use short ribs, which I did for some soups. It is difficult to know which is the most economical, as the prices of oxtail and neck bones seem to fluctuate and sometimes there is more meat on these bones than at other times.

Whatever bones you use for soup, be sure to brown them and the meat before you start the beef stock. It is a good idea to brown the onions, celery, and carrots for the stock, too. This helps the flavor and color because it is a brown stock you are making. Cook the stock over very low heat for 3 or 4 hours, then cool and strain it. Of course, you will want to save any meat which comes off the bones for the soup. Let the fat harden on top of the stock and discard it. Then store stock in the refrigerator.

Since grinding tough meat tenderizes it, the part of the animal from which a butcher's ground beef is taken is not significant. Too little fat in ground meat causes it to be dry and to have less flavor, so in my opinion, neither ground round nor ground sirloin is desirable. So-called "lean beef," which is sold in some stores, is often ground beef with some lean bull meat added to it. Sometimes this is labelled "ground chuck" or, with a little more bull meat added, "ground round." There's nothing wrong with bull meat, but I think the label should identify it honestly. The only ways to be sure what part of what animal your ground meat comes from are to grind it yourself or else buy the cut whole and watch the butcher do it.

Since stretching meat is what this book is all about, and since beef seems to be our favorite meat to stretch, I used my imagination in finding a variety of "stretchers" for ground beef. Recipes for meatballs and meat loaves use raw and cooked potatoes, buckwheat groats, mushrooms, soy grits, rice, oatmeal, wheat germ, raw turkey, raw beef heart, raw pork, and raw liver. I hope my discoveries inspire you to do some experimenting on your own.

Glossary of Meat Cookery Terms

Braise: to cook in steam which is trapped in a tightly covered container. The source of the steam is added liquid or the meat's own juices.

Broil: to cook by direct heat from a flame, electric unit, or glowing coals. Meat is cooked on one side at a time.

Pan Broil: to cook in an uncovered pan over low direct heat. Fat is drained off as it accumulates and meat is turned only when necessary.

Pan Fry: to cook meat with a small amount of fat in an uncovered pan over direct heat.

Pot Roast: to braise large cuts of meat. Pot roasting is done either in the oven or on top of the stove.

Roast: to cook by hot air in an uncovered pan and without liquid. Roasting is usually done in the oven.

Barbecue Sauce

2	tablespoons oil
½	cup water
1½	cups tomato juice
¼	cup cider vinegar
½	cup lemon juice
2	tablespoons tamari soy sauce
¼	cup honey

1	cup Tomato Catsup (see Index)
½	teaspoon paprika
¼	teaspoon black pepper
1	teaspoon dry mustard
1	teaspoon chili powder
1	medium-size onion, grated

Short Ribs

4	pounds beef short ribs
2	medium-size onions, cut into chunks
2	celery stalks, cut into chunks

1	carrot, cut into chunks
1	bay leaf
1	small bunch parsley

Cumin Potatoes

6	baking potatoes
6 to 8	tablespoons oil
cumin seeds	

1. Combine all intredients for barbecue sauce in a 1-quart bowl. Mix well and set aside.

2. Cover short ribs with water in a 5-quart pot. Add onions, celery, carrot, bay leaf, and parsley. Cover and simmer over medium-low heat for 1 hour. Preheat oven to 350°F.

3. While short ribs are simmering, prepare cumin seed potatoes. Slice unpeeled potatoes about 1-inch thick. Coat slices with oil, place them in a 13 x 9 x 2-inch baking pan, and sprinkle with cumin seeds. Set aside.

4. Remove short ribs from pot. Cut them into 6 equal portions and place them in a 13 x 9 x 2-inch roasting pan. Brush the barbecue sauce on all sides of the ribs. Bake for 1¼ hours, brushing ribs with more sauce every 15 minutes and turning them over after the first 30 minutes.

5. Bake cumin potatoes along with short ribs (1¼ hours). Serve with extra barbecue sauce.

Serves 6

6	cups cubed cooked potatoes	¼	teaspoon black pepper
2	cups diced cooked beef	¾	teaspoon dry mustard
9	green onions, sliced	1½	teaspoons dill weed
¾	cup coarsely chopped green peppers	⅓	cup chopped parsley
¾	cup coarsely chopped celery	3	hard-cooked eggs
½	cup oil		salad greens
¾	cup wine vinegar	1	cup Mayonnaise (see Index)
1	tablespoon honey	1	tablespoon Tomato Catsup (see Index)

1. Combine potatoes, beef, onions, green peppers, and celery in a 3-quart bowl.

2. Mix oil, wine vinegar, honey, and seasonings in a 1-pint bowl and pour over potato-beef mixture. Add parsley and toss lightly. Set aside at room temperature for at least 1 hour.

3. Before serving, coarsely chop 1½ hard-cooked eggs and add to salad. Mix lightly. Place in a salad bowl lined with the greens. Slice the remaining hard-cooked eggs and arrange them over the top of the salad.

4. Combine mayonnaise and catsup in a 1-pint bowl. Transfer to a serving dish. Serve salad accompanied by the dressing.

Serves 6

Beef Mushroom Burgers

1	pound ground chuck	6	tablespoons wheat germ
2	cups finely chopped mushrooms	¼	teaspoon black pepper
¼	cup tomato sauce	2	tablespoons oil

1. In a 2-quart bowl, combine ground chuck, mushrooms, tomato sauce, wheat germ, and black pepper. Blend well and form into 6 patties.

2. Heat oil in a large skillet and saute patties over medium-high heat until browned on both sides. Serve immediately.

Serves 6

1⅓	pounds beef from bottom round roast or top sirloin roast	10	tiny white onions
1	tablespoon cumin seeds	18	cherry tomatoes
½	cup lemon juice	12	chunks turnip, cut into 1-inch squares
1	garlic clove, crushed	18	chunks yellow summer squash, cut into 1-inch squares
⅛	teaspoon black pepper		
¼	cup water	6	water chestnuts, sliced in half
3	tablespoons oil	30	mushroom caps
18	small okra (or zucchini), cut into 1-inch squares	1	cup Beef Stock (see index)

1. Cut beef into 1-inch cubes.

2. Toast cumin seeds for several seconds in a dry, medium-sized skillet over medium-high heat, while stirring, until you can smell their rich aroma. Remove from heat.

3. In a 1-quart bowl, combine meat with toasted cumin seeds, lemon juice, garlic, black pepper, and water. Cover bowl and refrigerate for 12 to 24 hours.

4. In a large skillet, heat oil and saute all vegetables and mushrooms over medium-high heat for 1 to 2 minutes, turning vegetables to coat them evenly with the oil. Lift the mushroom caps out of the skillet and set aside.

5. Add stock and marinade to the skillet, cover, and steam over medium-low heat for 4 minutes. Lift vegetables out of the skillet and cool in a flat pan.

6. Preheat broiler. Pass skewers (5¼ inches in length) through beef, vegetables, and mushrooms alternately, fitting as many pieces on each skewer as possible. (Allow 3 kabobs per serving.) Place filled skewers in a 17¼ x 11½ x 2¼-inch shallow pan. Broil 6½ inches below the broiler unit for 4 minutes on each side, basting with the marinade as they are turned.

Serves 6

Remarks   Serve on a mound of cooked brown rice. Pour any remaining marinade from the broiler pan over the kabobs and rice.

1	bottom round roast (about 3¾ pounds)	1	large carrot, cut into ¼ x 3-inch sticks (about 27 sticks)
3	tablespoons Mustard (see Index)	1½	medium-size onions, cut into 9 wedges
2¼	cups soft whole grain bread crumbs	6	tablespoons rye flour or whole wheat flour
3	tablespoons chopped parsley	¼	cup oil
1	cup tomato juice	2	cups Beef Stock (see Index)
6	water chestnuts, halved and then thinly sliced	2	tablespoons cornstarch
		2	tablespoons cold water

1. Cut 9 slices, ¼-inch thick from the large end of the roast, cutting across the grain. The combined weight of the 9 slices should be about 30 ounces. Reserve what is left of the roast for future use in kabobs, stew, or steaks.

2. Trim off any fat and pound the slices, using a mallet, rolling pin, or the side of an ordinary saucer. Score the meat in both directions. The slices will look something like cubed steaks which have been through a meat tenderizing machine. (This pounding enlarges each slice and helps to tenderize the meat.)

3. Spread 1 teaspoon mustard over each slice.

4. Combine crumbs, parsley, and 6 tablespoons of the tomato juice. Put 2 tablespoons of this mixture at the widest end of the slice. Place about 2 teaspoons of water chestnut slices on top of crumbs, pressing them down. Then place three carrot sticks crosswise and then one wedge of onion on top of the stuffing.

5. Roll the beef slice as tightly as possible, starting at the stuffing end. Securely tie roll crosswise and lengthwise with string, to prevent the stuffing from falling out of the ends. Follow this procedure for each slice.

6. Dredge paupiettes in flour, patting off any excess flour. Brown in hot oil in a large skillet. Add stock and remaining tomato juice and simmer, covered, for 30 to 45 minutes, or until meat is tender.

7. Lift paupiettes out onto a platter, remove string, and keep warm. Dissolve cornstarch in water, add to stock, and stir until the liquid thickens. Pour sauce over paupiettes before serving.

Serves 6

1¼	pounds ground chuck	⅛	teaspoon black pepper
1½	cups cooked brown rice	6	tablespoons tomato sauce
¼	teaspoon allspice	2	tablespoons oil
¼	teaspoon mace		Tomato Catsup (see Index)

1. Combine chuck, rice, spices, and tomato sauce.

2. Knead mixture until well mixed. Then form into 6 patties.

3. Heat oil in a large skillet and brown patties over medium-low heat. Cover the skillet during the last minute of cooking time to be sure patties are cooked through. Serve with tomato catsup, if desired.

Serves 6

══════ Beef-Soy Stuffed Peppers ══════

6	tablespoons soy grits	1½	teaspoons basil
4	cups plus 2 tablespoons Beef Stock or Chicken Stock (see Index)	¾	teaspoon thyme
		¾	teaspoon paprika
		¾	teaspoon ground coriander
1	tablespoon oil	¼	teaspoon cinnamon
½	cup coarsely chopped onions	¼	teaspoon allspice
18	ounces ground chuck	6	medium-size green peppers
1½	cups cooked brown rice	3	tablespoons brown rice flour
¾	cup tomato sauce		

1. Combine soy grits and 1 cup plus 2 tablespoons stock in a 1-quart saucepan. Simer over medium heat for 3 minutes, stirring occasionally, until the stock is absorbed and the grits are soft. Set aside.

2. In a large skillet, heat oil and saute onions, then beef, until the pink has disappeared from the beef. Add the cooked soy grits, the rice, tomato sauce, herbs, and spices. Mix together well. Turn mixture out into a 2-quart bowl.

3. Cut green peppers in half, lengthwise. Cut out core, membrane, and seeds, keeping each half intact.

4. Fill each pepper half with beef-soy mixture, packing it in and rounding the top. Layer pepper halves in the skillet and pour in the remaining stock. Cover skillet and cook over medium-low heat for 10 minutes.

5. Move pepper halves to serving platter. Add the flour to the stock and cook until thickened. Pour sauce over peppers and serve.

Serves 6

Beef Short Ribs
with Acorn Squash

4	pounds beef short ribs	¼	teaspoon allspice
6	cups water	¼	teaspoon ground ginger
3	celery stalks with tops, cut into chunks	¼	teaspoon cinnamon
3	medium-size carrots, cut into chunks	2	tablespoons oil
4 or 5	sprigs parsley	4	tablespoons rye flour or whole wheat flour
1	bay leaf	3	tablespoons tamari soy sauce
2	medium-size onions	3	tablespoons tomato juice
3	acorn squash	1	tablespoon vinegar

1. Place short ribs and water in a 10-inch Dutch oven or 5-quart, heavy-bottom pot. Add celery, carrots, parsley, bay leaf, and 1 onion cut into chunks. Bring to a boil and simmer, covered, for 1 hour or until meat on ribs is fork-tender.

2. Cut each squash in half lengthwise, making 6 equal boat-shaped servings. Remove seeds.

3. When short ribs are fork-tender, lift them out of pot, place them in a shallow 17¼ x 11½ x 2¼-inch baking pan, and set aside. Strain stock from short ribs into a 2-quart saucepan, saving the vegetables. There should be about 3¾ cups stock. Chop vegetables coarsely and return to stock. Set aside.

4. Using the same pot in which short ribs were cooked, parboil squash pieces for 5 minutes, using as little water as possible. Drain and place squash in the baking pan. Sprinkle spices over squash. Preheat oven to 375°F.

5. Chop the remaining onion. Heat oil in a large skillet and brown the short ribs and chopped onion.

6. Place one portion of short ribs along with some onions on each piece of squash and bake for 30 minutes.

7. Beat flour into the vegetables and stock, using a wire whisk. (This works fine if stock is at room temperature.) Add tamari, tomato juice, and vinegar. Cook sauce until thickened.

8. Remove squash and short ribs from oven. Pour a little sauce over the ribs. Serve with the remaining sauce as an accompaniment.

Serves 6

6	tablespoons oil	3	cups thickly sliced carrots
1½	pounds chuck, cut into 1½-inch cubes	3	cups thickly sliced celery
2	cups coarsely chopped onions	3	cups mushroom halves or quarters
5	cups water	2	tablespoons cornstarch
2	bay leaves	¼	cup cold water
3	cups tomato juice		Potato Dumplings (see Index)

1. In a 5-quart Dutch oven or heavy-bottom pot, heat 2 tablespoons oil and brown beef cubes over medium-high heat. Add 1 cup onions and saute for about 1 minute. Then add water, bay leaves, and 1 cup tomato juice. Cover, reduce heat, and simmer stew for 2 hours or until tender.

2. In a large skillet, heat 2 tablespoons oil and saute remaining onions, carrots, and celery for about 2 minutes, stirring constantly. Then add to beef. Saute mushrooms in 2 tablespoons oil for 2 minutes and add to beef, along with remaining tomato juice. Simmer stew over low heat for 15 to 20 minutes or until vegetables are tender.

3. Dissolve cornstarch in water and add to stew, stirring until thickened. Serve with potato dumplings.

Serves 6

═══ Ginger Beef ═══

1	pound round steak	3	medium-size onions, sliced
¼	cup tamari soy sauce	3	cups sliced zucchini
2	tablespoons lemon juice	3	cups sliced yellow squash
2	tablespoons water	3	cups sliced mushrooms
3	garlic cloves, minced	1½	cups Beef Stock (see Index)
1	tablespoon minced ginger root	2	tablespoons cornstarch
6	tablespoons oil	6	tablespoons water

1. Cut beef across the grain into thin strips (about ½ x 2 inches).

2. Combine tamari, lemon juice, water, garlic, and ginger root in a 1-quart bowl. Marinate beef strips for 30 minutes.

3. Heat 2 tablespoons oil in a large skillet and saute beef strips over medium-high heat until pink disappears. Lift beef out of skillet and set aside.

4. Add remaining oil and saute onions, zucchini, squash, and mushrooms. Stir and toss constantly until vegetables are tender but still crisp.

5. Add stock, cover skillet, and cook for about 2 minutes.

6. Dissolve cornstarch in water and then add to skillet, stirring until thickened. Return beef to skillet, toss to combine, and serve immediately.

Serves 6

Black Bean Soup with Meatballs === 65

Soup

4	cups cooked black beans (about 2 cups dry)	6	cups Beef Stock (see Index)
4	cups tomato juice	½	cup lemon juice

Meatballs

6	ounces ground pork
10	ounces ground chuck
½	onion, grated
1	garlic clove, minced
¾	cup grated raw potato
¼	teaspoon ground ginger
⅛	teaspoon allspice
¼	teaspoon mace
⅛	teaspoon black pepper
3	tablespoons oat flour (rolled oats ground in a blender)

3	tablespoons buckwheat flour (buckwheat groats ground in a blender)
¼	cup raw wheat germ
1	egg
2	tablespoons lemon juice
1	tablespoon tamari soy sauce
2	tablespoons oil

1. In a blender, puree beans, tomato juice, and 2 cups of the stock in 2 batches.

2. Pour mixture into a 4-quart, heavy-bottom pot and heat over medium-low heat. Add remaining stock and lemon juice. While soup is simmering, make the meatballs.

3. Combine all meatball ingredients except the oil. Mix throroughly by hand.

4. Heat oil in a large skillet. Drop mixture by the teaspoonful into the skillet and brown on all sides. Then drop the meatballs into the simmering soup. Continue cooking over low heat, covered, for 30 minutes longer.

Serves 6

Stock

1	teaspoon oil	1	onion, cut into chunks
2	pounds beef short ribs	1	celery stalk with top, cut into
8	cups water		chunks

Borscht

1	pound beets (3 cups coarsely chopped)	2	teaspoons honey
½	cup tomato juice	¼	teaspoon dill weed
3	cups coarsely chopped cabbage (about ½ pound)	¼	teaspoon caraway seeds
		⅛	teaspoon black pepper
1	cup coarsely chopped onions	¼	cup raisins
¼	cup vinegar	¾ to 1	cup Yogurt (see Index)

1. In a medium-size skillet, heat oil and brown short ribs. Combine browned ribs, water, onion, and celery in a 4-quart soup pot and bring to a boil. Lower heat and simmer, covered, for 1½ hours or until meat is tender and comes away from the bones easily. Remove short ribs from pot. Cut meat into small pieces and set aside. Return bones to soup pot and continue to simmer stock while you prepare the borscht.

2. Scrub beets and cook in enough water to cover until tender. Measure beet liquid. If necessary, add enough stock to liquid to equal 1½ cups. Peel beets. Coarsely chop half of them (1½ cups) and place in a 3-quart, heavy-bottom pot. Place remaining beets in the container of a blender. Add tomato juice and beet liquid. Process for about 10 to 15 seconds or until beets are finely chopped. Empty contents of blender into the pot.

3. Place another 2 cups of stock into blender container. (Reserve remaining stock for future use.) Add half the cabbage and onions and process for 10 to 15 seconds or until cabbage is finely chopped. Add remaining cabbage and onions and process until all the vegetables are finely chopped. Empty contents of blender into pot.

4. Stir in beef, vinegar, honey, dill weed, caraway seeds, black pepper, and raisins. Bring to a boil, reduce heat, and simmer, covered, over low heat for 30 to 45 minutes or until cabbage is cooked and flavors are blended. Garnish each serving with a dollop of yogurt.

Serves 6

Buckwheat Meatballs with Greek Lemon Sauce

1¼	pounds ground chuck	4	tablespoons chopped parsley
½	cup light buckwheat groats	4	cups Chicken Stock or Beef
½	medium-size onion, minced		Stock (see Index)
3	garlic cloves, minced	1	tablespoon tamari soy sauce
1	tablespoon chopped mint or 1	1	tablespoon cornstarch
	teaspoon dried mint	1½	tablespoons lemon juice
⅛	teaspoon cinnamon	2	eggs, beaten
⅛	teaspoon ground cloves		

1. In a large bowl, combine ground chuck, buckwheat groats, onion, garlic, mint, cinnamon, and cloves with 3 tablespoons of the parsley and ⅓ cup stock. Mix well and form into meatballs about the size of a walnut.

2. Pour remaining stock into a 3-quart saucepan, season with tamari, and bring to a boil. Drop meatballs into stock and simmer, covered, until buckwheat at center of meatballs is tender (about 30 minutes).

3. Lift meatballs out of stock onto a platter and keep warm while making the sauce. Dissolve cornstarch in lemon juice, add eggs, and whisk slowly into simmering stock. Continue to cook over low heat until thickened, stirring constantly.

4. Pour sauce over meatballs. Garnish with the remaining chopped parsley.

Makes 30 meatballs

Hungarian Beef and Cauliflower Goulash

2	tablespoons oil	2	cups cooked tomatoes
1½	pounds chuck or bottom round,	3	pounds cauliflower, cut into 2-
	cut into 1-inch cubes		inch chunks
2	cups sliced onions	1	tablespoon cornstarch
4	teaspoons paprika	2	tablespoons cold water
2½	cups Beef Stock (see Index)	3	cups frozen peas

1. In a 5-quart Dutch oven or heavy-bottom pot, heat oil and brown beef and onions with paprika.

2. Stir in stock and tomatoes. Simmer, covered, over medium-low heat until meat is tender (about 1 hour).

3. Add cauliflower, cover, and cook for 5 to 10 minutes or until tender.

4. Dissolve cornstarch in water and stir into goulash. Add peas and cook about 2 minutes longer or until peas are done. Serve at once.

Serves 6

Stuffing

6	tablespoons butter		¼	teaspoon sage
½	cup chopped onions		¼	teaspoon marjoram
1	cup chopped celery		¼	teaspoon nutmeg
4	cups soft whole grain bread crumbs		⅛	teaspoon black pepper
			1	cup chopped cranberries
¼	teaspoon rosemary		2	teaspoons honey
¼	teaspoon thyme		½	cup Beef Stock (see Index)

Pot Roast

4 pounds boneless beef pot roast
2 tablespoons oil
2 cups Beef Stock (see Index)

Cranberry Sauce Gravy

3	cups cranberries		¼	cup cornstarch
2¼	cups water		3	cups Beef Stock (see Index)
½	cup honey			

1. In a large skillet, melt butter and saute onions, celery, and bread crumbs until vegetables are soft. Add herbs, spices, chopped cranberries, honey, and ½ cup stock. Mix well and set aside.

2. Make a deep pocket in the roast by cutting through the thickness from one side, leaving about an inch of the roast intact along the other side and at the ends.

3. Pack the stuffing into the pocket evenly and tie the roast together securely with clean string.

4. Heat oil in a 5-quart Dutch oven or heavy-bottom pot over medium-high heat and brown the roast on both sides. Add 2 cups stock, cover, and simmer over low heat for 1½ hours until meat is fork-tender.

5. While meat is cooking, make the cranberry gravy. Combine cranberries, 2 cups of the water, and honey in a 2-quart saucepan. Cover and simmer for 10 minutes or until all berries have popped. Set aside.

6. Transfer roast to carving board and keep warm. Dissolve cornstarch in remaining ¼ cup water and add to liquid in pot. Then add 3 cups beef stock and stir until thickened. Add 2 cups of the cranberry mixture to the gravy.

7. To serve, remove string from roast and carve into ½-inch slices. The stuffing will be in the center of each slice. Serve with the gravy.

Serves 6

Italian Beef Balls and Greens Casserole

Italian Sauce and Greens

4	teaspoons cornstarch		2	teaspoons basil
2	cups tomato juice		6	cups coarsely chopped spinach
3	cups cooked tomatoes, drained			(or Swiss chard or endive or
½	cup finely chopped onions			dandelion greens)
4	teaspoons vinegar		2	cups coarsely chopped
2	teaspoons honey			watercress

Beef Balls

1	pound ground chuck		2	tablespoons chopped parsley
2	cups soft whole grain bread		¼	teaspoon oregano
	crumbs		¼	teaspoon allspice
2	eggs		¼	teaspoon nutmeg
½	cup finely chopped onions		¼	teaspoon dry mustard
2	garlic cloves, minced		2	tablespoons oil
¼	cup milk			

1. In a small bowl, dissolve cornstarch in tomato juice. Combine tomatoes, onions, vinegar, honey, and basil in a 2-quart, heavy-bottom saucepan. Stir in the cornstarch mixture. Bring to a boil, reduce heat, and simmer for 15 minutes. Set aside.

2. Trim, wash, and chop greens. Leave to drain.

3. In a 2-quart bowl, combine all beef ball ingredients except oil. Blend mixture by hand until soft and "fluffy."

4. Rinse hands in cold water and form mixture into 1-inch balls, making 48 balls in all. Preheat oven to 350°F.

5. Layer half the greens in the bottom of a 3-quart casserole.

6. In a large skillet, heat the oil and brown beef balls as you form them. As balls are browned, transfer them to the casserole, making a layer of balls over the greens. Pour half the Italian sauce over the beef balls. Layer the remaining greens over this, then the remaining beef balls and sauce.

7. Cover casserole tightly and bake for 20 to 30 minutes until contents of casserole are bubbling.

Serves 6

Salad

2	tablespoons oil	½	cup chopped celery
8	cups boiling water	2	cups cooked corn
2	cups whole grain corn pasta shells (6 ounces) or whole wheat elbow macaroni	3	cups shredded romaine lettuce (about 1 small head)
1	pound ground chuck	2	cups grated medium-sharp cheddar cheese (about ½ pound)
2	garlic cloves, minced		
4	green onions, finely sliced	1	tablespoon chili powder
¾	cup chopped green peppers	1	teaspoon ground cumin
2	cups chopped tomatoes	1	teaspoon oregano

Salad Dressing

¾	cup Mayonnaise (see Index)	3	tablespoons oil
½	cup Yogurt (see Index)	3	tablespoons vinegar
¼	cup Tomato Catsup (see Index)		

1. Add oil to boiling water. Drop in pasta and boil over high heat, uncovered, for 13 to 15 minutes or until tender. Be sure all pasta separates during the cooking. Drain and then rinse with cold water.

2. Brown beef with garlic in a large dry skillet just until pink disappears. Drain and discard excess fat drippings.

3. In a 3-quart bowl, combine beef and garlic with remaining salad ingredients.

4. Combine all salad dressing ingredients in a small bowl and pour over salad. Toss gently.

Serves 6

Mexican Black Beans, Corn, and Beef

3	tablespoons oil		2	cups cooked corn
2	medium-size onions, minced		2	cups cooked tomatoes, drained
4	garlic cloves, minced		¼	cup Tomato Catsup (see Index)
1	cup chopped green peppers		¼	cup molasses
3	tablespoons ground cumin		2	tablespoons lemon juice
2½	cups cooked beef strips			
4	cups cooked black beans (about 2 cups dry)			

1. In a large skillet, heat oil and saute onions, garlic, and green peppers until onions are soft, adding the cumin during the sauteing process.

2. Stir in the beef, beans, corn, and tomatoes.

3. Add the catsup, molasses, and lemon juice. Simmer, covered, for 10 minutes and serve.

Serves 6

Remarks   This is a good dish to serve when you have leftover roast beef on hand.

Middle-Eastern Stuffed Eggplant

1¼	pounds ground chuck		3	tablespoons tomato paste
3	garlic cloves, minced		1	tablespoon chopped mint or ½ teaspoon dried mint
½	cup finely chopped green peppers		2	eggplants (about 2¼ pounds total weight)
½	teaspoon allspice		3	cups cooked tomatoes
½	teaspoon cinnamon			
⅛	teaspoon black pepper			

1. In a large skillet, brown meat with garlic and green peppers until meat is no longer pink. Drain and discard any excess fat drippings. Add spices, tomato paste, and mint. Set aside.

2. Cut each eggplant into six wedges, lengthwise, and then slit each wedge lengthwise, making a pocket. Steam eggplant for 4 minutes in a covered 3-quart saucepan, using as little water as possible. Drain.

3. Place eggplant wedges skin-side down in a 17¼ x 11½ x 2¼-inch baking pan. Stuff pockets with meat mixture and pour tomatoes over the top.

4. Bake in 350°F oven for 30 to 40 minutes until eggplant is tender. It is not necessary to preheat oven.

Serves 6

½	cup dried lima beans, soaked overnight in enough water to cover	½	cup sliced carrots
		½	cup sliced celery
		2	cups sliced zucchini
4 to 5	tablespoons olive oil	2	cups shredded cabbage
1½	pounds meaty beef neck bones	1	cup cooked tomatoes
7	cups water	¾	cup tomato sauce
1	cup coarsely chopped onions	2	tablespoons Tomato Catsup (see Index)
½	cup whole wheat elbow macaroni		
		1	tablespoon honey
3	cups boiling water	½	teaspoon basil
2	garlic cloves, minced	¼	teaspoon oregano

Garnish

¼   cup chopped parsley
¼   cup grated Parmesan cheese

1. Drain lima beans and discard soaking water.

2. In a 5-quart Dutch oven or heavy-bottom pot, heat 2 tablespoons olive oil and brown beef neck bones over medium-high heat. Add the drained beans, 7 cups fresh water, and ½ cup of the onions. Cover pot and bring to a boil. Reduce heat and simmer for 2½ to 3 hours or until beef comes away from the bones easily and lima beans are tender. Remove neck bones and separate meat from bones. Discard bones and return meat to soup pot.

3. In a 1½-quart saucepan, cook macaroni in boiling water for 20 minutes or until tender. Drain and set aside.

4. In a large skillet, heat 1 tablespoon olive oil and saute remaining onions, garlic, carrots, and celery for about 2 minutes. Add them to the soup pot. Saute zucchini and cabbage for 2 minutes, adding more olive oil if necessary, and then add to the soup pot. Stir in the cooked macaroni, tomatoes, tomato sauce, catsup, honey, basil, and oregano. Garnish with chopped parsley and Parmesan cheese before serving.

Serves 6

Russian Cabbage Soup ========73

2	tablespoons oil	3½	cups shredded white cabbage (about 9 ounces)
3	pounds oxtail		
1	medium-size onion, cut into chunks	3½	cups shredded red cabbage (about 9 ounces)
2	celery stalks with tops, cut into chunks	1	cup cooked tomatoes
		1	cup tomato juice
1	large carrot, cut into chunks	12	prunes
9	cups water	¼	cup raisins
2	tablespoons butter	2	teaspoons honey
2	cups sliced onions	2	tablespoons lemon juice
1	cup coarsely chopped celery		

1. In a 5-quart Dutch oven or heavy-bottom soup pot, heat oil and brown oxtail, then onions, celery, and carrots. Add water and bring to a boil. Reduce heat and simmer, covered, for 2 hours until meat is very tender.

2. Strain stock and set it aside. Remove meat from bones and cut into small pieces.

3. In the same 5-quart pot, melt butter and saute onions, celery, and cabbage until cabbage has wilted. Add 4 cups oxtail stock, the meat, tomatoes, tomato juice, prunes, and raisins. Cover and simmer 25 to 30 minutes. Before serving, add honey and lemon juice. Serve 2 prunes in each portion of soup.

Serves 6

Crepes

4	eggs	¾	cup cornmeal
1	cup milk	¾	cup rye flour
1	cup water	2 to 4	tablespoons oil

Filling

3	tablespoons oil	1¼	cups bean liquid
2	garlic gloves, minced	¾	cup tomato juice
4	cups cooked pinto beans	3	tablespoons vinegar
1	teaspoon ground cumin	1	cup finely chopped cooked beef
1	teaspoon chili powder		Hot Pepper Sauce (see Index)
¼	teaspoon cayenne pepper		

1. Combine crepe ingredients with 2 tablespoons oil in the container of a blender and process until smooth.

2. Generously oil an 8-inch skillet or crepe pan and heat over medium-high heat. Wipe out excess oil with paper towel. Pour ¼ cup of crepe batter into the pan, tilting it so as to spread batter evenly.

3. When crepe is nicely brown underneath, (about 40 to 45 seconds), flip crepe over, using a pancake turner, and brown the reverse side for about 30 seconds. Remove crepe, cover with a damp towel, and place in a warm oven until ready to fill.

4. Repeat steps 2 and 3 until all batter is used, re-oiling pan if necessary and wiping out any excess oil with paper towels. Crepes may be stacked one on top of the other.

5. To make filling, heat oil in a large skillet. Add garlic, then add the beans and mash them in the skillet with a potato masher.

6. Stir in spices, bean liquid, tomato juice, and vinegar, stirring constantly. Add the beef and mix well.

7. Place about 3 tablespoons of filling in the center of each crepe and fold both sides toward the center over filling.

8. Heat hot pepper sauce and pour a little over the crepes. Serve immediately with extra hot pepper sauce.

Makes 20 crepes (6 inches long) and 4 cups filling

Remarks   This is an excellent way to use up a small amount of leftover roast beef.

Spaghetti and Untomato Meat Sauce

1	pound beets	¼	cup lemon juice
½	pound carrots	2	teaspoons honey
Beef Stock (see Index)		1	teaspoon oregano
1 to 2	tablespoons oil	1	teaspoon basil
1	pound ground chuck	½	teaspoon mace
1	cup coarsely chopped onions	¼	teaspoon allspice
2	garlic cloves, minced	⅛	teaspoon black pepper
¼	cup light buckwheat flour (buckwheat groats ground in blender)	4	quarts water
		1	pound whole wheat spaghetti

1. Scrub beets and carrots and then cut them into chunks. Cook each vegetable in separate 2-quart saucepans in enough water to cover until tender. (There should be about 2¼ cups of each vegetable and 2¼ cups of the combined liquids after cooking. If necessary, add beef stock to the liquid to equal 2¼ cups.)

2. While vegetables are cooking, heat oil in a 3-quart, heavy-bottom pot and saute beef, onions, and garlic until meat is no longer pink. Drain and discard any excess fat drippings. Stir in flour and set aside.

3. Puree the beets, carrots, and their cooking waters in a blender. Pour puree into pot with beef mixture and heat slowly. Stir occasionally. Add lemon juice, honey, herbs, and spices, and simmer, covered, for 15 to 20 minutes.

4. Bring water to a boil in a 6-quart pot, add 1 tablespoon oil, then drop in spaghetti, stirring to keep strands separated. Boil, uncovered, for 15 to 20 minutes until tender. Drain and serve topped with the meat sauce.

Serves 6

1	pound ground chuck	1	tablespoon chili powder
1	medium-size onion, finely chopped	¼	cup brown rice flour
		2	cups tomato juice
1	cup finely chopped green peppers	¾	cup cornmeal
		2	tablespoons rye flour
2	cups cooked tomatoes	1½	teaspoons baking powder
2	cups frozen corn	1	egg
1	teaspoon ground cumin	6	tablespoons milk
¼	teaspoon cayenne pepper	1	tablespoon oil

1. In a large skillet, brown beef until pink disappears. Drain and discard any excess fat drippings.

2. Stir in onions, green peppers, tomatoes, corn, and spices. Dissolve brown rice flour in tomato juice and add to mixture. Cover skillet and simmer over low heat for 5 minutes.

3. Turn mixture out into a 3-quart casserole. Preheat oven to 425°F.

4. In a 1-pint mixing bowl, combine cornmeal, rye flour, and baking powder. Mix together egg, milk, and oil in another 1-pint bowl. Stir wet ingredients into dry ones, mixing well, and pour batter evenly over beef mixture in casserole. Bake for 20 to 25 minutes or until the cornbread is done.

Serves 6

══════════ **West African Groundnut Stew** ══════════

2	tablespoons oil	2	cups cooked tomatoes, drained
1	pound chuck or bottom round, cut into 1-inch cubes	2	teaspoons cornstarch
		½	teaspoon cayenne pepper
1	medium-size onion, chopped	1	cup unsalted ground peanuts (groundnuts)
5	cups Beef Stock (see Index)		
2	cups coarsely chopped green peppers	¼	cup peanut butter
		2	cups frozen peas
2	cups coarsely chopped celery		

1. Heat oil in a large skillet or a 3-quart, heavy-bottom pot and brown beef and onions. Add 4 cups stock and simmer, covered, until meat is tender (about 1 to 1½ hours).

2. Add green peppers, celery, and tomatoes and simmer, covered, 5 minutes longer.

3. Combine remaining 1 cup stock with cornstarch, cayenne pepper, ground peanuts, and peanut butter and add to simmering stew. Stir until thickened.

4. Stir in peas and simmer, covered, for 5 minutes.

Serves 6

Turkish Prune, Barley, and Beef Soup

1	teaspoon oil	½	cup coarsely chopped onions
2	pounds beef short ribs	1	cup coarsely chopped celery
10	cups water	1	cup coarsely chopped turnips
1	onion, cut into chunks	¼	teaspoon allspice
1	celery stalk with top, cut into chunks	¼	teaspoon cinnamon
½	cup barley	¼	teaspoon paprika
18	prunes	4	teaspoons lemon juice
		¼	cup chopped parsley

1. In a medium-size skillet, heat oil and brown short ribs. Combine browned ribs, water, onion, and celery in a 4-quart soup pot and bring to a boil. Reduce heat and simmer, covered, for 1½ hours or until meat is tender and comes away from the bones easily. Remove short ribs from pot. Cut meat into small pieces and set aside. Discard bones. Strain stock and set aside.

2. Wash and dry the skillet and toast barley over medium-high heat, stirring constantly, for about 1 minute or until the barley begins to darken. Then place in a blender and process until barley resembles coarse meal.

3. Place 3 cups of the stock in a 2-quart saucepan. (Reserve the remaining stock for future use.) Add prunes, barley meal, onions, celery, turnips, and spices. Cover and simmer over medium heat for 20 to 25 minutes or until barley is soft. Remove pits from prunes, then return prunes to pot. Add meat and simmer 5 minutes longer. Stir in lemon juice and parsley before serving.

Serves 6

Pork

Pork, after poultry, is the most economical meat available today. It also is a meat which lends itself to a great variety of preparations. If you instinctively reach out for the pork chops or spareribs when you approach the pork section in your market, expand your horizons and save yourself some money! With a little adventuring and a good sharp boning knife, you can make quick work of a picnic shoulder or blade roast and reduce it to versatile, valuable cubes of meat, ready for stewing, grinding, stir-frying, or kabobs.

I boned my first picnic shoulder while developing these recipes, and I assure you that it's within your capabilities, too. I didn't need a saw, just a good boning knife. You have to remove the skin and some fat first. The skin can be boiled with a pot of beans for that down-home flavor that comes no other way, or with a mess of collards or turnip greens. The fat can be saved and stored in your freezer for sausage-making.

Once the skin is off, you remove the hock (the pig's ankle). Wiggle the hock to find the joint and then cut right through to that point where the hock is joined to the arm bone. There is a small space between the bones. To remove the arm bone, cut down to and along the bone from one end to the other. Then cut around the bone and lift it out. Pork bones make good stock for your pork entrees. The somewhat sweet flavor of pork stock is prized by Chinese chefs for seafood dishes. To make pork stock, follow the recipe for Beef Stock (see Index).

If you want to serve thrifty pork cutlets instead of expensive chops, cut the larger muscles of the shoulder across the grain into slices to be breaded or sauteed. A picnic shoulder weighs between 4 and 6 pounds, and I found I could feed 14 people from a 5¾ pound roast, allowing ¼ pound per person. Divide the price of that size roast by 14 and you will see how little that meal costs per person. These cuts are priced extremely low at times. Fresh picnics are on "special" from time to time and you would be smart to buy one when you see it. Select one with lots of firm, fine-textured, lean meat and little fat and bone. The color of its flesh should be greyish pink to red.

If you prefer, you can simply roast the picnic shoulder in a 325°F oven, allowing 45 minutes to the pound. The skin will come off more easily and you can serve the roast and use what you need for the immediate meal, then bone what is left, divide it into portions, and freeze or refrigerate it to be used for casseroles, pilaf, hash, or pork and beans. Cooked pork can be stored in a refrigerator for up to 4 days; it will keep in the freezer for 3 months.

Whatever the method you use to cook pork, cook it slowly and thoroughly. Cook it slowly because pork, like all meat, can toughen and dry out at too high a temperature. If you brown pork chops, add a little stock or water, cover the skillet, and turn down the heat—I promise you, the chops won't be dry. Or, if you are roasting a pork butt, cover the roasting pan after adding a little stock or water to it, set the oven at 325°F and allow 30 to 45 minutes to the pound. You will have a succulent, tender roast.

Pork Must Be "Done"—How to Be Sure It Is

A meat thermometer helps take the guesswork out of meat cookery and assures you of safety where pork is concerned. We are all aware of the danger of trichinosis from eating undercooked pork. This disease nowadays is a clinical rarity in man but, because our government still does not require systematic microscopic inspection of pork, we would do well to take the precaution of making absolutely sure that any pork we eat has been sufficiently cooked. The trichina parasite is destroyed at 137°F, so the internal temperature of the pork must be at least that high. But for optimum flavor and juiciness, the correct internal temperature for fresh pork should reach 170°F. Many recipes continue to call for an internal temperature of 185°F, but this is not really necessary. Another way to test meat for doneness is to make a small cut in the meat next to

Timetable for Roasting Pork

Cut of meat[1]	Approximate weight (pounds)	Hours[2,3] (325°F)
Fresh		
Ham	12 to 16	5½ to 6
Ham, boneless, rolled	10 to 14	4⅔ to 5½
Loin, center cut	3 to 5	2 to 3⅓
Shoulder, Boston butt	4 to 6	3 to 4
Shoulder, Boston butt, boneless, rolled	3 to 5	2¼ to 3¼
Shoulder, picnic	5 to 8	3 to 4
Shoulder, picnic, boneless, rolled	3 to 5	2 to 3
Spareribs	3 to 4	2

[1]All cuts of meat listed in the table contain bone unless specified otherwise.
[2]Meat at refrigerator temperature at start of roasting.
[3]Cooking time is only approximate; a meat thermometer can be used to determine doneness. All pork should be cooked until the internal temperature reads 170°F.

SOURCE: *Pork in Family Meals: A Guide for Consumers*, Home and Garden Bulletin No. 160, United States Department of Agriculture, 1977.

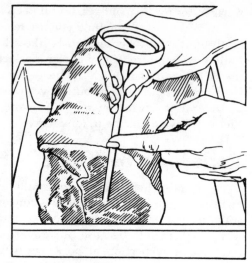

Place meat thermometer near the center of a roast and in the thickest part of the meat. The thermometer should not touch either bone or fat. This illustration shows one way to estimate how deep to insert the thermometer.

the bone or thickest part of the roast. If the juice that runs out is clear, it usually means the roast is done. If there is any pinkness or evidence of blood in the juice, the roast needs more cooking. Cooked pork flesh should be white or greyish, especially at the center of a large roast.

One more word of caution before we leave this subject. Never taste even a tiny bit of raw pork, bacon, or sausage, and make sure to wash your hands and to scrub with soap and hot water any knife, utensil, board, or surface which the raw pork has touched.

Pork butt and pork shoulder blade roasts are the next best buys after the picnic shoulder. Pork butt is from the shoulder and is sometimes called a Boston butt. It has a higher proportion of fat to meat and for this reason is marvelous for making sausage. (A fatless sausage is a dry, juiceless sausage.) Making your own sausage may seem to be complicated and difficult, but it really isn't, and if you are so inclined, it can be a lot of fun. This chapter provides meat-stretching recipes for sausage as well as instructions and information about equipment. You can save money and cut down on salt and other preservatives if you make your own sausage. Because fresh sausage can become rancid quickly, keep it for only 1 to 2 days in the refrigerator or 1 to 2 months in the freezer.

For soups such as split pea or lentil, or if you want to flavor a pot of beans, pork neck bones offer a better choice, to my way of thinking, than hocks or pigs' feet. There is very little meat on the feet and not a great deal on some hocks. And the hocks are a lot more expensive than the neck bones. Any cut of pork can be cooked on top of the stove if you prefer. It can be pot-roasted just like beef—browned first and then cooked in a Dutch oven with some stock or fruit juice. (See Beef chapter for braising tips.) In Sweden it is traditional to cook the dried peas right along with the pork shoulder blade roast in water with seasonings. Then the soup is served accompanied by slices of the pork.

You will notice that no recipes are included for ham, bacon, or smoked sausage. There is good reason for this. Sodium nitrite, which is widely used in the curing of these products, has been implicated as a carcinogen (cancer-causing substance). The USDA is now monitoring the use of nitrites with the idea of phasing out their use sometime in the future. Until that time comes, the sensible thing is to avoid the consumption of cured meats.

Best Buy — Blade End Loin

When it comes to pork loin, the part of the loin known as the blade end roast is apt to be one of the best pork buys at almost any time of year. The blade end is the end of the loin toward the front of the pig. Country-style spareribs are cut from this. The sirloin (next to the hind leg or ham), though leaner, does have a good proportion of bone and so is not very economical. The center of the loin is the least economical of all. This is where the premium pork chops come from. The quality of the meat is much the same from one end of the loin to the other, except the blade end has more fat but less bone than the sirloin end. Using your boning knife, you can work some magic with the blade end.

To make it worth your time, select two of the largest blade end roasts you can find and try to get them about the same size. The more ribs on them, the better. And if the backbone hasn't been cracked already, ask the butcher to do it for you.

Now place each roast, backbone down, on your board. Above the meaty portion on one side of the roast, you will see a bone. That is the blade bone, part of the shoulder blade. Carefully cut around that and remove it. Then cut along the ribs and backbone, separating them from the meat. Now cut between each of the ribs, leaving meat on the bones, and you will be surprised to see that you have not just a pile of bones, but spareribs! And of course, you also have two

Timetable for Braising Pork

Cut of meat	Approximate weight or thickness	Hours[1,2]
Chops, rib or loin	¾ to 1½ inches	¾ to 1
Cubes	1 to 1¼ inches	¾ to 1
Spareribs	2 to 3 pounds	1½
Steaks, shoulder	¾ inch	¾ to 1

[1]Meat at refrigerator temperature at start of braising.
[2]Cooking time is for meat braised at simmering temperature.

SOURCE: *Pork in Family Meals: A Guide for Consumers*, Home and Garden Bulletin No. 160, United States Department of Agriculture, 1977.

Pork Cuts

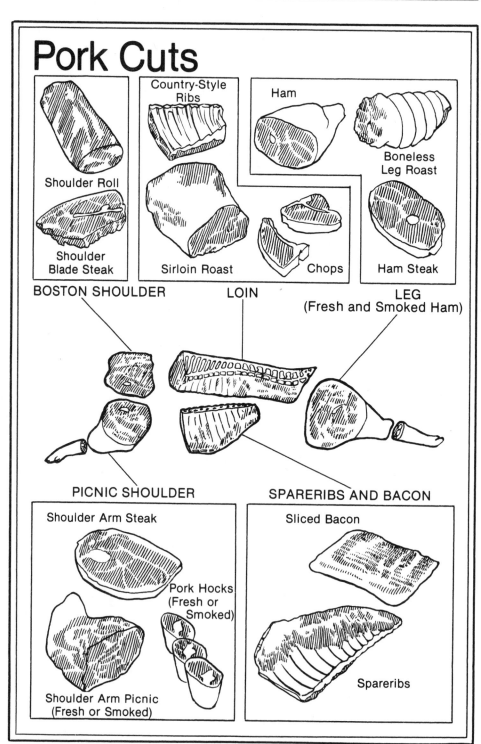

Shoulder Roll

Country-Style Ribs

Ham

Boneless Leg Roast

Shoulder Blade Steak

Sirloin Roast

Chops

Ham Steak

BOSTON SHOULDER

LOIN

LEG
(Fresh and Smoked Ham)

PICNIC SHOULDER

SPARERIBS AND BACON

Shoulder Arm Steak

Sliced Bacon

Pork Hocks
(Fresh or Smoked)

Shoulder Arm Picnic
(Fresh or Smoked)

Spareribs

Suggested Home Storage Periods to Maintain High Quality in Pork

	Refrigerator (days)	Freezer (months)
Fresh		
Chops	3 to 5	3 to 4
Roasts	3 to 5	4 to 8
Sausage	1 to 2	1 to 2
Variety meats	1 to 2	3 to 4
Cooked		
Cooked pork and pork dishes	3 to 4	2 to 3
Gravy and meat broth	1 to 2	2 to 3

SOURCE: *Pork in Family Meals: A Guide for Consumers,* Home and Garden Bulletin No. 160, United States Department of Agriculture, 1977.

nice pieces of boneless pork loin to roast for a festive occasion, saute as premium cutlets, or barbecue as kabobs, all for a modest price.

You can store raw pork roasts, chops, or stew meat in the refrigerator for up to 4 days if the pork is wrapped loosely so that air can get to it. Ground raw pork should only be refrigerated up to 2 days, so it is better to freeze it unless you plan to use it right away.

For those who love their spareribs and don't wish to do their own butchering, I have good news. I succeeded in stretching them in my recipes so that ½ pound of spareribs per person was ample instead of the usual allowance of 1 pound per person. I suggest parboiling the spareribs for 4 to 5 minutes before roasting, to save energy and to produce more tender meat.

I was delighted to learn that I could do just about everything with pork that is done with beef, and all for less money. Try the recipes for Orange-Braised Pork, Polynesian Pork Pilaf, and Pork Ragout with Cornmeal Dumplings and I know your "pork-horizon" will broaden as mine did.

Adobo
(Traditional dish
of the Philippines)

1½	pounds top loin pork roast	2	tablespoons water
2	garlic cloves, minced	2¼	cups brown rice
1	teaspoon slivered ginger root	4½	cups Chicken Stock (see Index)
1	bay leaf	1	cup finely chopped sweet red
1	teaspoon black pepper		peppers
2	tablespoons tamari soy sauce	1	cup frozen peas
½	cup vinegar		

1. Trim fat off pork and cut into 1½-inch cubes.

2. Combine garlic, ginger root, bay leaf, black pepper, tamari, vinegar, and water in a 2-quart saucepan. Add meat, coating it evenly with the marinade. Set aside for 2 to 3 hours.

3. An hour before the meal, bring meat and marinade to a simmer and cook, covered, over low heat for 45 minutes, until pork is tender.

4. While pork is simmering, combine rice and stock in a 2-quart, heavy-bottom pot. Bring to a boil, reduce heat, and simmer, covered, for 25 to 30 minutes or until rice is soft and stock is absorbed.

5. Five minutes before serving time, add red peppers and peas to meat mixture.

6. Pour off any liquid from meat and set liquid aside. Gently combine the meat-pepper mixture with the cooked rice, adding some of the liquid if desired. Serve immediately.

Serves 6

Polynesian Pork Pilaf

2	tablespoons oil	1½	cups chopped green peppers
1	cup sliced onions	1	cup unsweetened pineapple
3	cups cubed cooked pork		chunks, cut in halves
2	cups brown rice	½	cup raisins
4	cups Chicken Stock (see Index)	2	tablespoons minced ginger root

1. In a 5-quart, heavy-bottom pot, heat oil and saute onions until soft. Add pork, then rice. Stir thoroughly so that rice is evenly coated with the oil.

2. Add chicken stock, cover, and cook over low heat for 20 minutes.

3. Stir in green peppers, pineapple, raisins, and ginger. Cook, covered, for another 10 minutes or until rice is soft and stock is absorbed.

Serves 6

2	cups navy beans (about 1 pound)	6	tablespoons molasses
		3	tablespoons honey
1½	pounds pork with bone (pork loin roast, with 6 bony separate chops, is suitable)	1	tablespoon dry mustard
		3	tablespoons vinegar
		2	teaspoons tamari soy sauce
20	cups water	¾	cup thick tomato juice
½	cup coarsely chopped onions	2	cups Chicken Stock (see Index)

1. Soak beans for 8 hours in enough water to cover.

2. Roast pork in 325°F oven for 2 hours.

3. Drain beans and discard soaking water. Place beans in a 6-quart pot, add 8 cups water, and bring to a boil. Reduce heat and simmer, covered, for 30 minutes. Drain and discard cooking water. Add 12 cups water and bring beans to a boil again. Simmer for ½ to 1 hour or until soft. Drain and discard cooking water.

4. In a 3-quart casserole, mix beans with onions, molasses, honey, dry mustard, vinegar, tamari, and tomato juice. Add stock, submerge the pork in the mixture, cover casserole, and bake in 350°F oven for 1½ to 2 hours. Watch carefully and add more stock if necessary. Before serving, remove any bones from meat.

Slow Cooker Method

1. Roast pork, uncovered, in 325°F oven for 2 hours.

2. Cover beans with 8 cups water in a slow cooker. Cook on Low for 12 hours. Drain beans and discard cooking water.

3. Combine beans, onions, molasses, honey, dry mustard, vinegar, tamari, tomato juice, and 1 cup stock. Submerge the cooked pork in the bean mixture. Cook on Low for 12 hours. Remove bones from meat.

Serves 6

Remarks Discarding the soaking water and the cooking water after the beans have cooked for 30 minutes rids the beans of carbohydrates that can cause intestinal gas.

18	ounces Sausage, bulk (see Index)	1½	teaspoons baking powder
1½	cups buckwheat flour (buckwheat groats ground in blender)	3	egg yolks
		2	cups water
		1	tablespoon honey
¾	cup cornmeal	4 to 6	tablespoons oil
		3	egg whites

1. In medium-size skillet, brown sausage and set aside.

2. Combine flour, cornmeal, and baking powder in a 2-quart bowl.

3. In another 2-quart bowl, combine egg yolks, water, honey, and 2 tablespoons of the oil.

4. Beat egg whites until stiff but not dry. Stir wet ingredients into dry ones, add sausage, and gently fold in beaten egg whites.

5. Heat 2 tablespoons oil in a large skillet. Drop pancake batter into skillet by the tablespoonful and cook over medium-low heat. Turn pancakes when bubbles have formed over the surface and cook only a few seconds on the reverse side. Add more oil if necessary, but there should be no excess oil in the skillet. Keep pancakes in a warm oven until all the batter is used.

Serves 6

Remarks   Serve with warm Applesauce (see Index), if desired.

══════ Dilled Green Bean ══════ and Pork Casserole

3	tablespoons butter	½	teaspoon dill weed
¼	cup coarsely chopped onions	3	cups cubed cooked pork
6	tablespoons rye flour or whole wheat flour	4	cups cut cooked green beans (about 2 pounds)
1½	cups Yogurt (see Index)	1½	cups grated Swiss cheese
1½	cups sour cream	½	cup finely ground whole grain bread crumbs
4	teaspoons honey		

1. In a 2-quart saucepan, melt butter and saute onions. Stir in flour. Then add yogurt and sour cream. Stir until smooth. Cook over low heat, stirring constantly, until thickened. Add honey and dill weed.

2. Preheat oven to 350°F. In a 1½-quart casserole, arrange a layer of pork on the bottom, then a layer of green beans, and then a layer of 1¼ cups of the cheese. Pour the yogurt-sour cream sauce over this.

3. Mix the bread crumbs with the remaining ¼ cup grated cheese and sprinkle over the top of the casserole. Bake for 20 to 30 minutes or until bubbling and brown on top.

Serves 6

Farm Casserole 87

1	pound Sausage, bulk (see Index)	¼	cup Yogurt (see Index)
		1	teaspoon thyme
2	tablespoons oil	½	teaspoon sage
¼	cup finely chopped onions	4	cups cooked corn
1	cup finely chopped green peppers	2	cups cooked baby lima beans
		3	cups sliced tomatoes (4 to 5, medium-size)
2	tablespoons brown rice flour		
1	cup Chicken Stock (see Index)	½	cup whole grain bread crumbs
2	tablespoons cornstarch	1	tablespoon butter

1. Preheat oven to 350°F. Brown sausage meat in a medium-size skillet. Drain on paper towels and discard excess fat drippings.

2. In the same skillet, heat oil and saute onions and green peppers until onions are golden. Stir in flour, then stock. Combine cornstarch and yogurt and add to sauce, stirring until sauce has thickened. Add herbs.

3. Arrange a layer of corn in a 2-quart casserole, then a layer each of the sausage, the onions and pepper sauce, the lima beans, and the sliced tomatoes.

4. Sprinkle bread crumbs over the top and then dot with butter. Bake for 30 minutes.

Serves 6

Hot German Potato Salad

1¼	pounds Sausage, in casing (see Index)	1	cup pork stock or Chicken Stock (see Index)
2	pounds medium-size potatoes, quartered	6	tablespoons vinegar
		¼	cup chopped parsley
1	cup coarsely chopped onions	1	teaspoon caraway seeds
3	cups celery, cut crosswise on the slant into ½-inch slices		

1. Prick sausage with a fork to enable fat to escape during cooking. In a medium-size skillet, cook sausage in enough water to cover it halfway. Cover skillet and simmer for 10 minutes. Turn sausage over and simmer another 10 minutes. Discard excess water and fat drippings. Return skillet to low heat, uncovered, and brown sausage on both sides. Remove from heat. Drain sausage on paper towels and discard fat drippings. Cut sausage into ½-inch slices. There should be about 2 cups.

2. Cook potatoes until tender but not mushy. Drain and remove skins, unless the potatoes are new. Cut potatoes into ½-inch cubes. There should be about 4 cups.

3. In the same skillet used for the sausage, cook onions and celery in stock until celery is tender but firm. Add vinegar. Turn contents into a 3-quart mixing bowl. Add sausage, potatoes, parsley, and caraway seeds. Toss lightly and serve.

Serves 6

Sauce

2¼	cups unsweetened apple juice
½	cup honey
2	teaspoons dry mustard

4	teaspoons cider vinegar
1	pound winter pears, cored and sliced

Loaf

1	pound ground pork
1	pound ground beef
2	tablespoons grated onion
½	teaspoon dry mustard
½	teaspoon ground ginger
½	teaspoon allspice

3	eggs, beaten
⅓	cup brown rice flour
⅓	cup non-fat dry milk
1	teaspoon whole cloves
2	tablespoons cornstarch

1. In a 1-quart saucepan, combine 2 cups of the apple juice with honey, dry mustard, and vinegar. Reserve ¼ cup apple juice for later. Simmer for 10 minutes. Add pears, cover, and simmer the syrup 5 to 10 minutes or until pears are tender but still firm.

2. Meanwhile, combine pork, beef, onions, spices, eggs, flour, and non-fat dry milk in a 2-quart mixing bowl. Add ½ cup of the pear syrup and mix well.

3. Pack mixture into a 9½ x 5 x 3-inch loaf pan and insert the whole cloves over the surface of the meat loaf. Spoon ¼ cup syrup over loaf and bake in 350°F oven for 1¼ to 1½ hours. It is not necessary to preheat oven.

4. Dissolve cornstarch in reserved ¼ cup apple juice and add to simmering pears and syrup, stirring until thickened. Serve meat loaf with pear sauce.

Serves 6

======= Lentil Barley Soup =======

1½	pounds pork hocks
8	cups water
1	cup coarsely chopped onions
1	cup coarsely chopped celery
4	garlic cloves, minced
1	cup sliced carrots
½	cup barley

1½	cups lentils
1	teaspoon marjoram
1	teaspoon thyme
1	bay leaf
½	cup vinegar
¼	teaspoon black pepper

1. In a 5-quart Dutch oven or heavy-bottom pot, combine pork hocks, water, onions, celery, garlic, carrots, barley, lentils, and herbs. Bring to a boil and simmer, covered, for 1½ hours.

2. Just before serving, remove hocks. Separate skin and bones from meat; cut meat into smaller pieces and return to soup. Add vinegar and black pepper.

Yields 9 cups

Millet and Sausage Spoonbread 89

1½	cups water	6	tablespoons cornmeal
6	tablespoons millet	3	cups milk
¾	pound Sausage, bulk (see Index)	3	eggs, beaten
2	teaspoons olive oil	½	teaspoon oregano
⅓	cup coarsely chopped onions	¼	teaspoon ground coriander
½	cup coarsely chopped green peppers		

1. In the top portion only of a double-boiler, bring water to boil over medium-high heat. Stir in millet and bring to a boil again. Then set top portion on the bottom portion of double-boiler and cook millet, covered, over simmering water for 25 minutes over medium-low heat.

2. Form sausage into small balls (about ¾ inch in diameter) and brown in a large skillet over medium heat. When thoroughly cooked, drain sausage balls on paper towels and discard fat drippings.

3. In the same skillet, heat oil and saute onions and green peppers over medium-low heat for about 4 minutes.

4. In a 3-quart bowl, combine cooked millet, cornmeal, milk, and beaten eggs, in that order. Add sausage, onions and peppers, oregano, and coriander. Turn into an oiled 3-quart casserole and bake in a 325°F oven for 45 minutes to 1 hour or until a knife inserted into center comes out clean. It is not necessary to preheat oven.

Serves 6

Orange-Braised Pork

1½	pounds boneless pork from picnic shoulder	¼	cup honey
2½	cups orange juice	2	teaspoons wine vinegar
2	cups Beef Stock or Chicken Stock (see Index)	½	teaspoon ground ginger
1	teaspoon tamari soy sauce	¼	teaspoon dry mustard
1	garlic clove, minced	3	tablespoons oil
		1	tablespoon cornstarch
		2	tablespoons cold water

1. Remove skin from pork shoulder and trim fat. Cut meat into ¾-inch cubes.

2. In a 2-quart bowl, combine orange juice, stock, tamari, garlic, honey, wine vinegar, and spices. Marinate pork cubes in this mixture for 2 hours.

3. Drain pork cubes, reserving marinade. In a large skillet, heat oil and saute pork until browned. Add marinade, cover, and simmer over low heat for 30 to 45 minutes or until pork is tender.

4. Dissolve cornstarch in water and add to pork. Stir until liquid has thickened.

Serves 6

¾ pound Sausage, bulk (see
Index)
2 cups Chicken Stock or Beef
Stock (see Index)
3 cups diced rutabaga (or turnips)
2 cups sliced celery
½ cup coarsely chopped onions
2 tablespoons butter
¾ cup oat flour (rolled oats ground
in blender)

1 teaspoon water
2 teaspoons tamari soy sauce
¼ cup chopped parsley
½ teaspoon allspice
½ teaspoon cinnamon
2 hard-cooked eggs, coarsely
chopped

1. Form sausage into ½-inch balls. In a large skillet, saute sausage balls in their own fat over medium heat, taking care to brown them evenly. Drain sausage balls on paper towels.

2. Combine stock, rutabaga, celery, and onions in a 3-quart, heavy-bottom saucepan. Cook, covered, for 15 to 20 minutes or until rutabaga is soft.

3. In a small bowl, cut butter into flour with a pastry blender or two knives. Sprinkle in water and gently work it into the mixture with a fork.

4. Add sausage balls, flour mixture, tamari, parsley, and spices to vegetables and stock. Simmer over low heat about 2 minutes. Serve soup garnished with hard-cooked eggs.

Serves 6

══════════ Pork and Lima Bean Casserole ══════════

1 tablespoon oil
½ cup coarsely chopped onions
2 cups diced cooked pork
5½ cups cooked lima beans (about
2½ cups dry)
2½ cups pork stock or Beef Stock
(see Index)

⅓ cup raisins
⅔ cup tomato sauce
3 tablespoons honey
½ teaspoon dry mustard
¼ teaspoon cayenne pepper

1. In a large skillet, heat oil and saute onions and pork over medium heat for 2 minutes.

2. Empty contents of skillet in a 3-quart casserole. Add remaining ingredients and bake, uncovered, in a 350°F oven for 1 hour. Oven does not need to be preheated.

Serves 6

Plantain Puff = 91
with Pepper Pork

2	tablespoons oil	3	cups green beans, cut into 2-
1½	pounds boneless pork butt		inch lengths
2	medium-size onions, sliced	3	plantains (about 2 pounds)
3	garlic cloves, minced	¼	cup lemon juice
4½ to 5	cups Chicken Stock (see Index)	3	tablespoons brown rice flour
1½	cups large slices green peppers	6	tablespoons water
1½	cups large slices sweet red	¼	cup chopped parsley
	peppers		

1. Cut pork into 1-inch cubes. In a large skillet, heat oil and brown pork with onions and garlic. Add 3 cups stock and simmer, covered, for 25 minutes or until meat is tender.

2. Add green and red peppers and beans. Simmer, covered, for 10 to 15 minutes or until vegetables are tender but have not lost their color. Remove skillet from heat.

3. Peel plantains, cut into 2-inch slices, and cook in 1½ cups stock in a 2-quart saucepan for 20 minutes or until soft. Strain and add the liquid to the pepper-pork mixture.

4. Puree plantains. Stir in 1½ tablespoons of the lemon juice and keep warm in the top of a double-boiler.

5. Heat pepper-pork mixture to a simmer. Add more stock if needed. Dissolve flour in water, add to skillet, and cook until stock is thickened. Stir in remaining 2½ tablespoons lemon juice. Turn contents into a 2½-quart shallow dish or casserole. Evenly arrange 6 mounds of the banana puree over the top and garnish with chopped parsley.

Serves 6

Rice, Peas, and Pork Salad

1	cup diced cooked pork	¾	cup coarsely chopped celery
6	tablespoons wine vinegar	1	teaspoon tarragon
1½	cups cooked brown rice	¾	cup grated sharp cheddar
1½	cups cooked peas		cheese
¾	cup coarsely chopped green	6	tablespoons Mayonnaise (see
	and red peppers		Index)
3	tablespoons sliced green onions		salad greens
	with tops		

1. In a 1-quart bowl, combine pork and wine vinegar. Set aside.

2. In a 3-quart bowl, combine rice, peas, peppers, onions, celery, tarragon, and half of the grated cheese. Add marinated pork and mayonnaise. Toss gently to mix thoroughly.

3. Serve in a bowl lined with salad greens and sprinkle remaining grated cheese over the top.

Serves 6

2½ to 3	pounds spareribs	2	teaspoons minced garlic
2½	cups unsweetened apple juice	½	teaspoon ground ginger
2	pounds prune plums	2	cinnamon sticks
¼	cup honey	2	tablespoons lemon juice

Dressing

2	tablespoons oil	3	cups whole grain bread cubes
1	cup minced onion		(¼ inch)
2	cups finely chopped celery	¼	cup chopped parsley
3	cups cooked rice	2	tablespoons tamari soy sauce

1. Place spareribs in a 5-quart pot. Add enough water to cover and bring to a boil. Simmer for 5 minutes.

2. Preheat oven to 350°F. Drain spareribs and lay them on a rack in a 14 x 10 x 2-inch roasting pan. Roast for 10 minutes.

3. Combine apple juice, plums, honey, garlic, ginger, and cinnamon sticks in a 2-quart saucepan and simmer for 10 minutes or until plums are very soft. Add lemon juice. Lift plums out of syrup, remove the pits, and set aside.

4. Brush spareribs generously with the syrup. Continue to roast spareribs for another 30 minutes. Baste with the syrup at least once during roasting.

5. Meanwhile, make dressing. In a skillet, heat oil and saute onion and celery until soft. In a large bowl, mix together the rice, bread cubes, and parsley. Add the onion and celery. Combine 1 cup plum syrup with tamari and then add to dressing. Toss lightly and spoon into a shallow 2-quart casserole.

6. After spareribs have roasted 30 minutes, remove from oven and reduce heat to 300°F. Divide spareribs into 6 portions and place them on top of dressing. Spoon a little plum syrup over the ribs. Bake casserole for 10 minutes.

7. Puree the plums with the remaining syrup in a blender and serve as a sauce with the spareribs and dressing.

Serves 6

Pork Ragout
with Cornmeal Dumplings

Ragout

1½	pounds boneless pork from picnic shoulder	1	cup tomato juice
1	tablespoon oil	5	cups peeled, cubed sweet potatoes (about ¾-inch cubes)
½	teaspoon basil	1¼	cups water
¼	teaspoon marjoram	2	cups thickly sliced celery
¼	teaspoon allspice	3	cups coarsely chopped green peppers
½	teaspoon chili powder		
2	cups coarsely chopped onions	2	cups cooked tomatoes
4	cups Beef Stock or Chicken Stock (see Index)	2	tablespoons cornstarch

Dumplings

⅓	cup cornmeal	⅛	teaspoon allspice
½	cup whole wheat pastry flour	1½	teaspoons baking powder
⅛	teaspoon marjoram	1	egg, beaten
¼	teaspoon basil	2	tablespoons oil
⅛	teaspoon nutmeg	1	teaspoon honey
¼	teaspoon chili powder	2	tablespoons milk

1. Remove skin from pork shoulder and trim fat. Cut meat into ¾-inch cubes.

2. In a 4-quart, heavy-bottom pot, heat oil and brown pork over medium-high heat. Add herbs and spices to pork while it is browning. Add 1 cup onions, stirring to blend with seasonings. Then add the stock and tomato juice. Cover skillet, reduce heat, and simmer for 1 to 1½ hours or until pork is tender.

3. While pork is cooking, place sweet potatoes in a 4-quart saucepan. Add 1 cup water and cook until they are almost tender. Stir in remaining onions, celery, and green peppers. Cover and cook over low heat for 10 minutes.

4. When pork is tender, add cooked vegetables to it along with the tomatoes. Dissolve cornstarch in remaining ¼ cup water and add to ragout. Continue cooking over low heat, stirring constantly, until thickened. Remove from heat.

5. In a 1-quart bowl, combine cornmeal, flour, herbs, spices, and baking powder. In another 1-pint bowl, combine egg, oil, honey, and milk, then add to dry ingredients and mix thoroughly.

6. Bring ragout to a simmer over medium-low heat. Drop dumplings into ragout by the rounded teaspoonful, taking care to leave a little space between each one. Cover pot and cook for 10 minutes. Do not remove cover during this time. Serve ragout as soon as dumplings are done.

Serves 6

Pork, Sweet Potato, and Apple Casserole

4	cups cored and sliced apples	¼	teaspoon allspice
1½	cups apple juice	½	teaspoon cinnamon
4	cups cooked, peeled, and sliced sweet potatoes	4	teaspoons cornstarch
2	cups cubed cooked pork butt or shoulder	2	tablespoons cold water

1. Preheat oven to 350°F. Combine apples and apple juice in a 2-quart pot and simmer, covered, over medium heat for 5 minutes. Remove from heat and set aside.

2. Arrange a layer of the sweet potatoes on the bottom of a 3-quart casserole, then a layer of the pork. Sprinkle allspice over the pork. Lift apples out of saucepan and layer them over the pork. Sprinkle cinnamon over the apples.

3. Dissolve cornstarch in cold water and add to apple juice in saucepan. Simmer over low heat, stirring constantly, until liquid has thickened. Pour evenly over apples. Bake casserole, uncovered, for 30 minutes.

Serves 6

Potato, Green Pepper, and Sausage Frittata

3	pounds potatoes, cut into chunks	6 to 8	tablespoons oil
½	cup coarsely chopped onions	1½	cups chopped tomatoes
3	cups coarsely chopped green peppers	1	tablespoon oregano
½	pound cooked sausage links, cut into ¼-inch slices	½	teaspoon black pepper
		12	eggs, beaten

1. Cook potatoes, in enough water to cover, until tender but still firm. Drain. Peel and slice potatoes. There should be about 6 cups.

2. In a large skillet with a heavy bottom, saute onions, green peppers, sausage slices, and potatoes in as little oil as possible until potatoes are lightly browned. Add chopped tomatoes and spices.

3. Carefully turn out half of the contents of the skillet into mixing bowl. Pour half of the beaten eggs over the remaining mixture in the skillet and reduce heat. When frittata is lightly browned underneath, turn it out, bottom-side up, onto platter and keep warm. Add more oil to skillet, return remainder of potato-sausage mixture to skillet, and heat briefly. Then pour in remainder of eggs and repeat the process. Serve immediately.

Serves 6

Red Flannel Hash

3	cups cubed potatoes (about ½-inch cubes)	½	teaspoon paprika
3	cups cubed cooked beets (about ½-inch cubes)	½	teaspoon dry mustard
2¼	cups diced cooked pork from picnic shoulder	¾	teaspoon caraway seeds
6	cups shredded cabbage	4 to 5	tablespoons oil
		1½	cups coarsely chopped onions
		3	tablespoons wine vinegar

1. In a 1½-quart pot, cook potatoes in as little water as possible until tender but not mushy. Drain.

2. In a 3-quart bowl, combine cooked potatoes, beets, pork, cabbage, and seasonings.

3. In a large skillet, heat 2 tablespoons oil and saute half the onions for 1 minute. Add half the hash mixture and saute over low heat for about 5 minutes. Cover skillet during the last few minutes of cooking. Sprinkle 1½ tablespoons vinegar over hash and turn out onto serving platter. Place in a warm oven. Heat remaining oil and saute remaining onions, then remaining hash mixture. Sprinkle with 1½ tablespoons vinegar and add to platter. Serve immediately.

Serves 6

Stuffed Apples

¾	pound Sausage, bulk (see Index)	6	tablespoons lemon juice
6	large, tart cooking apples (6 to 7 ounces each)	6	tablespoons finely ground whole grain bread crumbs
		1½	cups unsweetened apple juice

1. Saute sausage in a large, dry skillet, stirring constantly, until pink disappears. Drain. There should be about 1½ cups cooked sausage.

2. Preheat oven to 350°F. Cut a ½-inch slice off the top of each apple. Core and scoop out the pulp with a teaspoon, leaving a shell ½-inch thick all around. Chop the pulp and put 1 tablespoon of it in the bottom of each apple, pressing down firmly to fill the hole.

3. Combine remaining apple pulp, sausage, lemon juice, and bread crumbs. Pack each apple with the stuffing, pressing down firmly.

4. Place apples in a 9 x 9-inch baking pan, add apple juice to the pan, and bake, uncovered, for 40 to 50 minutes or until apples are tender but still retain their shape. Before serving, baste apples with pan juices.

Serves 6

1	unbaked 9-inch Whole Wheat Pie Crust (see Index)	½	teaspoon paprika
		6	eggs
½	pound cooked Sausage, in casing (see Index)	½	cup non-fat dry milk
		1½	cups water
1	tablespoon oil	2	tablespoons rye flour or whole wheat flour
2	cups sliced onions		
½	teaspoon dry mustard		

1. First make the pie crust.

2. Cut sausage into slices ¼-inch thick.

3. In large skillet, heat oil and saute onions until soft and lightly browned. Spoon onions over bottom of pie shell. Place sausage slices evenly over onions and sprinkle with spices.

4. Preheat oven to 400°F. In a 2-quart bowl, beat eggs until light. Combine non-fat dry milk and water. Add a little of the reconstituted milk to the flour, making a paste, and then whip paste into remainder of milk with a wire whisk.

5. Whisk together eggs and milk, pour mixture carefully over sausage and onions, and bake for 10 minutes. Reduce oven to 350°F and continue baking for 20 minutes longer or until filling is set. Remove quiche from oven, place on wire rack, and leave at room temperature 10 minutes before cutting.

Makes 1 9-inch quiche

══════════ **Swedish Split Pea Soup** ══════════

1½ to 2	pounds pork blade shoulder roast or neck bones	1	bay leaf
		¼	teaspoon thyme
1¾	cups split peas (12 ounces)	¼	teaspoon marjoram
10	cups water	½	teaspoon ground ginger
1	cup coarsely chopped celery with tops	⅛	teaspoon black pepper
		2	tablespoons vinegar
1	cup sliced onions	2	tablespoons tamari soy sauce

1. Place pork roast or neck bones, split peas, and water in a 4-quart soup pot. Add celery, onions, and bay leaf. Bring to a boil, reduce heat to medium-low, cover, and simmer for 1½ hours or until meat comes away from bones easily and peas are soft.

2. Remove meat from pot and separate it from bones. Cut enough of the cooked pork into small pieces to measure 2 cups. Return this to soup. (Reserve remaining pork for another use.)

3. Add herbs, spices, vinegar, and tamari to soup before serving.

Serves 6

6	large white onions (about 12 ounces each)
4	cups water

Stuffing

1	pound ground pork	½	teaspoon thyme
1	tablespoon oil	1	teaspoon sage
½	cup diced carrots	1	teaspoon rosemary
1	garlic clove, minced	2	tablespoons chopped parsley
½	cup finely chopped mushrooms	2	tablespoons Parmesan cheese
1	cup soft whole grain bread crumbs	1	egg, beaten

Sauce

1 to 2	cups Chicken Stock (see Index)	1	tablespoon brown rice flour
1	tablespoon cornstarch	4	tablespoons cold water

1. Peel onions and place in a 5-quart Dutch oven. Add water and simmer, covered, for 40 to 45 minutes until tender but firm.

2. Drain onions. Cut center out of each, leaving enough of a shell and bottom to hold the stuffing. Reserve ¾ cup of the onion centers to add to the stuffing; the remainder can be stored for future use in soup. If onions do not sit straight, shave the bottoms.

3. Preheat oven to 350°F. In the same pot used to cook the onions, brown the pork. Drain excess fat drippings. Then add oil, carrots, garlic, and mushrooms and saute for 5 to 10 minutes.

4. Chop the ¾ cup onion centers and add to pork mixture. Stir in bread crumbs, herbs, cheese, and egg. Mix lightly to combine.

5. Using a teaspoon, fill each onion, mounding the stuffing on top. Place stuffed onions in a 9 x 9-inch roasting pan. Pour 1 cup stock into pan and bake 1 to 1½ hours or until onions are nicely browned.

6. To make sauce, measure the remaining liquid in the roasting pan and add more stock if necessary to equal 2 cups. Dissolve cornstarch and flour in cold water and stir into boiling stock. Cook until thick. Serve with the stuffed onions.

Serves 6

3   pounds spareribs (not country-style)

Marinade

3	tablespoons lemon juice	2	tablespoons tamari soy sauce
3	garlic cloves, minced	1	tablespoon honey
½	cup finely chopped onions	½	cup oil
3	tablespoons slivered ginger root		

Cabbage Rolls

3½ to 4	pound head of cabbage	1½	teaspoons ground cumin
2¼	cups cooked brown rice	¾	cup tomato sauce
2¼	cups cooked black beans	2	cups Chicken Stock (see Index)
¼	cup wheat germ	1	cup tomato juice
1½	teaspoons chili powder		

1. Cut spareribs into 6 portions and parboil in enough water to cover for 4 minutes, then drain. Lay sparerib portions in a 13 x 9 x 2-inch roasting pan.

2. Combine marinade ingredients and heat in a 1-quart saucepan. Brush marinade on spareribs and set aside.

3. Cut out the bottom core of the cabbage. Hold head bottom-side up under running water, letting the weight of the water loosen the leaves from the head so they can be removed without tearing. Remove 12 large leaves and place them in a 4-quart pot.

4. Pour enough boiling water over cabbage leaves to cover them and simmer, covered, for 5 minutes. Drain and set aside. Coarsely chop 3 cups raw cabbage and place in bottom of a 4-quart casserole. Reserve remaining raw cabbage for future use.

5. Combine rice, beans, wheat germ, seasonings, and tomato sauce. Put 6 tablespoons of this mixture at the core end of each cabbage leaf. Fold in sides of leaf and roll tightly toward outer edge of leaf. Lay each roll in casserole on top of chopped cabbage, seam-side down, using a toothpick to secure roll if necessary. Pour in stock and tomato juice and cover casserole.

6. Bake spareribs and cabbage rolls in 350°F oven for 50 to 60 minutes until meat is brown and tender. Baste spareribs at least once during this time. Serve spareribs on top of cabbage rolls, pouring any remaining pan juices over the top.

Serves 6

Pie

½   cup bulgur
1   cup water
3   cups coarsely grated zucchini
    (about 1 pound)

1   cup grated mozzarella cheese (1 pound)
½   cup grated Parmesan cheese
3   eggs, beaten

Topping

1   tablespoon oil
1   medium-size onion, chopped
1   garlic clove, minced
1   cup sliced mushrooms
1   cup cooked tomatoes, drained
¼   teaspoon oregano

¼   teaspoon basil
¼   teaspoon rosemary
1   cup (½ pound) thinly sliced cooked Sausage, in casing (see Index)

1. Preheat oven to 350°F. Bring bulgur and water to boil, reduce heat, and simmer, uncovered, for 10 minutes, stirring frequently. Water should be almost completely absorbed.

2. Combine zucchini with ½ cup of the grated mozzarella cheese and all of the Parmesan cheese. Add the eggs, then the cooked bulgur. Mix lightly.

3. Turn zucchini-bulgur mixture into an oiled 9 x 1¼-inch pie pan, hollowing out the center slightly, and bake for 35 minutes until set and dry on top.

4. While pie is baking, make topping. Heat oil in a large skillet and saute onions, garlic, and mushrooms until lightly browned. Add tomatoes, herbs, and sausage slices. Simmer, uncovered, over low heat until thick and quite dry.

5. Place the pie under the broiler until the top is lightly browned. Leave oven at broil temperature, remove pie, and top it with tomato-sausage mixture. Sprinkle remaining ½ cup cheese over the top and return pie to oven, placing it well below the broiler unit, until the cheese on top has bubbled and browned slightly. Serve at once.

Serves 6

SAUSAGE

Making Your Own Sausage

Sausage Stuffing Technique and Equipment

Pork, beef, or lamb intestines are used as fresh sausage casings. These are available from wholesale supply companies or from butchers. They usually come cleaned and packed in salt.

1. Rinse off the salt.
2. Soak casings in water (with a little vinegar added) for 30 minutes before stuffing them.
3. Run cold water through each casing several times.
4. Fit one end of the casing over a funnel with a wide spout. Gather entire casing over spout to within 2 inches of the end. Tie with a string and cut the casing below the knot.
5. Using the long handle of a wooden spoon, stuff sausage mixture through funnel, easing the casing off the spout gradually as the sausage meat is packed into the casing evenly and tightly. If air pockets appear in the casing as you stuff, simply prick with a sterilized needle. Be gentle when squeezing the casings to avoid tearing. If a hole develops, cut the casing at that point and tie above it.
6. When filled, slide the casing off the funnel and tie the end securely. You can make one long link and curl it around in a circle, or make several smaller sausages, if you prefer. If you prepared more casings than needed, simply place table salt and casings into a small plastic bag, seal, and refrigerate. Stored this way, the casings will keep indefinitely.

Storage

Sausage will stay fresh in the refrigerator for 1 to 2 days. If it is to be stored any longer, freeze it; sausage is highly perishable.

Procedure for Cooking Sausage in Casings

1. Pierce casings with a fork in several places to allow fat to escape during cooking.
2. In a large skillet (for 2 pounds of sausage), cook sausage in enough water to reach halfway up the sides of the sausage. Cover skillet and cook for 3 to 5 minutes. Turn sausage over and cook another 3 to 5 minutes. (Pork Soybean Sausage—requires no more than 3 minutes cooking time on each side in water. Longer cooking can produce a dry sausage. Continue to brown as in the following step. Sausage Gravy is suggested for Pork Soybean Sausage.)
3. Remove lid and pour off and discard most of remaining liquid. Let sausage cook in its own juices over low heat for about 5 minutes longer. Turn frequently to allow even browning. Drain on paper towels and serve.

Procedure for Cooking Sausage Patties

Saute patties in a dry skillet over medium-low heat until brown on both sides. Drain on paper towels and serve.

Sausage Gravy

Sausage gravy can be made by stirring a little milk into the pan juices after sausage is browned. Gravy can be thickened or not, as desired.

1¼	pounds boneless pork butt	½	cup parsley sprigs
¾	pound pork fat	2	garlic cloves, crushed
¾	cup soybeans	¼	teaspoon dry mustard
1	cup water	1	teaspoon thyme
2	tablespoons vinegar	½	teaspoon sage
½	medium-size onion	1	teaspoon paprika

1. Grind pork, then pork fat, using coarse, large-holed disc of grinder. Combine meat and fat in a 2-quart bowl.

2. In a 1-quart saucepan, combine soybeans, water, and 1 teaspoon of the vinegar. Boil, uncovered, for 5 minutes.

3. Drain soybeans and then grind them using the fine, small-holed disc of the grinder. Then grind onion and parsley. Add to meat and fat.

4. Mix garlic, spices, and remaining vinegar into meat and fat, kneading by hand until well blended.

5. Stuff sausage into casings or form into patties. Refrigerate for several hours before cooking. (See Index for sausage stuffing technique and equipment and for procedure for cooking sausage.)

Yields 2 pounds sausage (uncooked)

══════════ Sweet Spicy Sausage ══════════

1	pound boneless pork butt	¼	teaspoon allspice
½	pound boneless beef chuck	¼	teaspoon mace
1	small onion, grated	⅛	teaspoon black pepper
1	garlic clove, crushed	⅓	cup water
¼	cup soy flour	2	tablespoons honey
⅓	cup brown rice flour	1	tablespoon vinegar
¼	teaspoon ground ginger		

1. Grind pork and beef separately, using the coarse, large-holed disc of grinder.

2. In a 2-quart bowl, combine ground pork, ground beef, and all remaining ingredients. Knead by hand to blend thoroughly.

3. Stuff sausage into casings or form into patties. Refrigerate for several hours before cooking. (See Index for sausage stuffing technique and equipment and for procedure for cooking sausage.)

Yields 2 pounds sausage (uncooked)

Lamb

I probably owe my love of lamb to my association with non-American cooks in the early days of my training as a chef. Lamb is far more appreciated in the rest of the world than it is in America, or at least middle-America where I grew up.

One of my favorite lamb recipes, a Greek lamb pilaf, was passed on to me and my fellow trainees by a Greek tennis champion who personally supervised the preparation. A special recipe for lamb curry was demonstrated for us by a labor leader from Pakistan. I will never forget the way he enthusiastically tackled that leg of lamb, cutting it up for his pilau. Another fond memory I have is shopping in London, as per instruction, for "best end of neck," so as to have the proper cut of lamb for preparing an authentic Irish stew. There is no question where the lamb-laden Scotch Broth originated, and Lamb Cassoulet has become a popular import from France.

If your supermarket is anything like mine, you are most likely to find frozen legs of lamb from New Zealand and, once in awhile, domestic fresh lamb legs. What will surprise you is the difference in price. In my area, the domestic leg is twice the price per pound of the New Zealand lamb. Odd that the imported product would cost less! None of the butchers I asked about this could give me a good reason for the price difference, though they hinted that it might be a matter of inferior quality and an undesirable taste in the New Zealand product.

I decided to hold my own comparison test. I purchased two legs of lamb, one from New Zealand, the other a domestic one, and I prepared and cooked each of them in exactly the same way. My family and I could not find any difference in the taste of the two legs. Both were delicious.

Buying Young, Tender Lamb

The term "spring lamb" made sense at one time, but that time has passed. For one thing, spring in New Zealand is autumn here. "Milk-fed" lamb is 3 to 5 months old; "grass-fed, grain-finished" lamb is 5 months to 1 year old. After 1 year of age, lamb becomes mutton. Actually, good, young, tender lamb is equally available during every season, although the price is often higher in the fall. Because all lamb is young and therefore tender, almost every part of the animal can be cooked with dry heat, except, I hasten to add, the "best end of

Lamb Cuts

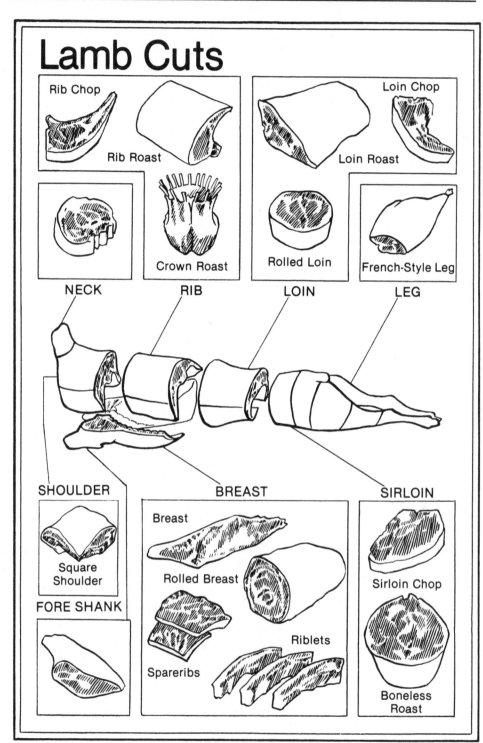

Rib Chop

Rib Roast

Crown Roast

NECK

Loin Chop

Loin Roast

Rolled Loin

LOIN

French-Style Leg

LEG

RIB

SHOULDER

Square
Shoulder

FORE SHANK

BREAST

Breast

Rolled Breast

Spareribs

Riblets

SIRLOIN

Sirloin Chop

Boneless
Roast

neck." That requires 2 to 3 hours stewing in a moderate oven (350°F), or 1½ hours on top of the stove. (See Beef chapter for roasting and braising tips.)

The appearance of fresh lamb is an important guide to quality. Young lamb should have pink, firm, and fine-textured meat and cross sections of bone that are red, moist, and porous. The meat in older lambs looks light red and the bones appear drier, harder, and less red than in the very young ones. The fat layer should be firm, but its color will vary with the breed. Color of the fat is not a good indication of quality.

Some people say there is an unpleasant odor from roasting lamb. I have never found the smell to be anything but good—in fact, irresistible. I roast lamb at 350°F for 20 to 25 minutes per pound, though official recommendations start at 325°F (see table on next page). Results are fine either way. I always insert slivers of garlic in the fat under the skin at various places on the leg, and I like to sprinkle rosemary liberally all over it.

A good buy in lamb chops sometimes comes your way, as I joyfully discovered one day. Usually called lamb leg sirloin chops, these chops come from the loin end of the leg, as the name implies. Often the leg will be sold with these three or four chops still attached. However, I purchased the chops separately for a modest price, and six chops (2 pounds) fed six people amply. I titled that recipe Lamb Chop Celebration, because it was! These chops may go by other names: large loin lamb chops, leg chops, lamb steak, chump chops, sirloin steaks, or loin end steaks.

I find 4½ ounces per person to be ample in recipes using lamb chops, shoulder as well as leg sirloin chops, if I simply cut the chops into portions after they are cooked. That makes these dishes economical, especially if the chops are on sale.

On one occasion, the butcher in a supermarket was glad to cut a frozen

Timetable for Braising Lamb

Cut of meat	Approximate weight or thickness	Hours[1,2]
Breast, boneless, rolled	1½ to 2 pounds	1½ to 2
Breast, stuffed	2 to 3 pounds	1½ to 2
Neck slices	¾ inch	1
Pieces for stew	1½ inches	1½ to 2
Riblets		1½ to 2
Shanks	¾ to 1 pound each	1½ to 2
Shoulder chops	¾ to 1 inch	¾ to 1

[1]Meat at refrigerator temperature at start of braising.
[2]Cooking time is for meat braised at simmering temperature.

SOURCE: *Lamb in Family Meals,* Home and Garden Bulletin No. 124, United States Department of Agriculture, 1976.

Timetable for Roasting Lamb

Cut of meat	Approximate weight (pounds)	Hours[1,2] (325°F)
Leg	5 to 8	3 to 4
Leg, boneless, rolled	3 to 5	2 to 3
Rib (rack)	4 to 5	3 to 3⅓
Shoulder	4 to 6	2⅓ to 3
Shoulder, boneless, rolled	3 to 5	2¼ to 3⅓
Shoulder, cushion-style	3 to 5	1¾ to 2½

[1]Meat at refrigerator temperature at start of roasting.
[2]Cooking time is for meat roasted until well done. A meat thermometer can be used to determine doneness. For well done, the internal temperature should be 180°F; for medium, 170°F.

SOURCE: *Lamb in Family Meals,* Home and Garden Bulletin No. 124, United States Department of Agriculture, 1976.

leg of lamb in half for me. I chose the loin end, which has more tender meat though there is more bone in it. The shank end is easier to carve but is a bit less tender. Both halves remained the same price per pound.

A Lot from a Leg

If you are like me, you think twice before buying a costly piece of meat, so I felt a bit guilty the first time I brought home a whole leg of lamb to prepare the recipes for this book. I was especially pleased to discover that I had been able to feed ten people from one (6-pound) leg, including a roast lamb meal for five. That may not sound like much, but that first meal was not a "stretch-the-meat" meal. From another leg which was a bit smaller (5 pounds, 12 ounces), I fed 14 people, this time using "stretching" recipes. From another half leg—one that weighed 3 pounds before being boned—I made the recipe for Rolled Lamb Leg with Prune and Walnut Stuffing and served six people.

Boning a leg of lamb is not difficult, in spite of what you may have heard. The best place to begin is with the aitchbone (hip bone) at the large end of the leg. Cut down behind this bone, keeping your knife blade as close to the bone as possible. Try to move the bone a bit, as you cut, and you will find the place where it is joined to the leg bone at the hip socket. Cut between these two bones, through the space between the joints. Now it will be easier to cut the aitchbone out. Next, cut along the leg bone to the knee joint and then on along the shank bone to the end of the leg. Once you have exposed the bones, trim away the meat around and underneath them and lift out the bones. Wrap and store the bones in the freezer or in the refrigerator, for making stock.

Now you have some beautiful boned lamb to use for curry, pilaf, kabobs,

Suggested Home Storage Periods to Maintain High Quality in Lamb

	Refrigerator (days)	Freezer (months)
Fresh		
Chops and steaks	3 to 5	6 to 9
Ground	1 to 2	3 to 4
Roasts	3 to 5	6 to 9
Stew meat	1 to 2	3 to 4
Variety meats	1 to 2	3 to 4
Cooked		
Cooked lamb and lamb dishes	3 to 4	2 to 3
Gravy and meat broth	1 to 2	2 to 3

SOURCE: *Lamb in Family Meals,* Home and Garden Bulletin No. 124, United States Department of Agriculture, 1976.

or fancy stew. Or, you may want to grind some of the lamb for meatballs. I allowed ¼ pound boned lamb per person for recipes such as these.

There is no harm in re-freezing lamb, or any meat for that matter, which has remained below 40°F and still contains ice crystals. If the lamb leg was frozen when purchased, thaw it in the refrigerator. Keep the thawed lamb refrigerated until you bone it. Cut and package the meat as it is boned, in amounts convenient for your needs.

When you are ready to make lamb stock, brown the bones in a 400°F oven before simmering them in water. Proceed from there just as you would to make Beef Stock (see Index). One big advantage to boning your own lamb leg is that you have all that bone to make a rich stock. In this section you will find recipes for several soups you can make with lamb stock, so keep a supply of the stock in the freezer.

Certain spices, such as coriander, cinnamon, and allspice, as well as herbs like mint, basil, bay leaves, dill, marjoram, savory, tarragon, thyme, and rosemary, do wonderful things for lamb. They seem to impart a Middle-Eastern flavor, particularly appropriate to lamb. I carried out this theme in several entrees, choosing eggplant, lentils, bulgur, and yogurt as suitable ingredients to be combined with lamb.

I don't feel guilty buying a leg of lamb anymore. I'm ready to do it anytime the price is right! With a little ingenuity, lamb becomes affordable—a bargain, in fact.

2	eggs	½	teaspoon paprika
½	cup lamb stock, Beef Stock (see Index), or Chicken Stock (see Index)	4	teaspoons lemon juice
		2	teaspoons Mustard (see Index)
		2	tablespoons oil
2	cups cooked brown rice	¼	cup finely chopped onions
2	cups chopped or ground cooked lamb	¼	cup finely chopped green peppers
½	cup wheat germ	2	tablespoons butter
¼	cup chopped parsley	2	cups lamb gravy or Tomato Brown Sauce (see Index)
1	teaspoon dry mustard		
2	teaspoons dill weed		

1. Beat eggs and stock together in a 2-quart bowl. Add rice, lamb, ¼ cup of the wheat germ, herbs, spices, lemon juice, and mustard. Mix well.

2. Preheat oven to 350°F. In a medium-size skillet, heat oil and saute onions and green peppers until soft. Then add to rice and lamb mixture.

3. Mix all ingredients together thoroughly and turn into a 1½-quart casserole. Sprinkle remaining ¼ cup wheat germ over the top and dot with butter. Bake for 30 minutes. Serve with lamb gravy or tomato brown sauce.

Serves 6

======= Lamb and Barley Stew =======

3	pounds lamb neck bones	2	cups turnip chunks
11	cups water	1½	teaspoons thyme
¾	cup barley	¾	teaspoon caraway seeds
1½	cups sliced onions	3	tablespoons lemon juice
1	cup sliced celery	¼	cup chopped parsley
2	cups carrot chunks		

1. Combine lamb neck bones, water, and barley in a 5-quart Dutch oven or heavy-bottom pot.

2. Add onions, celery, carrots, turnips, thyme, and caraway seeds. Cover and bring to a boil. Reduce heat and simmer over low heat for 1½ hours or until lamb is cooked and comes away from the bones easily.

3. Separate meat from bones. Discard bones, return meat to stew, and add lemon juice. Serve garnished with chopped parsley.

Serves 6

Remarks This dish is very simple to prepare since it is not necessary to brown the neck bones first.

Eggplant Roulades ══════ 109

Eggplant

2	eggplants (about 1 pound each)	1¼	cups rye flour
2	eggs, beaten	6 to 8	tablespoons oil
1	cup milk		

Filling

2	garlic cloves, minced	¼	cup whole grain bread crumbs
1	tablespoon butter	¼	cup tomato sauce
2	cups minced cooked lamb		

Sauce

2	tablespoons butter	½	teaspoon oregano
2	cups sliced mushrooms	4	teaspoons cornstarch
2	tablespoons rye flour	¼	cup cold water
1	cup lamb stock or Beef Stock (see Index)	2	teaspoons lemon juice
		¼	cup tomato sauce
1	cup tomato juice	¼ to ½	cup grated Parmesan cheese
½	teaspoon basil	¼	cup chopped parsley

1. Peel eggplants and slice each one lengthwise into about 9 slices ¼-inch thick.

2. Combine eggs, milk, and ¾ cup of the flour in a pie plate or similar-size shallow pan. Place remaining ½ cup flour in another pie plate.

3. Heat 2 tablespoons oil in a large skillet. Dredge eggplant slices in flour, then dip in batter and saute over medium-low heat just until golden brown and soft enough to be rolled. Add more oil to skillet as needed. As slices are sauteed, stack them one on top of the other in a 13 x 9 x 2-inch pan and set aside.

4. In a 2-quart, heavy-bottom saucepan, saute garlic in butter over low heat. Add the lamb, bread crumbs, and tomato sauce. Stir to combine, then remove from heat.

5. Preheat oven to 375°F. Place about 1½ tablespoons of the lamb filling on the large end of each eggplant slice and roll as tightly as possible toward the smaller end. Place rolls seam-side down in a 3-quart casserole.

6. In the same saucepan, melt butter over medium heat and saute mushrooms for 1 minute. Stir in flour. Gradually add stock, tomato juice, and herbs, stirring to make a smooth sauce. Dissolve cornstarch in water and add to sauce, stirring until thickened. Blend in lemon juice and tomato sauce.

7. Pour sauce over eggplant roulades and sprinkle Parmesan cheese over the top. Bake for 15 minutes. Garnish with chopped parsley and serve.

Serves 6

½	cup barley	2	cups cubed cooked lamb
6	cups lamb stock	⅔	cup Yogurt (see Index)
½	cup coarsely chopped onions	¼	cup chopped parsley
½	cup diced celery	1	tablespoon chopped mint or 1
1	cup diced carrots		teaspoon dried mint

1. Bring barley and stock to a boil in a 3-quart pot. Reduce heat and simmer, partially covered, for 30 minutes. Then add onions, celery, and carrots and continue to cook for 15 to 30 minutes longer or until barley is soft.

2. Stir in lamb, yogurt, parsley, and mint. Simmer over very low heat for 15 to 20 minutes before serving.

Serves 6

══════ Lamb Shoulder Chops ══════
with Stuffed Mushrooms and Turnips

4	cups sliced turnips or potatoes	24	mushroom stems, finely chopped
2	cups lamb stock, Beef Stock (see Index), or Chicken Stock (see Index)	1	cup soft whole grain bread crumbs
3	tablespoons brown rice flour	½	cup finely chopped tomatoes
2 to 4	tablespoons butter	¼	cup chopped parsley
2 to 4	tablespoons oil	1	teaspoon basil
¼	cup finely chopped onions	1	teaspoon ground coriander
4	garlic cloves, minced	1½	pounds lamb shoulder chops
24	large mushroom caps		

1. In a 2½-quart saucepan, cook turnips in stock until tender. Lift out turnips and arrange them on the bottom of a 3-quart casserole. Add brown rice flour to stock with a wire whisk and simmer until thickened. Pour over turnips.

2. In a medium-size skillet, melt 1 tablespoon of the butter in 1 tablespoon of the oil and saute onions, garlic, and mushroom stems until soft. Add bread crumbs, tomatoes, parsley, basil, an coriander. Set aside.

3. Preheat oven to 350°F. In a large skillet, brown lamb chops, using only as much butter and oil as is necessary. Lay mushroom caps in skillet, top-side down, and brown for 1 to 2 minutes while lamb chops are browning. Lift mushroom caps out onto a tray and stuff them with the sauteed mixture.

4. When chops are brown, trim off any fat and cut into 6 portions, removing bones if desired. Arrange chops on top of the turnips and top with stuffed mushrooms.

5. Cover casserole and bake for 30 minutes.

Serves 6

Lamb Cassoulet

2	cups white navy beans or baby lima beans	6	whole cloves
½	pound Sausage, in casing (see Index)	1 to 2	tablespoons oil
		1	pound lamb shoulder chops or neck bones
4	cups water	1¼	pounds chicken (about 2 wings
4	cups lamb stock, Beef Stock (see Index), or Chicken Stock (see Index)		and 2 legs separated at the joint)
1	bay leaf	1	cup coarsely chopped onions
½	teaspoon thyme	2	garlic cloves, minced
¼	teaspoon marjoram	1½	cups sliced carrots
3	sprigs parsley	¾	cup tomato sauce
½	cup chopped celery leaves	½	cup whole grain bread crumbs
		3	tablespoons melted butter

1. Soak beans for 8 hours in enough water to cover. Drain and discard water. In a 5-quart pot, bring beans to a boil in enough fresh water to cover. Reduce heat and simmer, partially covered, for 30 minutes. Drain and discard water.

2. Prick sausage with a fork in five or six places on both sides to allow fat to escape during cooking. In a large skillet, place sausage in enough water to reach halfway up its sides. Cover and simmer for 5 minutes. Turn sausage over after half the cooking time has elapsed. Pour off the fat and water, and then brown sausage on both sides over low heat for a few minutes.

3. Bring beans, 4 cups water, and stock to a boil in the same 5-quart pot. Add sausage, herbs, parsley, celery leaves, and cloves. Cover and simmer over low heat for 30 minutes.

4. In the same skillet used to cook the sausage, heat oil and brown lamb chops and chicken pieces. Set meat aside. Saute onions, garlic, and carrots until lightly browned, using more oil if necessary.

5. Remove sausage from beans after the 30-minute cooking time has elapsed and set aside. Add lamb, chicken, and vegetables to beans and continue to cook, covered, for 30 minutes longer. Skim fat from top and discard.

6. Transfer lamb and chicken from pot to cutting board. Remove bones from meat and cut into serving portions, keeping pieces fairly large. Slice sausage.

7. Drain any excess liquid from the beans. (Reserve for future use in soup.) Stir tomato sauce into beans. Layer half the beans on the bottom of a 3-quart casserole. Then arrange a layer of half the lamb, chicken, and sausage. Then layer the remaining beans and finally the remaining meat.

8. Combine bread crumbs with melted butter and sprinkle over the top of the casserole. Bake in 300°F oven for 30 to 45 minutes until top is crusty.

Serves 6

6 tablespoons oil

1½ cups coarsely chopped onions

4 garlic cloves, minced

1 pound mushrooms, separated into caps and stems (4 cups)

1½ cups coarsely chopped green peppers

2 pounds shoulder or leg sirloin lamb chops

3 tablespoons chopped mint or 2 teaspoons dried mint

1 teaspoon mace

¼ teaspoon black pepper

1¼ cups lamb stock, Beef Stock (see Index), or Chicken Stock (see Index)

2 cups sliced carrots (¼-inch thick on diagonal)

1½ cups cubed potatoes (½-inch cubes)

4 cups cubed zucchini (½-inch cubes)

2 tablespoons cornstarch

¼ cup lemon juice

1. In a large skillet, heat oil and saute onions, garlic, and half of the mushrooms for about 2 minutes. Add half the green peppers and saute for about 1 minute. Clear a space in the center of the skillet and brown half of the chops on both sides. Combine seasonings in a 1-pint bowl and sprinkle one-quarter of the amount over the chops.

2. Lift chops and vegetables out of skillet and place in a 2-quart bowl. Set aside. Then saute remaining mushrooms and green peppers and brown remaining lamb chops. Add one-quarter of the seasonings to the chops.

3. Return the reserved lamb chops and vegetabels to skillet, keeping all the chops on the bottom of the pan. Add 1 cup of the stock, then all the carrots, potatoes, and zucchini. Then add the remaining half of the seasonings. Cover skillet and simmer over very low heat for 20 to 25 minutes or until chops are fork-tender.

4. Lift chops from skillet, remove bones, cut lamb into suitable serving portions, and return meat to skillet. (Bones may be saved for stock.)

5. Dissolve cornstarch in remaining ¼ cup cold stock and add to lamb mixture. Stir over low heat until sauce has thickened. Stir in lemon juice just before serving.

Serves 6

Remarks Serve with cooked brown rice.

Lamb Hash Patties 113

3	cups diced potatoes	½	cup fine whole grain bread
½	cup coarsely chopped onions		crumbs
3	cups diced cooked lamb	4 to 6	tablespoons oil
4 to 6	tablespoons lamb stock, lamb		
	gravy, or tomato sauce		

1. Combine potatoes and onions in a 2-quart saucepan and cook in as little water as possible over medium heat for 10 minutes. Drain.

2. Mash potatoes and onions, then combine them with the lamb in a 3-quart bowl. Add enough stock, gravy, or tomato sauce (about 4 tablespoons) to bind lamb and potatoes together.

3. Form mixture into 12 patties (about 2 inches in diameter and ¾-inch thick) and coat with bread crumbs. In a large skillet, heat oil and saute patties over medium heat until brown and crisp on both sides. Add more oil if necessary to prevent patties from sticking.

Serves 6

Remarks Serve with Tomato Catsup (see Index).

Lamb Oatmeal Soup

1	cup rolled oats	1	teaspoon basil
2	cups diced rutabagas	2	tablespoons butter
4	cups lamb stock	¼	cup coarsely chopped onions
1	cup cooked tomatoes	1	cup thinly sliced zucchini
1	cup tomato juice	2	teaspoons tamari soy sauce
2	cups diced cooked lamb	¼	cup chopped parsley
¼	teaspoon marjoram		

1. In a medium-size dry skillet, toast rolled oats over medium heat, stirring constantly, until they are lightly browned. Set aside.

2. Place rutabagas and lamb stock in a 3- or 4-quart soup pot and simmer, covered, until tender.

3. Add tomatoes, and tomato juice, rolled oats, lamb, and herbs to rutabagas and stock.

4. In the same skillet used for the oats, melt butter and saute onions and zucchini until onions are soft and zucchini is lightly browned. Add to soup and simmer over very low heat for 5 to 10 minutes. Stir in tamari and parsley before serving.

Serves 6

2	cups cubed potatoes	4	whole cloves
2	cups sliced carrots	¼	teaspoon thyme
2	cups cubed turnips	4	cups lamb stock
1	cup coarsely chopped onions	¼	cup brown rice flour
2	teaspoons ground coriander	2	cups cubed cooked lamb
½	teaspoon allspice		Whole Wheat Pie Crust (see Index)
½	teaspoon cinnamon		

1. Combine potatoes, carrots, turnips, onions, spices, and stock in a 3-quart pot. Simmer, covered, for 5 minutes or until vegetables are tender. Drain liquid into a 2-quart bowl. Stir in brown rice flour with a wire whisk.

2. Turn vegetables out into a shallow 2-quart baking pan. Add the lamb and pour thickened stock over vegetables. Set aside.

3. Preheat oven to 425°F. Make pie crust dough. Roll it out and lay it on top of lamb mixture. Make a fluted edge around the pie and several small slits in the crust to allow steam to escape. Bake the pie for 12 to 15 minutes or until crust is lightly browned.

Serves 6

===== Lamb Prune Pilaf =====

2	tablespoons oil	2	teaspoons ground coriander
1¼	pounds lamb leg, cut into 1 x ½-inch pieces	¼	teaspoon black pepper
		3 to 4½	cups lamb stock, Beef Stock (see Index), or Chicken Stock (see Index)
1	medium-size onion, sliced		
2	garlic cloves, minced		
1	cinnamon stick, broken in half	12	prunes
¾	teaspoon allspice		

Pilaf

½	cup finely chopped onions	2¼	cups brown rice
2	tablespoons butter	4	tablespoons chopped parsley

1. In a large skillet, heat oil and brown lamb, onions, garlic, and spices.

2. Add 3 cups of the stock and the prunes and simmer, covered, over low heat for 30 minutes or until lamb is tender. Remove prunes and set aside. Pour off liquid and measure it. Add enough additional stock to make 4½ cups. Set lamb aside and keep warm.

3. In a 3-quart, heavy-bottom pot, melt butter and saute onions in it. Add rice and stir thoroughly to evenly coat with the butter. Stir in the 4½ cups stock, cover, and cook over low heat for 35 to 40 minutes or until liquid is absorbed.

4. Combine cooked rice with lamb, tossing gently. Serve pilaf topped with prunes and garnished with chopped parsley.

Serves 6

Lamb Tabouli 115

1½	cups bulgur	¾	cup chopped parsley
3	cups boiling water	¼	cup chopped mint or 4
¾	cup finely chopped onions		teaspoons dried mint
¾	cup finely chopped green	½	teaspoon black pepper
	peppers	½	cup lemon juice
¾	cup finely chopped tomatoes	6	tablespoons oil
2	cups diced cooked lamb		romaine lettuce

1. Combine bulgur and boiling water in a 3-quart bowl. Set aside for 15 minutes. Drain water and dry bulgur between paper towels, pressing firmly to remove all moisture. Return bulgur to bowl.

2. Add all remaining ingredients except lettuce. Toss gently and chill mixture in the refrigerator. Serve in a salad bowl lined with lettuce.

Serves 6

Lamb-Vegetable Curry

3 to 4	tablespoons oil	2	teaspoons cilantro or parsley
2	cups sliced onions	2	teaspoons ground cumin
2	garlic cloves, minced	1¼	pounds lamb leg, cut into 1 x
2	cinnamon sticks, broken in half		½-inch pieces
6	whole cloves	3	cups sliced cauliflower
2	teaspoons minced ginger root	4	cups cubed eggplant
1	teaspoon chili powder	2	cups tomato juice
⅛	teaspoon cayenne pepper	1	cup lamb stock, Beef Stock (see
1	teaspoon ground cardamom		Index), or Chicken Stock (see
2	teaspoons dried mint		Index)
1	bay leaf	2	cups frozen peas
3	teaspoons ground coriander		

1. In a 5-quart Dutch oven or heavy-bottom pot, heat oil and saute onions and garlic with spices and herbs until soft. Add lamb and continue cooking until browned. Stir frequently.

2. Add cauliflower, eggplant, tomato juice, and stock. Cover, reduce heat, and simmer for 30 minutes or until lamb is tender.

3. Stir in peas and cook for an additional 5 minutes.

Serves 6

Remarks The curry, which is best served with cooked brown rice, becomes a truly festive dish when accompanied by small dishes of shredded coconut, raisins, almonds, chutney, and yogurt.

9 cups lamb stock or Beef Stock (see Index)
¾ cup lentils
1 cup coarsely chopped onions
1 garlic clove, minced
¾ cup sliced celery
1½ cups cooked tomatoes
1 cup cubed potatoes (about ½-inch cubes)

1½ teaspoons ground coriander
1½ teaspoons tarragon
1 tablespoon honey
1 cup diced cooked lamb
1 cup sliced zucchini
2 tablespoons lemon juice

1. Combine stock, lentils, onions, garlic, and celery in a 4-quart soup pot and simmer over medium heat for 40 minutes.

2. Add tomatoes, potatoes, coriander, tarragon, and honey. Simmer another 10 minutes.

3. Finally, add lamb and zucchini and simmer 10 minutes longer. Stir in lemon juice before serving.

Serves 6

========= **Orange Lamb Salad** =========

3 cups coarsely sliced cauliflower
1 cup frozen peas
⅔ cup Yogurt (see Index)
⅓ cup oil
1 tablespoon honey
⅓ cup frozen orange juice concentrate
2 cups cubed cooked lamb
3 cups peeled and quartered orange slices

½ cup sliced onions
1 cup coarsely chopped green peppers
1 cup coarsely chopped celery
1½ cups watercress
4 teaspoons ground coriander
¼ teaspoon black pepper
2 teaspoons dried mint
romaine lettuce

1. Simmer cauliflower and peas together in as little water as possible over medium heat, covered, for 2 minutes. Drain and set vegetables aside in a 3-quart bowl to cool.

2. In a 1-quart bowl, combine yogurt, oil, honey, and frozen orange juice concentrate.

3. Add all remaining ingredients, except lettuce, to vegetables.

4. Pour dressing over salad. Toss gently. Serve in a salad bowl lined with lettuce.

Serves 6

Rolled Lamb Leg 117
with Prune and Walnut Stuffing

3	pounds lamb leg (sirloin end)		⅓	cup coarsely chopped walnuts
9	prunes		1⅔	cups Chicken Stock or Beef
⅔	cup boiling water			Stock (see Index)
2	tablespoons butter		¼	teaspoon allspice
½	cup coarsely chopped onions		⅛	teaspoon black pepper
½	cup coarsely chopped celery		¼	teaspoon rosemary
1	garlic clove, minced		4	teaspoons cornstarch
1⅓	cups soft whole grain bread cubes (¼-inch cubes)		3	tablespoons cold water

1. Bone lamb leg. Save bone for future use in soup.

2. Soak prunes in the boiling water for 30 minutes. Drain. Remove pits and chop prunes.

3. Preheat oven to 375°F. In a medium-size skillet, melt butter and saute onions, celery, and garlic for about 2 minutes. Add bread cubes, walnuts, prunes, ⅓ cup of the stock, and seasonings. Mix gently but thoroughly.

4. Pack stuffing into cavity left by bone and tie meat together with clean string, making a rolled roast.

5. Roast in a 10 x 10-inch pan for 15 minutes. Reduce oven temperature to 350°F and roast for 25 minutes longer or until leg is nicely browned. Cover with foil and continue to roast for another 30 to 35 minutes.

6. Lift roast onto carving board. Pour remaining 1⅓ cups stock into roasting pan and loosen the drippings. Pour the stock and drippings into a 1-quart saucepan and heat. Dissolve cornstarch in water and add it to the saucepan. Simmer over medium heat until thickened. Serve sliced lamb and stuffing accompanied by the gravy.

Serves 6

6	medium-size potatoes	1	cup lamb gravy or Tomato
1½	cups ground lamb		Brown Sauce (see Index)
2	tablespoons oil	½	teaspoon rosemary
½	cup finely chopped onions	½	teaspoon paprika
1	cup finely chopped green	1	egg yolk, beaten
	peppers	1	egg white
1½	cups grated or ground carrots	3	tablespoons butter
½	cup lamb stock, Beef Stock (see	½	cup milk
	Index), or Chicken Stock (see	¼	teaspoon nutmeg
	Index)		

1. Cook potatoes until tender, using as little water as possible.

2. While potatoes are cooking, brown lamb in a large skillet and then move to a 2-quart bowl. In the same skillet, heat oil and saute onions, green peppers, and carrots until soft. Add stock, cover, and cook for 5 minutes.

3. Add the vegetables to the lamb. Stir in gravy or tomato brown sauce. Add the seasonings and turn out into a 3-quart casserole.

4. Preheat oven to 350°F. Drain the potatoes and put them through a ricer into a 2-quart bowl. Mix in beaten egg yolk. Add butter, milk, and nutmeg, beating until potatoes are fluffy. Beat egg white until stiff but not dry and fold into potato mixture. Spread over lamb mixture, sprinkle with a little more nutmeg, and bake for 20 minutes.

Serves 6

Remarks   Serve with Tomato Catsup (see Index) or extra tomato brown sauce.

═══ Spaghetti and Spicy Lamb Sauce ═══119

Sauce

2	tablespoons butter		1	cup drained and chopped cooked tomatoes
1	medium-size onion, minced		1	cup lamb stock, Beef Stock (see Index), or Chicken Stock (see Index)
2	garlic cloves, minced			
½	teaspoon ground ginger			
½	teaspoon ground cumin			
1	teaspoon ground coriander		¼	cup lemon juice
¼	teaspoon turmeric		3	tablespoons honey
⅛	teaspoon cayenne pepper		1	tablespoon molasses
¼	teaspoon black pepper		2	teaspoons tamari soy sauce
¼	cup brown rice flour		½	cup vinegar
1	cup tomato sauce		1½	cups cubed cooked lamb
1	cup tomato juice			

Spaghetti

4	quarts water		1	pound whole wheat spaghetti
1	tablespoon oil		¼	cup chopped parsley

1. In a 2½-quart, heavy-bottom saucepan, melt butter and saute onions, garlic, and spices for 2 minutes. Stir in brown rice flour, then add tomato sauce, tomato juice, tomatoes, and stock, stirring until thickened. Add lemon juice, honey, molasses, tamari, vinegar, and lamb. Keep warm over low heat.

2. Bring water to a boil in a 6-quart pot. Add oil, then drop in spaghetti, stirring to keep strands separated. Boil, uncovered, for 15 to 20 minutes or until tender. Drain.

3. Serve spaghetti topped with the sauce and garnish with chopped parsley.

Serves 6

2	tablespoons oil		2	tablespoons rosemary
1	pound ground lamb		4	teaspoons oregano
1	medium-size onion, chopped		2	tablespoons cornstarch
4	garlic cloves, minced		2	tablespoons cold water or stock
6	cups cooked white beans		4	green onions, thinly sliced
3	cups sliced white turnips			
3	cups Chicken Stock or Beef Stock (see Index)			

1. In a 10-inch Dutch oven or a 5-quart, heavy-bottom pot, heat oil and brown lamb with onions and garlic.

2. Add cooked beans, turnips, stock, and herbs. Cover pan and simmer until turnips are tender.

3. Dissolve cornstarch in cold water or stock and add to the simmering mixture. Stir until thickened.

4. Turn contents of skillet into a 3-quart casserole and garnish with green onions before serving.

Serves 6

¾	cup Yogurt (see Index)	3	tablespoons oil
¼	cup unsweetened pineapple juice	16	carrot chunks (about ½ inch)
2	garlic cloves, minced	24	zucchini chunks (about 1 x 1 inch)
¼	teaspoon ground ginger	34	green pepper chunks (about 1 x ½ inch)
⅛	teaspoon cayenne pepper		
⅛	teaspoon black pepper	14	onion chunks (about 1 x 1 inch)
⅛	teaspoon celery seeds	2	cups lamb stock, Beef Stock (see Index), or Chicken Stock (see Index)
¼	teaspoon ground cumin		
½	teaspoon ground coriander		
¼	teaspoon cinnamon	22	pineapple chunks (about ¾ x ¾ inch)
⅛	teaspoon ground cloves		
½	teaspoon dried mint	24	banana chunks (about ¾ inch)
¼	pounds lamb, cut into 1-inch cubes		

1. In a 2½-quart bowl, combine yogurt, pineapple juice, garlic, and spices. Add lamb. Mix by hand in order to coat lamb evenly with marinade. Cover and refrigerate for 24 hours.

2. Heat oil in a large skillet. Saute carrots over medium heat for 3 minutes. Then add zucchini, green peppers, and onions and saute for 2 minutes longer, turning vegetables to coat them evenly with the oil.

3. Add stock, cover, and cook vegetables over medium-low heat for 4 minutes. Remove skillet from heat. Drain stock and let vegetables cool, uncovered. Reserve stock for some future use.

4. Pass skewers (5¼ inches in length) through lamb, vegetables, pineapple, and bananas alternately, fitting as many pieces on each skewer as possible. (Allow 3 kabobs per serving.) Place in a 17¼ x 11½ x 2¼-inch shallow pan. Set oven rack 5 to 6 inches below broiler unit and broil kabobs for 5 to 10 minutes on both sides or until browned, basting with the marinade as they are turned.

Serves 6

Remarks Serve on a mound of cooked brown rice. Pour any remaining marinade from the broiler pan over the kabobs and rice.

Organ Meats

The organ meats (sometimes called variety meats) are among the most nourishing of all meats. They are, for the most part, cheaper than others, and they provide a welcome change from the usual beef, pork, or chicken routine. Years ago, butchers virtually gave organ meats away, but the sophisticated palates of today have elevated them to a new level of desirability. A smart shopper stocks up on these meats at every opportunity.

Tongue, heart, kidney, and liver are generally available if you keep an eye out for them. Ask, if you don't see them displayed. Good tripe is hard to find; brains and sweetbreads are even more elusive—but well worth the hunt. Fresh tongue is scarcer than smoked tongue, but I search out the fresh because I want to avoid the sodium nitrite used in the curing process. (See Pork chapter.)

The markets seem to have a constant supply of frozen beef kidneys, but if you keep a sharp lookout, you sometimes see a lamb or veal kidney. If you do, buy it by all means. Freeze it for a "mixed broil." Both veal and lamb kidneys are tender enough to be cooked by dry heat.

Generally speaking, the organ meats are rich depositories of the B vitamins, vitamin A, and of certain minerals, particularly iron, that are lacking in most ordinary diets. For those who lack B_{12}, liver and kidneys offer from 10 to 200 times the amount found in an equal serving of muscle meats.

The "Best" Kind of Liver

Somehow the idea persists that calves' liver or "baby beef" liver is vastly superior to any other kind. This old wives' tale should be laid to rest. The major difference among the livers is price. Calves' liver costs the most, baby beef liver is next, then beef liver, and, finally, pork liver, which is often just about half the price of beef liver. I will happily settle for beef and pork livers. Some say the flavor of the latter is too strong. I honestly don't notice it, and I think you will agree, particularly if you use it in my recipes for liver entrees which combine the liver with vegetables, spices, sauces, and grains. Start with Curried Pork Liver and Rice Pilaf, which begins by marinating the liver in yogurt and spices.

In the Liver Pate, I enhanced the flavor by adding pork liver to the beef liver. That's what they do to perk up liverwurst. I was trying to produce my own version of liverwurst but without the additives and salt, and I think I came awfully close! It's smooth and flavorful, and it can be sliced for use as a luncheon meat or works well as a spread on bread or crackers.

I used to think there was only one way to cook liver (sauteed quickly over medium-high heat), but I have discovered something new—Oven-Fried Herbed Liver Strips. They just might become my new favorite! The liver is "fried" in the oven for just 15 minutes without any fat at all. You simply dip the strips of liver in milk and then in a crumb and spice mixture, lay them on a rack, and let the oven do the work. They come out crunchy on the outside and moist inside.

Liver in a dumpling was an idea that intrigued me. Leave it to the Pennsylvania Dutch—who else would think of mixing raw liver with bread stuffing, then cooking it by dropping it into soup! A most satisfying meal, simple and fun to make. Raw ground liver also makes a very good "stretcher" for ground beef in Liver and Beef Burgers. Oven-Fried Liver Roll-Ups were inspired by the experience of making Beef Paupiettes. Could the same thing be done with liver slices? It could—another pleasant surprise.

Old-Timer: Tripe

Whenever I told anyone that I was experimenting with recipes for tripe, the response was often a nostalgic smile and a wistful remark such as, "My mother made wonderful pickled tripe," or "I haven't had tripe for years. We used to eat it creamed when we were kids." It seems that in the "olden days," Americans really ate a lot of tripe.

Basic Preparation of Variety Meats

Heart: Wash in warm water. Trim away gristle and the large blood vessels. Braise or simmer with sauce or stuffing.

Kidney: Peel off the outer membrane. Split in half to remove the inner white fat and tubes. Wash in cold water. Simmer or braise beef and pork kidneys before using them in your favorite recipe.

Liver: Cut away heavy blood vessels and outside membrane. Wash. Braise older beef and pork liver, then use in a favorite recipe. Pan broil or broil lamb liver.

Sweetbreads and Brains: Wash in cold water. Remove clotted blood, blood vessels, and excessive connective tissue. Pan broil, simmer, or broil. Use cooked brains or sweetbreads in a tasty scalloped dish recipe, smother with tomato or cream sauce, or add to scrambled eggs.

Tongue: Wash. Cook in simmering water, then cut away skin, bones, and gristle. Use in a favorite tongue recipe.

Tripe: Simmer until tender. Prepare in a tasty tripe recipe.

Honeycomb tripe, named for its texture, is the muscular lining of the first and second stomachs of the beef. There is also a smooth kind of tripe, which comes from other parts of the beef stomach but is only available from those who slaughter their own beef.

All tripe is cooked before it is sold; nevertheless, it requires additional cooking once purchased. It will tenderize in 2 hours if simmered over low heat, but the texture will remain a bit chewy, a texture preferred by some people. Tripe will become really soft if cooked in the pressure cooker at 15 pounds pressure for 30 minutes. Then it can be cut into desirable sizes and cooked according to your choice of recipe.

Tongue Is Delicate and Tender

Tongue must be simmered slowly and long enough so that the skin and root-end bones can be easily removed. Strain the stock and cool it, then refrigerate with the tongue in it. And when you freeze tongue, freeze it in the stock to keep it moist. The meat of tongue is tender and delicate. There's nothing rich or heavy about it. It lends itself nicely to salads, adding its unique flavor and texture to vegetables, both cooked and raw. Tongue, as it is prepared with a cranberry glaze in the recipe in this section, is a dish fit for a celebration.

Low-Calorie Heart

Heart is a more solid, earthy meat. Stuffed heart is a gourmet's delight, providing a contrast in textures and seasonings which complement the flavor of the meat. Veal and beef hearts are equally delicious, differing only in the length of cooking time required (1 hour for veal, 2 to 3 hours for beef). Heart supplies a large proportion of low-calorie protein per pound of meat, due to its low fat content. Because it is so firm, the cooked meat can be used very successfully in salad or hash without becoming stringy. Raw heart is an economical and nourishing "stretcher" for ground beef in patties or a meat loaf.

All organ meats are highly perishable, more so than any other meat. If purchased fresh, they must be used within 2 days. If frozen when purchased, they will keep that way for 4 months. Frozen organ meats should be thawed in the refrigerator and, should you wish to grind the liver or heart, they should be used quickly or refrozen while still cold.

Kidneys Are Elegant, Underrated Fare

Beef kidneys are the least expensive of any organ meats, probably because they are not as fully appreciated in America as they are abroad. Beef, pork, veal, and lamb kidneys are all delicate and elegant fare when properly prepared. The fatty white center should be snipped out because enzymes convert nitrogen in this white tissue into ammonia, and that is what causes the unpleasant odor often associated with kidney. After washing the kidneys, many cooks choose to rinse them in vinegar to neutralize any remaining ammonia.

Don't cook kidneys over high heat. Not only does it toughen them and make them rubbery, but it encourages the production of more ammonia which then evaporates, leaving behind an unappetizing odor.

Veal and lamb kidneys are especially suitable for grilling. Unlike beef and pork kidneys, they should *not* be washed or soaked prior to being cooked. Just split them and remove the core of white tissue. They are tender and should be broiled only until the pink disappears. The veal kidney is surrounded with a delicate and delicious fat which enhances the flavor when broiled, so if you fancy that taste, don't remove the fat.

As you try the kidney entrees in this book, I think you'll be surprised at how quickly you can prepare them, how delicious they are, and how little they cost.

By using particular care in preparation and in cooking, we can spread the organ meat "renaissance" I mentioned earlier, an enlightened frame of mind which sees these unique meats as the delicacies they truly are.

HEART

Because the heart is a much-used muscle, it calls for some tenderizing in the cooking process. Time may be a factor in which method you choose.

Methods of Cooking Beef Heart

1	beef heart (about 2 pounds)		1	large carrot, cut into chunks
3 to 4	cups water		1	small bunch parsley
1	medium-size onion, cut into chunks		1	bay leaf
2	celery stalks with tops, cut into chunks			

1. Place heart in a 4-quart pot, add 4 cups water, and bring to a boil. Add remaining ingredients, reduce heat to low, and simmer, covered, for 2 to 3 hours or until heart is fork-tender.

2. Strain stock. Cool and then refrigerate heart and stock.

Pressure Cooker Method

1. Combine heart, 4 cups water, vegetables, and herbs in a 4-quart pressure cooker. Cook at 15 pounds pressure for 45 minutes. Remove from heat and let pressure drop.

2. Strain stock. Cool and then refrigerate heart and stock.

Slow Cooker Method

1. Combine heart, 3 cups water, vegetables, and herbs in a 3½-quart slow cooker. Cook on Low for 9 hours.

2. Strain stock. Cool and then refrigerate heart and stock.

Basic Stuffed Beef Heart 127

1	medium-size onion, minced	1	teaspoon oregano
4	celery stalks, chopped	1	teaspoon thyme or basil
4	cups cubed dried bread	2	cups Beef Stock (see Index)
6	tablespoons oil	1	beef heart
1	teaspoon poultry seasoning		

1. In a large skillet, heat 4 tablespoons oil and saute onion, celery, and then bread cubes. Add poultry seasoning and herbs. Gradually stir in 1 cup stock, then set aside.

2. Cut heart open so that it will lie flat. Remove large tubes from inside. Spoon stuffing onto heart and then wrap heart around the stuffing, securing it with skewers or toothpicks. In another skillet, heat 2 tablespoons oil and carefully brown outside of stuffed heart. Place in Dutch oven with remaining cup of stock and cook until heart is tender (about 1 to 2 hours).

3. Thicken broth, if desired, to make gravy. Slice heart and serve with gravy.

Serves 4 to 6

Beef Heart, Potato, and Apple Salad

8	medium-size potatoes (about 2 pounds), peeled and cut into ½-inch cubes	3	cups coarsely chopped celery
		3	tart red apples, cored and cut into small slices
¼	cup vinegar	½	cup Mayonnaise (see Index)
3	cups chopped cooked beef heart (½-inch cubes) (See Index for methods of cooking beef heart)	1½	teaspoons Mustard (see Index)
		¾	cup Yogurt (see Index)
		1	tablespoon honey
		2	tablespoons lemon juice
6	green onions, finely sliced	1½	teaspoons celery seeds

1. Cook potatoes in enough boiling water to cover until tender but firm. Drain. Coat cooked potatoes with vinegar and set aside to cool.

2. In a 4-quart bowl, combine heart, onions, celery, and apples.

3. In a 1-quart bowl, combine mayonnaise, mustard, yogurt, honey, lemon juice, and celery seeds.

4. Add cooled potatoes to heart mixture, then add dressing and toss lightly.

Serves 6

3	pounds potatoes	¾	cup tomato sauce
4	cups diced cooked beef heart	1	tablespoon oregano
	(see Index for methods of	¾	teaspoon allspice
	cooking beef heart)	6	tablespoons oil
1	cup coarsely chopped onions		Tomato Catsup (see Index)

1. Scrub potatoes and remove any rough spots. Then grate them. (There should be about 8 cups.)

2. Combine grated potatoes with heart, onions, tomato sauce, and seasonings.

3. Heat 3 tablespoons oil in a large iron skillet over medium-low heat, add half the mixture, cover, and cook for about 5 minutes or until brown underneath. Turn portions of the mixture over until the hash has a brown crust on both sides.

4. Turn out of skillet onto a platter and place in a warm oven.

5. Heat remaining oil in skillet and brown the remaining mixture as above. Serve with tomato catsup.

Serves 6

━━━━━ Spoon Beef Heart Loaf ━━━━━

½	pound veal or beef heart	2	teaspoons chili powder
1	pound ground chuck	2	teaspoons basil
1	medium-size onion, chopped	1½	cups rolled oats
2	garlic cloves, minced	1	cup tomato juice
½	cup chopped green peppers	1	cup cooked tomatoes

1. Grind heart, using the coarse, large-holed disc of grinder.

2. Combine all ingredients in a 3-quart bowl, mixing thoroughly by hand.

3. Transfer to a 3-quart casserole and bake, uncovered, in a 350°F oven for 1 hour or until liquid is absorbed and top is browned. Serve with a spoon.

Serves 6

Veal Heart with 129
Prune and Apple Stuffing

2	veal hearts (3½ pounds total weight)	1	celery stalk with tops, cut into chunks
4	cups water	1	carrot, cut into chunks
1	medium-size onion, coarsely chopped	1	bay leaf

Stuffing

12	prunes	2	cups soft whole grain bread crumbs
3	tablespoons butter		
½	cup finely chopped onions	½	teaspoon allspice
1	cup finely chopped celery	½	teaspoon nutmeg
¼	cup sunflower seeds	1	tablespoon cornstarch
1	cup finely chopped apples	2	tablespoons cold water

1. Cut hearts in half, lengthwise. Place in a 3-quart pot, add water, and bring to a boil. Add onions, celery, carrots, and bay leaf. Reduce heat and simmer, covered, for 1 hour or until hearts are fork-tender.

2. To make stuffing, add prunes to simmering hearts during the last 15 minutes of cooking time. In a large skillet, melt butter. Add onions, celery, sunflower seeds, apples, bread crumbs, and spices and saute until onions are soft.

3. Preheat oven to 350°F. Lift the hearts out of the stock and arrange them in a 13 x 9 x 2-inch baking pan. If necessary, make slits in the hearts to open each one just enough to be stuffed.

4. Lift prunes out of the stock, remove pits, chop, and add to stuffing along with ½ cup of stock. Mix well and mound stuffing on top of each half.

5. Pour 2 cups stock into baking pan, cover with foil, and bake for 30 minutes.

6. Before serving, cut each stuffed half crosswise, making 8 portions.

7. Pour liquid from baking pan into a 1-quart saucepan and place over medium-high heat. Dissolve cornstarch in water and add to hot liquid, stirring until thickened. Serve sauce with stuffed heart.

Serves 6

KIDNEY

Buckwheat Kidney Pilaf

2	beef kidneys (about 2 pounds total weight)	1	cup coarsely chopped celery
3	tablespoons vinegar	1	cup coarsely chopped green peppers
3	tablespoons oil	1½	cups buckwheat groats
½	cup coarsely chopped onions	1½	cups Chicken Stock or Beef Stock (see Index)
2	garlic cloves, minced		
1½	cups thinly sliced carrots	1½	cups tomato juice

1. Using kitchen shears, snip out fatty centers from kidneys and discard. Cut kidneys into ½-inch pieces and wash in cold water. Place kidneys in a 1-quart bowl, add vinegar, and mix thoroughly.

2. Then wash vinegar off kidneys and dry with paper towels. In a large skillet, heat oil. Add kidneys, onions, and garlic and saute until lightly browned.

3. Add the remaining vegetables, then the buckwheat groats. Stir thoroughly so that groats and vegetables are evenly coated with the hot oil. Saute over low heat for about 1 minute, stirring constantly.

4. Add stock and tomato juice. Cover skillet and cook over low heat for 15 minutes or until the buckwheat is cooked and the liquid is absorbed. Serve immediately.

Serves 6

Creamed Kidneys and Mushrooms on Toast

3	beef kidneys (about 3 pounds total weight)	2	cups Chicken Stock (see Index)
¼	cup vinegar	1	cup milk
4 to 6	tablespoons butter	2	tablespoons cornstarch
1	medium-size onion, coarsely chopped	2	tablespoons cold water
3	cups sliced mushrooms	½	teaspoon nutmeg
6	tablespoons rye flour or whole wheat flour	6	slices whole grain toast

1. Using kitchen shears, snip out fatty centers of kidneys and discard. Cut kidneys into ½-inch pieces, wash in cold water, and then combine with vinegar in a 1-quart bowl. Set aside.

2. In a large skillet, melt 4 tablespoons butter. Saute onions and mushrooms for 5 to 10 minutes. Lift from skillet and set aside.

3. Wash vinegar off kidneys and pat dry between paper towels. Roll kidneys in flour and saute, while stirring, just until pink disappears. Add more butter if needed. Do not overcook kidneys.

4. Return onions and mushrooms to skillet. Add stock and milk, stirring to make a smooth sauce. Dissolve cornstarch in water and add to skillet. Stir until thickened. Add nutmeg and serve over whole grain toast.

Serves 6

5 lamb kidneys (about 1¼ pounds total weight)
6 teaspoons tamari soy sauce
6 tablespoons wine vinegar
½ teaspoon dry mustard
3 tablespoons oil
18 small white onions
18 radishes, trimmed
2 medium-size green peppers, cut into 1½-inch squares (about 24 pieces)

5 to 6 celery stalks, cut into 2-inch lengths (about 24 pieces)
1½ cups yellow summer squash, cut into 1-inch pieces (about 18 pieces)
18 large mushroom caps
1 cup Beef Stock (see Index)

1. Using kitchen shears, snip out the white fatty centers of kidneys and discard. Cut kidneys into 1-inch pieces and wash in cold water.

2. In a 1-quart bowl, combine 5 teaspoons tamari, 5 tablespoons wine vinegar, and dry mustard. Marinate kidney pieces in mixture for 12 to 24 hours.

3. Heat oil in a large skillet. Add vegetables and mushroom caps and saute over medium-high heat for 1 to 2 minutes, turning frequently to coat the vegetables evenly with the oil. Lift out mushrooms and green peppers and set aside.

4. Add stock and the remaining 1 teaspoon tamari and 1 tablespoon wine vinegar to vegetables in skillet. Cover and steam over medium-low heat for 4 minutes. Lift out vegetables and cool on a flat pan or tray.

5. Preheat broiler. Pass skewers (5¼ inches in length) through kidneys, vegetables, and mushrooms alternately, fitting as many pieces on each skewer as possible. (Allow 3 kabobs per serving.)

6. Place filled skewers in a 17¼ x 11½ x 2¼-inch shallow pan. Broil 6½ inches below the broiler unit for 5 minutes. Brush the browned side of the kabobs with the stock mixture, turn, and broil 4 minutes. Then brush the reverse side with the stock mixture.

Serves 6

Remarks   Serve on a mound of cooked brown rice. Pour any remaining stock mixture from the broiling pan over the kabobs and rice.

3	beef kidneys (3 pounds total weight)	4	cups coarsely chopped cauliflower
¼	cup vinegar	4	cups coarsely chopped broccoli
6	tablespoons oil	3	tablespoons minced ginger root
2	medium-size onions, sliced	6	tablespoons tamari soy sauce
4	garlic cloves, minced	1½	cups Beef Stock (see Index)
2	cups sliced green peppers	6	tablespoons cornstarch
2	cups sliced zucchini	6	tablespoons cold water

1. Using kitchen shears, snip out fatty centers of kidneys and discard. Cut kidneys into ½-inch pieces and wash in cold water. Then combine with vinegar in a 1-quart bowl and set aside.

2. In a large skillet, heat 2 tablespoons oil over medium-high heat and stir-fry onions, garlic, and green peppers for 2 minutes. Turn vegetables out of skillet into casserole and keep warm in oven set at 200°F.

3. Heat 2 tablespoons oil. Stir-fry zucchini, then cauliflower, then broccoli, turning each vegetable out into casserole as it is ready. Remove skillet from heat and set aside.

4. Wash vinegar off kidneys and pat dry between paper towels. Heat 2 tablespoons oil in skillet and stir-fry kidneys just until they are firm and the pink disappears. (Overcooking causes kidneys to become rubbery.)

5. Add ginger root, tamari, and stock. Dissolve cornstarch in water and then add to the stock, stirring until sauce has thickened.

6. Pour kidneys and sauce over vegetables in casserole and serve immediately.

Serves 6

Remarks   Serve with cooked brown rice.

3 to 4	pork kidneys (about 1 pound)	3	tablespoons potato flour or rye flour
4	teaspoons vinegar		
4	tablespoons oil	1½	cups Chicken Stock or Beef Stock (see Index)
½	cup chopped onions		
½	cup chopped celery	3 to 4	tablespoons chopped parsley
1	garlic clove, minced	¼	teaspoon black pepper
1	cup sliced carrots	1	cup chopped mushrooms

1. Preheat oven to 350°F. Cut kidneys lengthwise. Before washing, carefully snip white tissue out of kidneys using kitchen scissors. Then wash with cold water, dice, and mix with vinegar.

2. Heat 3 tablespoons oil in skillet and saute diced kidneys over medium heat, pushing to one side as they brown. Add onions, celery, garlic, and carrots. Continue to saute 10 minutes longer.

3. Sprinkle flour over kidney-vegetable mixture and mix together to blend. Gradually stir in the stock, mixing constantly to prevent lumping. Add 2 tablespoons chopped parsley and the pepper. Simmer 15 minutes.

4. Meanwhile, saute chopped mushrooms in remaining 1 tablespoon oil for 5 minutes. Add to kidney-vegetable mixture.

5. Turn mixture into a lightly oiled, 2-quart, oven-proof casserole and bake, covered, for 1 hour or until kidneys are tender. Garnish with remaining parsley before serving.

Serves 4 to 5

Sesame Kidney Salad 135

3	veal or beef kidneys (2½ to 3 pounds total weight)	2	tablespoons chopped parsley
¼	cup cider vinegar	1¼	cups finely chopped celery
3	cups Beef Stock (see Index)	1¼	cups finely chopped water chestnuts
¼	cup unhulled sesame seeds	6	hard-cooked eggs, coarsely chopped
6	green onions, finely sliced		
2	tablespoons tamari soy sauce	2	tablespoons wine vinegar

1. Using kitchen shears, snip out fatty centers of kidneys and discard. Cut kidneys into ¼-inch pieces. Wash in cold water and then combine with cider vinegar in a 1-quart bowl. Set aside for at least 30 minutes.

2. Bring stock to a boil. Wash vinegar off kidneys, add to the stock, and simmer for 1 minute or just until they are firm. Lift kidneys out of the stock and return to 1-quart bowl. Reserve stock for soup, if desired.

3. Roast sesame seeds in a dry skillet over medium-high heat until you can smell their rich aroma. Stir them or shake the pan to prevent burning.

4. Add green onions, tamari, parsley, celery, water chestnuts, hard-cooked eggs, sesame seeds, and wine vinegar to kidneys. Toss lightly, cover, and refrigerate until ready to serve.

Serves 6

Remarks For a luncheon, serve this salad in lettuce cups on individual salad plates accompanied by thin slices of buttered bread.

Sauce

2	beef kidneys (2 pounds total weight)	¾	cup chopped green peppers
3	tablespoons vinegar	¾	cup coarsely chopped celery
4 to 6	tablespoons oil	2¼	cups drained and coarsely chopped cooked tomatoes
¾	cup coarsely chopped onions	1½	cups tomato juice

Omelet

6	eggs	1½	teaspoons baking powder
6	tablespoons milk	3	tablespoons butter

1. Using kitchen shears, snip out fatty centers of kidneys and discard. Cut kidneys into ½-inch pieces and wash in cold water. Then combine with vinegar in a 1-quart bowl and set aside.

2. In a large skillet or a 3-quart, heavy-bottom pan, heat 2 tablespoons oil. Saute onions, green peppers, and celery until soft. Add tomatoes and tomato juice and simmer, covered, for 5 to 10 minutes. Set aside.

3. Wash vinegar off kidneys and pat dry between paper towels. In a separate skillet, heat remaining oil and saute kidneys just until they are firm and the pink disappears. (Overcooking causes kidneys to become rubbery.) Add kidneys to the sauce and keep warm while you make the omelets.

4. Separate eggs. In a 1-quart bowl, combine egg yolks, milk, and baking powder. Then, in a 2-quart bowl, beat egg whites until stiff but not dry. Fold yolk mixture carefully into beaten whites.

5. Melt 1½ tablespoons butter in a large skillet over medium-low heat. Pour half the omelet mixture into skillet. Cover and cook for 5 minutes, making slits in the omelet with a knife to permit the heat to penetrate to the surface. Then place skillet in a 350°F oven, uncovered, for 5 minutes. (Do not preheat oven.) Cut omelet into 3 equal pie-shaped portions and turn out onto plate, bottom-side up. Keep it warm while you make the second omelet.

6. Melt remaining 1½ tablespoons butter in skillet, add remaining omelet mixture, and proceed as above. Serve each portion topped with sauce.

Serves 6

Steak and Kidney Pie ════════ 137

1	beef kidney (about 1 pound)	1	cup sliced turnips
¾	pound round steak	2½	cups sliced carrots
4	teaspoons vinegar	¾	teaspoon summer savory
6	tablespoons oil	½	teaspoon rosemary
4½	cups Beef Stock (see Index)	¾	teaspoon thyme
1½	cups coarsely chopped onions	4	tablespoons brown rice flour
2½	cups sliced mushrooms	6	tablespoons water

Pastry

1⅓	cups whole wheat flour
⅓	cup butter
5 to 6	tablespoons water

1. Using kitchen shears, snip out fatty center of kidney and discard. Cut kidney into ½-inch pieces, wash in cold water, and then mix with vinegar in a 1-quart bowl. Set aside.

2. Cut round steak across the grain into strips (½ x 2 inches).

3. Heat 2 tablespoons oil in a large skillet. Add beef strips and saute over medium-high heat until browned. Transfer to a 3-quart casserole and set aside.

4. Wash vinegar off kidneys, pat dry with paper towels, and saute until pink has disappeared, adding more oil as needed. Lift kidneys from skillet and add to beef strips. Pour some stock into skillet to loosen brown bits and add to kidneys and beef.

5. Add remaining oil to skillet and saute onions, mushrooms, turnips, and carrots over medium heat for 2 minutes. Add remaining stock and herbs. Cover skillet and simmer for 5 minutes.

6. Dissolve brown rice flour in water, stir into stock, and cook until thickened. Then empty contents of skillet into the casserole.

7. Preheat oven to 400°F. To make pastry, place flour in a 1-quart bowl. Add butter and cut it into the flour with a pastry blender or two knives until the flour is completely moistened by the butter and the mixture resembles fine crumbs. Add water gradually, mixing it in lightly until the dough forms into a ball.

8. Flatten dough slightly and roll out between 2 pieces of wax paper, lightly floured, until it is about ⅛-inch thick. Remove top piece of wax paper and slit dough in several places to allow steam to escape. Wet rim of casserole. Invert pastry over casserole and remove the second piece of wax paper. Flute edges and bake for 15 minutes.

Serves 6

LIVER

Baked Beef Liver Pate

1	tablespoon oil	½	cup whole grain bread crumbs
10	ounces sliced beef liver	⅛	teaspoon oregano
1	small onion, minced	⅛	teaspoon sage
2	garlic cloves, minced	⅛	teaspoon ground cumin
¾	cup Chicken Stock (see Index)	⅛	teaspoon cayenne pepper
1	cup tofu	1	teaspoon tamari soy sauce
½	cup chopped parsley	1½	teaspoons lemon juice

1. Preheat oven to 350°F. In a large skillet, heat oil and saute liver, onions, and garlic until liver is browned. Cool and cut liver into chunks, removing any gristle. There should be approximately 1½ cups.

2. Combine sauteed onions, garlic, and the liver with stock and tofu in container of blender and process until smooth.

3. Scrape mixture out into a 2-quart bowl and add parsley, bread crumbs, herbs, spices, tamari, and lemon juice. Mix well.

4. Spoon pate into individual Pyrex cups or a 1½-quart casserole and bake for 20 minutes or until a knife inserted in center comes out clean. Cool and store, covered, in refrigerator or freezer until ready to use.

Yields 3½ cups

Remarks　This pate makes a fine spread for crackers or bread.

Cabbage, Kasha, and Liver

1	egg	2	teaspoons cumin seeds
1	cup dark buckwheat groats	½	teaspoon celery seeds
2	cups boiling water	1½	pounds beef liver
8 to 10	tablespoons oil	¾	cup rye flour
1	cup coarsely chopped onions	2	cups water
8	cups coarsely chopped cabbage	1	cup Yogurt (see Index)
	(about 1½ pounds)	½	cup tomato sauce

1. In a 1½-quart saucepan, stir egg into dry buckwheat groats over medium-high heat until egg is absorbed. Add water, stirring constantly. Cover saucepan and cook over low heat for 15 to 20 minutes or until buckwheat is tender and water is absorbed. Take care not to overcook groats. Set aside 2 cups kasha for this recipe and reserve remaining 2 cups for future use.

2. In a large skillet, heat oil and saute onions, then cabbage with spices, until cabbage is limp but not soft. (The cabbage will have to be cooked in two batches. Be sure to cook some of the spices with each batch.) Remove from skillet and set aside.

3. Cut liver into 2 x 1 x ¼-inch pieces and dredge in ½ cup of the flour. In the same skillet, saute liver until brown, adding more oil as needed. Remove liver from skillet and keep warm.

4. Pour water into skillet and loosen brown bits in pan. Dissolve remaining ¼ cup flour in ½ cup of the yogurt and then add to liquid in skillet, stirring constantly. Add remaining yogurt and cook over low heat until sauce has thickened. Stir in tomato sauce.

5. Return cabbage mixture and kasha to skillet and blend well. Add liver, toss gently to combine, and serve at once.

Serves 6

8	chicken gizzards	2½	cups coarsely chopped
8	chicken hearts		mushrooms
3½	cups Chicken Stock (see Index)	1¼	cups brown rice
1	teaspoon thyme	¼	cup finely chopped water
1	teaspoon marjoram		chestnuts
6	tablespoons butter	12	chicken livers
½	cup coarsely chopped onions	5	tablespoons tomato sauce
½	cup coarsely chopped celery	¼	cup chopped parsley

1. In a 2-quart saucepan, bring chicken gizzards and hearts to a boil in 3 cups of the stock. Add the herbs, reduce heat, and simmer, covered, for 30 minutes or until giblets are tender. Remove giblets. Trim all inedible parts from gizzards and dice them. Cut each heart in half. Set aside and keep warm. Reserve the stock.

2. In a 5-quart, heavy-bottom pot, melt 3 tablespoons butter and saute onions, celery, and mushrooms for about 2 minutes, stirring constantly.

3. Add the rice, stirring to coat it evenly with butter. Add the water chestnuts and the stock from the gizzards. Reduce heat and simmer, covered, for 30 minutes.

4. In a large skillet, melt remaining 3 tablespoons butter and saute chicken livers until they are brown and firm and the pink has disappeared. Set aside and keep warm.

5. When rice is soft, gently combine it with the gizzards, hearts, and livers. Heat remaining ½ cup chicken stock in the skillet in which livers were sauteed, loosening any brown bits that may be in the pan. Add tomato sauce and blend well. Pour over Risotto before serving. Garnish with chopped parsley.

Serves 6

Gizzard Chili

1¼	pounds chicken gizzards	2¾	cups cooked pinto or kidney
2	tablespoons oil		beans
1	large onion, chopped	2	cups cooked tomatoes
1	garlic clove, minced	⅛	teaspoon black pepper
		3	teaspoons chili powder

1. Simmer gizzards in enough water to cover until tender. Drain and grind. There should be about 3 cups.

2. In a large skillet, heat oil and saute onion and garlic until soft and lightly browned. Add ground gizzards and saute 5 minutes longer. Then add remaining ingredients and simmer for 10 minutes. Serve immediately or set aside to be reheated.

Serves 4 to 6

Remarks This dish improves after a day or two when the flavors have blended.

3 tablespoons butter
1½ pounds chicken livers, cut into halves
1 medium onion, chopped

1 pound fresh spinach or 1 package (10 ounces) frozen chopped spinach, thawed
4 cups cooked brown rice
¼ cup Chicken Broth (see Index)

1. Preheat oven to 350°F. In a large skillet, melt butter and lightly brown livers and onions.

2. Wash spinach thoroughly and steam it (in just the water that clings to the leaves) until wilted. Then chop spinach. (If using frozen spinach, precooking is not necessary.)

3. Spread the spinach on the bottom of an oiled 3-quart casserole. Mix together the livers, onion, and rice and spoon the mixture on top of the spinach. Drizzle the broth over all. Cover and bake for 25 minutes or until livers are cooked through but are not dry.

Serves 4 to 6

Oven-Fried Liver Roll-Ups

5 tablespoons butter
¼ cup minced onions
¾ cup minced celery
1½ cups soft whole grain bread crumbs
¼ teaspoon thyme
¼ teaspoon sage
⅛ teaspoon marjoram

3 tablespoons Chicken Stock or Beef Stock (see Index)
1½ teaspoons Mustard (see Index)
1¼ pounds thinly sliced beef liver (3 large slices or 6 smaller slices)
¼ cup rye flour

1. Preheat oven to 375°F. In a medium-size skillet, melt 3 tablespoons of the butter and saute onions and celery over medium-high heat for 2 minutes. Turn contents into a 2-quart bowl. Mix in bread crumbs, herbs, and stock.

2. Melt remaining butter in the same skillet and set aside. Spread mustard over liver slices, then spread an equal amount of stuffing over each slice, and roll, jelly roll fashion, as tightly as possible. Tie each roll with string.

3. Coat liver roll-ups with the flour, then pat them with melted butter using a pastry brush. Place them on a rack set in a shallow 14 x 10 x 2-inch baking pan, allowing a little space between each.

4. Bake 15 to 30 minutes or until liver is tender. Remove strings and serve immediately.

Serves 6

½	teaspoon cumin seeds	½	teaspoon whole cloves
½	teaspoon fennel seeds	½	teaspoon ground cardamom
1	pound pork liver	2	tablespoons butter
⅓	cup Yogurt (see Index)	2	medium-size onions, thinly
2	tablespoons lemon juice		sliced
¼	cup oil	2	garlic cloves, minced
¾	teaspoon ground coriander	1½	cups brown rice
½	teaspoon turmeric	3	cups Beef Stock or Chicken
¼	teaspoon cayenne pepper		Stock (see Index)
½	teaspoon cinnamon	1½	cups frozen peas

1. Toast cumin seeds and fennel seeds in a medium-size dry skillet, stirring constantly, until you smell their rich aroma. Grind seeds using a mortar and pestle, or place seeds on a board between sheets of wax paper and pound with a mallet until they are pulverized.

2. Cut liver into strips approximately 1½ x ¾ x ¼ inches, trimming any inedible parts. Combine liver strips with yogurt, lemon juice, 2 teaspoons of the oil, and spices in a 2-quart bowl. Set aside to marinate at room temperature for 30 minutes.

3. In a large skillet, heat 1 tablespoon oil and 1 tablespoon butter and saute onions and garlic over medium heat until onions are evenly browned. Turn garlic and onions out of skillet into a 1-pint oven-proof dish and place in a warm oven. Set skillet aside.

4. In a 2½-quart, heavy-bottom pot, heat 1 teaspoon oil and 1 tablespoon butter and saute rice for about 30 seconds. Using your fingers, strip as much marinade from liver as possible and add all marinade to the rice along with the stock. Cover pot and simmer over low heat for 30 to 35 minutes until liquid is absorbed and rice is soft. Add frozen peas for the last 5 minutes, spreading them on top of the rice. Do not stir into rice.

5. In the same skillet, heat 2 tablespoons oil and saute liver strips over medium-high heat until brown on both sides.

6. Combine cooked rice and peas with sauteed liver and serve, topped with the sauteed garlic and onions.

Serves 6

Remarks   This is an exceptionally good curry dish.

Levverknepp Supp ===143
(Pennsylvania Dutch Liver Dumpling Soup)

Dumplings

2	small onions (about ½ cup after grinding)
4	celery stalks (about ½ cup after grinding)
3	tablespoons butter
1	pound beef liver

¼	cup parsley leaves
1	cup whole grain bread crumbs
2	eggs, beaten
½	teaspoon poultry seasoning
¼	teaspoon black pepper

Soup

8	cups Beef Stock or Chicken Stock (see Index)
¾	cup coarsely chopped celery

¾	cup coarsely chopped carrots
1½	cups shredded cabbage

1. Put onions and celery through meat grinder, using the coarse, large-holed disc of grinder. Together they should measure 1 cup. In a large skillet, melt butter and saute ground onions and celery for about 5 minutes.

2. Grind liver, using the coarse, large-holed disc, and then grind parsley. Add both to sauteed vegetables in skillet. Stir in bread crumbs, eggs, and seasonings, mix well, and set aside.

3. Bring stock to a boil in a 5-quart soup pot. Add celery, carrots, and cabbage. Reduce heat.

4. Drop liver mixture into simmering soup by the teaspoonful, taking care to keep each dumpling separate. Do not cover pot. When dumplings rise to the surface, continue cooking for about 8 minutes. Serve immediately.

Serves 6

6	ounces beef liver	2	tablespoons tomato sauce
18	ounces ground chuck	6	medium-size onions
¼	teaspoon allspice	1 to 2	tablespoons oil
½	teaspoon dry mustard		

1. Grind liver using the coarse, large-holed disc of grinder.

2. In a 2-quart bowl, combine ground chuck with ground liver. Add spices and tomato sauce. Mix well and form into 6 patties.

3. Slice onions as thinly as possible. Heat oil in a large skillet and saute onions until they are soft and golden brown. Cover with a lid for 1 to 2 minutes at the beginning to steam them slightly. Remove from skillet and keep warm.

4. In the same skillet, heat a little additional oil, if needed, and saute the patties until they are brown on both sides. Cover the skillet toward the end of cooking time to be sure the burgers are cooked through. Serve topped with the sauteed onions.

Serves 6

======== **Liver Creole** ========

1½	pounds beef liver	3¾	cups shredded cabbage
3	tablespoons rye flour	3	cups stewed tomatoes
4 to 6	tablespoons oil	¾	cup tomato juice
1½	medium-size onions, chopped	1½	teaspoons basil
2	cups finely chopped green peppers	4	teaspoons cornstarch
		2	tablespoons cold water

1. Cut liver into pieces about 2 x 1½ x ¼ inches and dredge in the flour. Heat 2 to 3 tablespoons oil in a large skillet and saute liver over medium-high heat until crisp and brown. Transfer to a 14 x 10 x 2-inch oven-proof dish and place in a warm oven.

2. In the same skillet, heat an additional 2 to 3 tablespoons oil and saute onions, green peppers, and cabbage for about 2 minutes.

3. Add tomatoes, tomato juice, and basil and simmer, covered, for 5 minutes. Dissolve cornstarch in water and add to vegetables. Stir constantly until thickened.

4. Turn creole vegetable sauce into a 3-quart bowl or casserole, place liver on top, and serve immediately.

Serves 6

Remarks Serve with cooked brown rice.

2	tablespoons oil	½	cup water
½	pound sliced pork liver	2	tablespoons unflavored gelatin
½	pound sliced beef liver	½	teaspoon dry mustard
1	medium-size onion, cut into chunks	¼	teaspoon paprika
1	celery stalk, cut into chunks	¼	teaspoon black pepper
1	medium-size carrot, cut into chunks	½	teaspoon ground coriander
½	cup cornmeal	¼	teaspoon ground cloves
¾	cup Chicken Stock or Beef Stock (see Index)	2	tablespoons lemon juice
		2	tablespoons Tomato Catsup (see Index)

Garnish

salad greens
parsley sprigs
radish roses or cherry tomatoes

1. In a large skillet, heat oil and saute pork and beef liver, onions, celery, and carrots until liver is brown and vegetables are tender. Put vegetables through meat grinder using the fine, small-holed disc, then put liver through grinder twice.

2. Combine cornmeal and stock in a 1-quart, heavy-bottom saucepan and simmer over low heat for 5 to 10 minutes, stirring occasionally, until thick.

3. Place water in a 1-pint saucepan, sprinkle gelatin over water, and leave to soak for 5 minutes. Set pan over low heat and stir soaked gelatin until it has melted.

4. In a 2-quart mixing bowl, combine cooked cornmeal and melted gelatin with the ground liver and vegetables. Add spices, lemon juice, and catsup. Mix thoroughly and turn into an oiled 7⅜ x 3⅝ x 2¼-inch loaf pan.

5. Refrigerate, covered, for several hours. To unmold, run hot water over outside of loaf pan, loosen sides with a table knife, and turn out onto a small platter lined with salad greens. Garnish with parsley sprigs and radish roses or cherry tomatoes.

Makes 1 loaf

Remarks   This pate may be served as an hors d'oeuvre, as a sandwich spread, or as sliced luncheon meat.

½	cup whole grain bread crumbs	1½	teaspoons oregano
⅓	cup ground almonds	1	teaspoon dry mustard
¼	cup oat flour (rolled oats ground in blender)	1½	teaspoons paprika
		1½	pounds beef liver
1½	teaspoons thyme	½	cup milk

1. Preheat oven to 375°F. In a 1-quart bowl, combine bread crumbs, ground almonds, oat flour, herbs, and spices.

2. Cut liver into strips about 2½ x ½ x ¼ inches and cover with milk in another 1-quart bowl.

3. Dredge each liver strip in bread crumb mixture until evenly coated. Place breaded strips on a rack in a shallow 17¼ x 11½ x 2¼-inch baking pan. Leave space between each strip to permit even cooking. Bake for 15 minutes. Serve immediately.

Serves 6

══════ Tuxedo Liver Saute ══════

½	cup plus 1 tablespoon rye flour	1	tablespoon ground coriander
1	teaspoon ground ginger	1¾	cups Beef Stock or Chicken Stock (see Index)
½	teaspoon black pepper		
6 to 8	tablespoons oil	¼	cup water
6	medium-size onions, cut lengthwise into about 12 chunks	1	tablespoon tamari soy sauce
		2	pounds pork liver, cut into 2 x 3 x ¼-inch pieces
3	medium-size green peppers, cut into 2 x ½-inch strips	6	medium-size potatoes, cut into 2½ x ½-inch pieces

1. Combine flour, ginger, and black pepper in a pie plate or shallow dish.

2. In a large skillet, heat 2 tablespoons oil and saute onions and green peppers for 1 minute. Add coriander and stock, cover, and steam for 2 minutes.

3. Combine water and tamari. Dissolve 3 tablespoons of the flour mixture in the liquid and then stir into the onions and green peppers. Cook until thickened, then transfer to a 2-quart oven-proof dish and place in a warm oven.

4. Dredge liver in remaining flour mixture. Heat 2 to 3 tablespoons oil in a clean skillet and saute liver pieces until brown. Remove liver from skillet and place in a warm oven.

5. Heat 2 to 3 tablespoons oil in a clean skillet and saute potatoes until golden brown. Cover skillet and steam until tender.

6. Serve onions and peppers surrounded by liver and potatoes.

Serves 6

Spicy Avocado
Liver Saute

1	pound beef liver	3	tablespoons butter
2	avocados (1½ pounds total	½	teaspoon allspice
	weight)	½	teaspoon nutmeg
6	tablespoons lemon juice	6	green onions, finely sliced
10	cups water	¾	cup Beef Stock or Chicken
1	tablespoon oil		Stock (see Index)
2½	cups whole grain noodles	¾	cup tomato sauce

1. Cut liver into strips about ½ x 2 x ¼ inches.

2. Peel and cut avocados into slices that are ½-inch thick. Coat avocado slices with lemon juice in a 1-pint bowl.

3. Bring water to a boil in a 4-quart pot, add oil, and stir in noodles. Boil, uncovered, for 10 minutes or until noodles are soft. Set aside.

4. Melt butter in a large skillet and saute liver strips and avocado slices over medium-low heat until liver is brown on both sides, sprinkling with spices as they saute. Shake pan rather than stir, to avoid breaking avocados.

5. Push avocados and liver gently to one side and add green onions, stock, tomato sauce, and 2 tablespoons of the surplus lemon juice from the avocados. Loosen the brown bits in bottom of skillet and blend ingredients thoroughly. Simmer about 2 minutes.

6. Drain noodles. Serve liver, avocados, and sauce over noodles.

Serves 6

TONGUE

Tongue is delicate and delicious, but it calls for thorough cooking to make it tender. Use any method that suits your convenience.

Methods of Cooking Tongue

1	beef tongue (about 3 pounds)	1	celery stalk with top, cut into chunks
3 to 4	cups water		
1	medium-size onion, cut into chunks	1	large carrot, cut into chunks
		1	bay leaf

1. Place tongue in a 4-quart pot, add 4 cups water, and bring to a boil. Add onion, celery, carrot, and bay leaf. Reduce heat and simmer, covered, for 2 to 2½ hours or until tongue is fork-tender.

2. Remove outer skin from tongue. Strain stock. Cool tongue in stock before refrigerating both.

Pressure Cooker Method

1. Combine tongue, 4 cups water, vegetables, and bay leaf in a 4-quart pressure cooker. Cook at 15 pounds pressure for 45 minutes. Remove from heat and let pressure drop.

2. Open cooker, remove tongue, and strain stock. Remove outer skin from tongue and cool tongue in stock before refrigerating both.

Slow Cooker Method

1. Combine tongue, 3 cups water, vegetables, and bay leaf in a 3½-quart slow cooker. Cook on Low for 7 hours.

2. Strain stock and remove outer skin from tongue. Cool tongue in stock before refrigerating both.

3 cups cranberries	2 teaspoons grated orange rind
2 cups water	2 pounds cooked beef tongue
¾ cup honey	(see Index for methods of
2 tablespoons frozen orange juice	cooking tongue)
concentrate	

1. Preheat oven to 425°F. Combine all ingredients, except the tongue, in a 2-quart saucepan and simmer for 10 minutes. Set aside.

2. Cut tongue in half, lengthwise, and place, flat-sides down, in a 14 x 10 x 2-inch baking pan.

3. Pour the cranberry glaze over tongue halves and bake for 20 to 25 minutes, basting twice.

4. Slice tongue and serve topped with cranberry glaze.

Serves 6

======== **Russian Tongue Salad** ========

Salad

3 cups diced cooked beef tongue	1 cup cooked green peas
(see Index for methods of	8 green onions, including tops,
cooking tongue)	finely sliced
2 cups diced cooked beets	1 cup chopped sweet red peppers
1 cup diced cooked potatoes	1 cup chopped celery
1 cup diced cooked carrots	

Salad Dressing

⅓ cup wine vinegar	1 teaspoon caraway seeds
½ cup Yogurt (see Index)	2 teaspoons basil
¾ cup Mayonnaise (see Index)	salad greens

1. Combine all salad ingredients in a large bowl.

2. Combine all salad dressing ingredients and pour over salad. Toss lightly. Serve on a bed of salad greens.

Serves 6

1½	tablespoons unflavored gelatin	9	whole cloves
2½	cups tongue stock (see Index under methods of cooking tongue)		pinch black pepper
		½	cup finely chopped green and sweet red peppers
1½	tablespoons lemon juice	½	cup finely chopped celery
3	tablespoons vinegar	¾	pound cooked beef tongue, tip end (see Index for methods of cooking tongue)
2	teaspoons honey		
2	teaspoons grated onion		salad greens
1	cinnamon stick		

1. Sprinkle gelatin over ¼ cup cold tongue stock. Set aside to soften.

2. Combine remaining stock, lemon juice, vinegar, honey, onion, and spices in a 1-quart saucepan and simmer for 5 minutes.

3. Rinse out an 8½ x 4½ x 2½-inch loaf pan with cold water. Strain stock mixture into loaf pan and stir in peppers and celery.

4. Starting at the tip end of the tongue, cut ¼-inch slices on the diagonal. (There should be about 2 cups firmly packed slices.) Stand the slices in the loaf pan in the same order they are cut, allowing even distribution of stock, celery, and peppers between each slice. Cover the pan with plastic wrap, place a table knife on the slices to keep the tongue covered with stock, and refrigerate until set.

5. To serve, unmold loaf, then turn it right-side up and place on an oval platter lined with salad greens. To make individual portions, cut between the tongue slices and serve on a bed of salad greens.

Makes 1 loaf

Remarks Mustard (see Index) is a nice accompaniment to this dish.

===== **Two–Bean, Rice, and Tongue Salad** =====

1½	cups cooked pinto beans	½	cup finely shredded red cabbage
1½	cups cooked green beans		
1½	cups cooked brown rice	½	cup oil
3	cups diced cooked beef tongue (see Index for methods of cooking tongue)	½	cup cider vinegar
		1	teaspoon oregano
		¼	teaspoon dry mustard
1	small onion, minced	¼	teaspoon paprika
1	cup chopped celery		salad greens
1	cup chopped green peppers		

1. Combine all ingredients and toss lightly.

2. Serve in a bowl lined with salad greens.

Serves 6

===== Sliced Tongue with Spanish Sauce ===== 151

2 to 2½ pounds cooked beef tongue
(see Index for methods of
cooking tongue)
¼ cup olive oil
2 small onions, chopped
2 green peppers, chopped

2 cups coarsely chopped
tomatoes
1 teaspoon chili powder
pepper to taste
1 cup Beef Broth (see Index)
1 tablespoon cornstarch

1. Preheat oven to 350°F. Cut tongue on the diagonal into ½-inch thick slices.

2. In a large skillet, heat oil and saute onions and peppers. Add tomatoes, chili powder, and pepper and bring sauce to a boil. Mix beef broth with cornstarch until smooth. Gradually add broth mixture to tomato mixture, stirring constantly. Cook until thickened.

3. Arrange tongue slices in a casserole and pour sauce over the top. Bake, covered, for 30 minutes.

Serves 4 to 6

===== Tongue and Mushroom Ragout =====

¼ cup butter
3 cups thickly sliced mushrooms
1 medium-size onion, coarsely
chopped
2 cups Chicken Stock or Beef
Stock (see Index)
¼ teaspoon allspice
½ teaspoon paprika

2 tablespoons orange juice
2 teaspoons honey
4 teaspoons cornstarch
4 teaspoons cold water
1 pound (about 3½ cups) cooked
beef tongue, sliced (see Index
for methods of cooking tongue)
¼ cup chopped parsley

1. In a large skillet, melt butter. Add mushrooms and onions and saute over medium-high heat about 2 minutes. Stir in stock, spices, orange juice, and honey.

2. Dissolve cornstarch in water and then add the mixture to the sauce, stirring constantly.

3. Add sliced tongue and simmer, covered, for about 10 minutes. Serve garnished with parsley.

Serves 6

Remarks Serve over cooked whole wheat noodles.

TRIPE

Tripe must be thoroughly cooked before you can use it as an ingredient in another recipe. Here are two ways to prepare it.

Methods of Cooking Honeycomb Tripe

1	honeycomb tripe (about 2½ pounds)
3 to 6	cups water

1. Place tripe in a 4-quart pot. Add 6 cups water and cook over low heat for 2 hours. (Cooking over high heat will toughen it.) The tripe will be tender but chewy.

2. Drain tripe and discard water. Wash tripe in cold water and refrigerate.

Pressure Cooker Method

1. Combine tripe and 3 cups water in a 4-quart pressure cooker.

2. Cook at 15 pounds pressure for 30 minutes. Remove from heat and let pressure drop.

3. Drain tripe and discard water. Wash tripe in cold water and refrigerate. The tripe will be tender and soft rather than chewy.

Fried Tripe 153

2¼   pounds cooked honeycomb
     tripe (see Index for methods of
     cooking honeycomb tripe)

¼   cup oil
    vinegar or Hot Pepper Sauce
    (see Index)

1. Wash tripe in cold water. Pat dry between paper towels and cut into strips ½ x 2 inches.

2. Heat oil in a large skillet over medium-high heat. Fry strips of tripe, about 1½ cups at a time, stirring frequently so that each strip browns on all sides and becomes crisp. Lift out and drain on paper towels as they are done. Keep warm and serve with vinegar or hot pepper sauce.

Serves 6

Pickled Tripe

1½   pounds cooked honeycomb
     tripe (see Index for methods of
     cooking honeycomb tripe)
1   jalapeno pepper
2   medium-size onions, coarsely
    chopped
1½   cups Chicken Stock or Beef
     Stock (see Index)

1½   cups cider vinegar
2   tablespoons honey
¼   teaspoon mustard seeds
¼   teaspoon celery seeds
¼   teaspoon dry mustard
¼   teaspoon turmeric
¼   teaspoon allspice
6   whole cloves

1. Wash tripe in cold water and then cut it into 2-inch cubes.

2. Cut jalapeno pepper in half, holding it under cold running water. Remove seeds and center and discard. (To avoid stinging, wash hands immediately in cold water after handling peppers.)

3. In a 2-quart saucepan, combine onions, stock, vinegar, honey, and spices with peppers and tripe and simmer, covered, for 30 minutes. Cool and refrigerate in a covered container.

Yields 3 cups

No-Meat Dishes Will Help Stretch the Meat Budget

A meal with a meatless entree can be a flavorful, wholesome, and welcome change from those with meat. For many of us, such meatless meals evoke fond memories of simple, tasty foods that were childhood favorites: baked macaroni and cheese, open-face toasted cheese and tomato sandwiches, baked beans with brown bread.

Best of all, dishes based on grains, nuts, and legumes offer opportunities for a greater variety of textures, colors, shapes, and flavors than those built around meat. Think of the grains you have to choose from—not only wheat, rye, oats, and rice, but the less familiar millet, buckwheat, amaranth, barley, bulgur, cornmeal, and triticale. Let your imagination run to the hearty beans, peas, and lentils as well as to the bright vegetables—tomatoes, broccoli, cauliflower, carrots, greens, eggplant, to name a few—available in the market. Just imagine the endless number of delightful menu combinations possible with nuts, seeds, herbs, spices, eggs, yogurt, cheese, and fruit.

Obviously, serving meatless meals more than occasionally will help to make a little meat go further still. If you are accustomed to eating a lot of meat, try serving one no-meat meal a week. Then, gradually increase the number of meatless meals until such meals are a regular part of your weekly menu cycle. At the same time, expand the variety of grains, nuts, seeds, legumes, and dairy products used in the entrees and side dishes at these meals. Eating a wide range of foods helps to ensure a healthy balance of protein, vitamins, and minerals in your diet.

Variety Is Essential for Protein Balance

A look at the makeup of protein clearly shows why variety is so important. Protein consists of 22 amino acids. Thirteen of those amino acids can be manufactured by our bodies, but nine of them (called essential amino acids) must be obtained from outside sources. Animal protein—meat—has a good concentration of all the essential amino acids and is, therefore, a high quality protein that our bodies can utilize efficiently. Plant protein, on the other hand, is low in one or more of the essential amino acids, so we use it less efficiently. But by combining several plant proteins we can create an amino acid quality similar to that of meat, and then our bodies can make full use of plant protein. Simply serve in one meal two foods with complementary proteins (a food low in one or more essential amino acids is served with a food that's high in the lacking amino acids). Grains or seeds eaten with legumes, and dairy products teamed with grains, nuts, or seeds are two good examples of complementary protein combinations.

Roasting Nuts and Seeds

For rich flavor and even browning, coat nuts with one teaspoon oil to each cup of nutmeats; then, spread the nuts (or seeds) in a shallow baking pan. Roast them in a 350°F oven until they're just barely browned. While they're roasting, stir them occasionally.

Once browned, remove them quickly from the oven, since nuts and seeds continue to cook and darken even after being taken from the heat. Cool them on a linen towel or absorbent paper.

Beans, Grains, and Seeds

Beans (and other legumes) have been called the "meat that grows on vines" because of their high protein levels—20 to 40 percent! They are also fine sources of the B vitamins, calcium, iron, and fiber; contain little fat; are low in sodium; and cost less than any other protein. Dried legumes can be stored for months in any cool, dry place. Cooked and frozen, beans will keep for several weeks in the refrigerator or freezer.

You can use cooked beans to add body and nourishment to salads, soups, stuffed peppers, cabbage rolls, and rice dishes. If you puree them, legumes make dips, spreads, sauces, and dressings thick and substantial. Try more than one variety of legumes, since each type makes its own unique flavor and texture contribution to a dish. One of my favorites is the soybean.

Among the legumes, the soybean reigns supreme with a 30 to 40 percent protein content that closely resembles the amino acid pattern of animal protein. Though its popularity is just dawning in the western countries, the Chinese and the Japanese have recognized its worth for centuries. From this small bean, those Oriental peoples have created a fermented soy sauce (tamari) and a seasoning (miso) as well as soy milk products and flours. I feature several of the soy products in my recipes.

Tofu is a pulpy, custard-like soy product that is particularly useful for those cutting back on meat. Submerged in liquid, tofu will remain fresh for about a week. The uses for tofu are myriad: sauteed for adding to soups, sandwiches, salads, main dishes; whipped as the base for mayonnaise, dips, or

[Continued on page 158]

Cooking Dried Beans

- Sort through the beans and remove any little stones, twigs, or damaged beans.
- Soak the beans in cold water (three to four times their volume) for 6 to 8 hours, or boil them (also in three to four times the water) for 2 minutes and then let them soak in the hot water for 1 hour. (If you're using a pressure cooker, eliminate the soaking step.)
- Add 1 to 2 tablespoons oil to water to reduce foaming when cooking soybeans.
- Cook the beans in simmering water or in a pressure cooker according to the time recommended in the chart. Then use in a favorite recipe.
- Store unused, cooked beans in the refrigerator or freezer.

Approximate Cooking Time for Beans

Bean	Soaked beans Regular method	Unsoaked beans Pressure cooker (15 pounds pressure)
Adzuki	45 to 50 minutes	15 to 20 minutes
Black-eyed pea	1 hour	20 to 25 minutes
Black turtle	1 to 1½ hours	30 to 35 minutes
Chick-pea	3 hours	45 minutes
Fava	45 to 60 minutes	not recommended
Lentil	30 minutes	10 to 15 minutes
Lima	1 to 2 hours	not recommended
Lima, baby	45 to 60 minutes	not recommended
Mung	1½ hours	8 to 10 minutes
Pinto	1½ to 2 hours	25 to 30 minutes
Red kidney	1½ to 2 hours	25 to 30 minutes
Soybean	3 hours	35 minutes
Split Pea	35 to 60 minutes	not recommended
White bean, small	1 to 2 hours	25 minutes

Note: Flatulence sometimes follows eating legumes. To lessen its effects, discard the soaking water and cook the beans in fresh water. After 30 minutes of cooking (or half the cooking time in the pressure cooker), discard that water and finish the cooking in another potful of fresh water. The process does reduce some nutrients but it also rids the beans of oligosaccharides, the culprits of the gas problem.

Cooking Grains
Regular Method
- Rinse grains *only* if they seem gritty. Grains contain B vitamins which are readily washed away.
- Measure the amount of cooking liquid (it can be water, broth, or juice) suggested in the chart and bring the liquid to a full boil. Since grains swell by two to four times during cooking, use a large pot.
- Add the grains to the boiling liquid and stir once.
- Allow the liquid to return to a boil, then reduce the heat. Cover the pot and slowly cook the grains until they are soft and the liquid has been absorbed.
- Use the taste test to determine if the grains are done. They should be somewhat chewy, not tough or hard.
- Keep cooked grains in the refrigerator or freezer.

Approximate Cooking Time for Grains

Grain (1 cup)	Amount of liquid (cups)	Cooking time	Cooked volume (cups)
Amaranth	3	20 to 25 minutes	2½
Barley	3	1¼ hours	3
Brown rice	2	45 minutes	3
Buckwheat groats	2 to 5	15 minutes	2½
Bulgur wheat	2	15 to 20 minutes	2½
Cornmeal	4	25 minutes	3
Cracked wheat	2	25 minutes	2⅓
Millet	3	45 minutes	3½
Oats	3	30 to 40 minutes	3½
Rye	2	1 hour	2⅔
Sorghum	3	45 minutes	3½
Triticale	4	1 hour	2½
Wheat	3	2 hours	2⅔
Wild rice	3	1 hour	4

Pilaf Method
- In hot oil, saute the grain along with onion (and garlic, parsley, or mushrooms).
- Add the liquid—approximately twice as much liquid as grain—and cover the pan.
- Cook the grain over medium heat until the liquid is absorbed and the grain is tender.

salad dressings; crumbled for blending with meat in meatballs; and cubed for making bread pudding. In my recipes, I have used from 1 to 3 ounces of tofu per person. Served in this quantity, tofu is a bargain protein. It's available in the produce section of many large supermarkets and natural food stores.

Hearty, whole grains are right up with beans when it comes to providing outstanding plant protein. Wheat, amaranth, and oats, for example, are almost 15 percent protein. And, if you combine them with beans, legumes, or dairy products, the protein quality is high.

When buying grains, look for those that have received a minimum of processing and still have the bran and germ intact. Whole grains provide the best nutrition. Keep them in the refrigerator or the freezer so that the oil in the germ does not turn rancid.

You can serve grains in a number of appealing ways. Breads—flat, quick, and yeast—are probably the most popular use. Yet grains are also exceptionally tasty and satisfying entrees when simply simmered in water or broth and topped with chopped nuts. As pastas, they're both scrumptious and filling when sauced or used as stuffing. Sauteed for a pilaf, grains take on a nut-like, chewy texture and flavor that makes it difficult to stop with one helping. For breakfast, cooked porridges provide creamy warmth and sustenance on cold winter mornings.

Nuts and seeds are the third major source of plant protein for meatless meals. Peanuts (which are actually legumes) are the best, with 26 percent; walnuts and pistachios have about 20 percent; others have slightly less. A nutritional profile shows that, besides protein, a good part of each nut and seed is made up of fiber, vitamins B and E, and several minerals. Though these tiny pieces of food are packed with nutrients, you should be aware that nuts and seeds are rich in fat. Instead of making nuts the mainstay of meals, use them for boosting protein quality, flavor, and crunch of other foods.

In cooking, you can put nuts and seeds to work in limitless ways. Sliced, ground, chopped, or whole, they perk up ordinary batters and doughs, pilafs and stews, salads and sauces. They're an unexpected surprise that sends protein levels to great heights when folded into a souffle. Granolas and cooked grains have added appeal with chopped cashews, almonds, or pumpkin seeds. Sprinkle ground almonds, walnuts, or whole sesame seeds over steamed green beans or sliced chilled tomatoes to give a new dimension to familiar stand-bys.

It only takes a little forethought and imagination to create superb meatless menus that will whet your appetite for more no-meat meals.

Apple, Cheese, and Walnut Salad 159

1	cup Mayonnaise (see Index)	3	cups cooked soybeans
3	tablespoons lemon juice	2	cups diced sharp cheddar
3	tablespoons honey		cheese (6 ounces)
1	tablespoon Mustard (see Index)	1½	cups coarsely chopped celery
1	tablespoon basil	6	green onions, finely sliced
¼	teaspoon paprika	¾	cup chopped walnuts
¼	teaspoon dry mustard		romaine lettuce
3	cups chopped tart apples		

1. In a 2-quart bowl, combine mayonnaise, lemon juice, honey, mustard, basil, paprika, and dry mustard.

2. Add apples and mix thoroughly to prevent them from turning brown.

3. Add soybeans, cheese, celery, green onions, and walnuts. Toss gently to combine. Serve in a salad bowl lined with lettuce.

Serves 6

Baked Green Peppers with Corn and Tofu Filling

6	medium-size green peppers	3	cups cooked corn
2	tablespoons butter	½	teaspoon thyme
¼	cup coarsely chopped onions	½	teaspoon oregano
6	ounces tofu	1	cup grated cheddar cheese
¾	cup tomato juice	1	tablespoon wheat germ

1. Preheat oven to 350°F. Remove top and center from each pepper. Rinse peppers to remove seeds. Stand peppers in 1 inch of water in a 9 x 9 x 2-inch baking pan.

2. In a medium-size skillet, melt butter and saute onions until soft. Set aside.

3. Combine tofu and tomato juice in container of blender and process until smooth. Pour into a 2-quart bowl.

4. Add the corn, herbs, ¾ cup of the cheese, and the sauteed onions, to the tofu mixture. Mix well.

5. Spoon corn-tofu mixture into each pepper. Combine remaining ¼ cup of cheese with the wheat germ, top each pepper with some of the mixture, and bake, uncovered, for 1 hour.

Serves 6

Remarks Serve with Tomato Brown Sauce (see Index), if desired.

2	tablespoons butter	2	tablespoons honey
¼	cup coarsely chopped onions	¼	teaspoon ground cloves
2	cups peeled and chopped tart apples	½	teaspoon dry mustard
		4	cups cooked soybeans
1	cup apple juice	6	tablespoons bread crumbs
2	tablespoons molasses	3	tablespoons butter

1. Preheat oven to 350°F. In a medium-size skillet, melt butter and saute onions and apples until soft.

2. Combine apple juice, molasses, honey, and spices in a 2-quart bowl. Add soybeans and sauteed onions and apples. Mix together lightly and turn into a 1½-quart casserole. Sprinkle with bread crumbs, dot with butter, and bake, covered, for 30 minutes.

Serves 6

═══════ **Cabbage Cashew Soup** ═══════

3	tablespoons butter	1½	cups cooked soybeans
¾	cup sliced onions	1	cup finely chopped cooked tomatoes
1	cup peeled and chopped apples		
2	cups diced rutabaga	2	cups tomato juice
2	cups coarsely shredded cabbage	3	cups Beef Stock or Chicken Stock (see Index)
1	cup coarsely chopped endive (chicory)	2	teaspoons honey
		2	teaspoons molasses
1	cup finely chopped celery	½	teaspoon ground cloves
¼	cup raisins	½	teaspoon dry mustard
½	cup coarsely chopped raw cashew nuts		

1. Melt butter in a 5-quart Dutch oven or heavy-bottom pot and saute onions, apples, rutabaga, cabbage, endive, celery, raisins, and cashew nuts for about 5 minutes.

2. Add soybeans, tomatoes, tomato juice, stock, honey, molasses, and spices. Cover and simmer over low heat for 45 minutes to 1 hour.

Serves 6

Remarks   Try this unusual combination of flavors for a unique and delicious dish.

Buckwheat Cheese Blintzes 161

Blintzes

¾	cup buckwheat flour (buckwheat groats ground in blender)	3	eggs, beaten
		1½	cups milk
		¾	cup water
¾	cup whole wheat pastry flour	6 to 8	tablespoons oil
1½	teaspoons baking powder	3	tablespoons honey

Filling

2¼	cups cottage cheese		
3	egg yolks	2 to 3	tablespoons oil
1	tablespoon honey	2 to 3	tablespoons butter
¼	teaspoon nutmeg	Yogurt (see Index)	

1. In a 1-quart bowl, combine both flours with baking powder.

2. Combine eggs, milk, water, 3 tablespoons oil, and honey in another 1-quart bowl. Then stir into dry ingredients. Blend well.

3. Heat 2 tablespoons oil in a large skillet. Drop batter into skillet, allowing about 2 tablespoons per blintz, and cook over medium-low heat. Turn blintzes when bubbles form over the surface and cook only a few seconds on the reverse side. Add more oil if necessary, but there should be no excess oil in the skillet. Transfer blintzes from skillet to pie plate or tray, stacking them one on top of the other, light-side up.

4. Combine cottage cheese, egg yolks, honey, and nutmeg in a 1-quart bowl. Place 1 tablespoon of cheese filling in the center of each blintz. Fold both sides over the filling and roll, sealing in the filling.

5. In the same skillet, heat 1 tablespoon oil and 1 tablespoon butter over medium-low heat. Saute the filled blintzes about 30 seconds on each side to heat them through and keep in a warm oven until all the blintzes are sauteed. Add more oil and butter if needed. Serve immediately topped with yogurt.

Makes about 24 blintzes, 4 inches long

¾	cup cooked soybeans	½	teaspoon thyme
1	cup cooked bulgur	1	teaspoon chopped parsley
½	cup chopped onions	2	teaspoons dry mustard
2	eggs, beaten	2	tablespoons tamari
1	cup milk		soy sauce
1	tablespoon chopped chives		

1. Grind soybeans using the fine, small-holed disc of grinder.

2. Preheat oven to 325°F. Combine all ingredients and turn into an oiled loaf pan. Bake about 1 hour or until browned.

Serves 6

═══════ Cabbage Leaves Stuffed ═══════
with Tofu Cheese and Rice

1	head cabbage (3½ to 4 pounds)	½	teaspoon dry mustard
2	tablespoons butter	3	cups cooked brown rice
1	cup finely chopped onions	2	eggs
2	garlic cloves, minced	1	cup tofu (10 ounces)
1	teaspoon fennel seeds	½	cup cottage cheese
1	teaspoon sage	3	cups coarsely chopped cabbage
1	teaspoon paprika	6	cups tomato sauce

1. Cut bottom core out of cabbage head. Hold head under running water and let the weight of the water running into the cabbage loosen the leaves so they can be removed without tearing them. Remove 12 large leaves and place them in a 5-quart pot. Pour boiling water over them and simmer, covered, for 5 to 10 minutes. Drain and set aside.

2. In a medium-size skillet, melt butter and saute onions, garlic, herbs, and spices for 1 to 2 minutes. Then combine mixture with cooked rice in a 2-quart mixing bowl.

3. Place eggs and tofu in container of blender and process until smooth. Add to rice mixture along with cottage cheese. Preheat oven to 350°F.

4. Put about ¼ cup of the tofu-cheese filling on each cabbage leaf near the core end. Roll core over filling toward center, fold sides in over center, and continue rolling toward outside edge of leaf.

5. Arrange a bed of the chopped cabbage on the bottom of a 4-quart casserole and place the 12 cabbage rolls on top, seam-side down. Pour tomato sauce over the rolls, cover, and bake for 40 minutes.

Serves 6

Cashew Carrot Soup 163

4	tablespoons oil	5	cups Beef Stock (see Index)
2	medium-size onions, sliced	2	tablespoons tomato paste
2	cups coarsely shredded cabbage, turnip greens, or Swiss chard	⅓	cup brown rice
		½	cup coarsely chopped cashew nuts
2	cups grated carrots	½	cup raisins
1	cup chopped apples	1 to 1½	cups yogurt

1. In a Dutch oven or heavy-bottom pot, heat oil and saute onions. Stir in greens and saute a few minutes longer. Then add the carrots and cook a minute or so longer. Stir in apples, stock, and tomato paste. Bring mixture to a boil and add rice. Simmer, covered, for 35 to 40 minutes or until carrots are tender and rice is cooked.

2. Add cashew nuts and raisins and cook until raisins are "plumped." Serve each bowl of soup topped with a generous dollop of yogurt.

Serves 4 to 6

Celery Mushroom Casserole

2	cups finely chopped celery	¼	cup finely chopped parsley
2	cups coarsely chopped mushrooms	6	tablespoons butter
		6	tablespoons whole grain bread crumbs
2½	cups Chicken Stock or Beef Stock (see Index)	6	tablespoons rye flour or whole wheat flour
½	cup soy grits		
½	cup slivered almonds	½	cup Yogurt (see Index)
1	cup sliced water chestnuts	½	cup grated Parmesan cheese

1. Combine celery, mushrooms, and 1 cup stock in a 2-quart, heavy-bottom saucepan. Bring to a boil, reduce heat, cover, and simmer for 5 minutes.

2. Add soy grits to the celery-mushroom mixture and let soak for 5 minutes.

3. Turn contents of saucepan into a 3-quart bowl. Add almonds, water chestnuts, and parsley.

4. Preheat oven to 350°F. In the same saucepan, melt butter. Place 2 tablespoons of the melted butter in a 1-pint bowl, mix in the bread crumbs, and set aside. Stir flour into butter in saucepan and cook over low heat for 1 minute. Add 1½ cups stock, stirring until smooth. Add yogurt and blend to make a smooth sauce.

5. Add sauce to celery-mushroom mixture. Stir in cheese and mix thoroughly.

6. Turn mixture into a 2-quart casserole, top with buttered crumbs, and bake for 15 to 20 minutes until bubbling and golden brown.

Serves 6

with Grated Potato Crust

1 tablespoon butter	½ cup chopped walnuts
3 medium-size mature potatoes, grated (about 3 cups)	1¼ cups grated sharp cheddar cheese
1 small onion, grated	¼ teaspoon dry mustard
⅛ teaspoon black pepper	¼ teaspoon paprika
⅛ teaspoon nutmeg	⅛ teaspoon cayenne pepper
4 eggs	1 cup milk

1. Preheat oven to 375°F. Place butter in a 9-inch pie plate and set in oven to melt. Coat bottom and sides of pie plate with melted butter.

2. In a 3-quart bowl, combine grated potatoes, grated onion, black pepper, and nutmeg with 1 egg. Mix seasonings and egg into potatoes by hand. Pat potato mixture into buttered pie plate, building up the sides to make a crust.

3. Arrange a layer of the chopped walnuts over the potato crust, then a layer of the grated cheese over that.

4. Beat the remaining eggs in a 1-quart bowl. Add dry mustard, paprika, cayenne, and milk. Mix well. Pour this mixture over the cheese layer.

5. Bake for 40 to 45 minutes until filling is set and crust is cooked and crispy. Let pie cool at room temperature for 10 minutes before cutting.

Serves 6

═══════════════════ **Garlic Soup** ═══════════════════

6 garlic cloves, minced	6 cups Chicken Stock (see Index), Beef Stock (see Index), or lamb stock
3 tablespoons butter	
3 cups toasted whole grain bread cubes	12 ounces tofu
	1 tablespoon tamari soy sauce
	6 tablespoons chopped parsley

1. In a 3-quart saucepan, saute garlic in butter until soft. Add cubed bread, stirring to coat on all sides with garlic and butter. Set aside.

2. Combine half of the stock and half of the tofu in the container of a blender and process until smooth. Add to bread in saucepan. Process remaining stock and tofu in blender and add to bread.

3. Stir in tamari. Cook over low heat, stirring constantly. Do not let soup boil. When hot, add parsley and serve.

Serves 6

Remarks This is a surprisingly delicious and attractive soup—and very nourishing, too.

Cheesy Vegetable Pie === 165

1	unbaked 9-inch Whole Wheat Pie Crust (see Index)	1½	cups grated medium-sharp cheddar cheese	
1⅓	cups frozen baby lima beans	½	teaspoon dill weed	
2½	cups cauliflower florets	½	teaspoon nutmeg	
1⅓	cups sliced carrots	½	teaspoon paprika	
2	cups water	¼	cup brown rice flour	
2	tablespoons butter	1	tablespoon lemon juice	
¼	cup soy flour	¾	cup drained cottage cheese	
1	cup milk			

1. Make the pie crust. Set aside.

2. Combine lima beans, cauliflower, and carrots in a 2-quart saucepan. Add the water and bring to a boil. Reduce heat and simmer, covered, for 10 minutes. Drain cooking water into measuring cup. There should be 1 cup. Set aside.

3. Preheat oven to 400°F. In another 2-quart saucepan, melt butter and stir in soy flour, using a wire whisk to avoid lumping. Gradually add the milk, then the vegetable cooking water, stirring with a whisk to make a smooth sauce. Add grated cheese, dill weed, and spices and then whisk in brown rice flour. Stir in lemon juice.

4. Spread drained cottage cheese on bottom of unbaked pie crust. Arrange vegetables on top of the cottage cheese and pour the sauce over the vegetables.

5. Bake for 10 minutes, reduce oven to 350°F, then bake for 25 minutes longer. Cool pie on rack for 5 to 10 minutes before cutting and serving.

Serves 6

Soybean Soup

2	tablespoons butter	⅔	cup tomato sauce
¾	cup sliced onions	1	tablespoon honey
1	cup sliced carrots	1	tablespoon molasses
3	cups coarsely chopped Chinese cabbage (if unavailable, substitute cabbage)	2	tablespoons tamari soy sauce
		1	tablespoon summer savory
		1½	teaspoons basil
6	cups Chicken Stock or Beef Stock (see Index)	½	teaspoon marjoram
		1	tablespoon Mustard (see Index)
3	cups cooked soybeans		

1. Melt butter in a 3-quart, heavy-bottom pot and saute onions, carrots, and Chinese cabbage for 2 minutes.

2. Add remaining ingredients, cover, and simmer for 30 minutes.

Serves 6

3	tablespoons oil	1½	cups coarsely chopped cooked
1	cup coarsely chopped onions		tomatoes
1	garlic clove, minced	1	tablespoon honey
1	cup coarsely chopped green	¼	teaspoon oregano
	peppers	¼	teaspoon marjoram
4½	cups Beef Stock (see Index)	¾	teaspoon ground cumin
6	tablespoons brown rice	¾	teaspoon chili powder
2¼	cups cooked pinto beans	¼	teaspoon nutmeg
2¼	cups tomato juice	¼	teaspoon allspice

1. In a large skillet, heat 1 tablespoon oil and saute onions, garlic, and green peppers for 2 minutes.

2. Combine sauteed vegetables, stock, and rice in a 4-quart pot. Bring to a boil, reduce heat, and simmer, covered, over medium heat for 30 to 40 minutes or until rice is cooked.

3. In the same skillet, heat 2 tablespoons oil over low heat and saute pinto beans for 1 minute. Mash them with potato masher and then mix in ¾ cup of the tomato juice.

4. Add mashed bean mixture to soup, along with remaining tomato juice, tomatoes, honey, herbs, and spices. Let soup simmer for 15 to 20 minutes over low heat until flavors are blended.

Serves 6

═══════════ Eggplant Fritters ═══════════

6 to 8	tablespoons oil		
2	small eggplants, peeled and cut	3	cups whole grain bread crumbs
	into ½-inch cubes (about 5⅓	2	eggs
	cups)	1	teaspoon oregano
4	garlic cloves, minced	¼	cup grated Parmesan cheese
2	medium-size onions, minced	3	cups Tomato Brown Sauce (see
2	cups cooked soybeans		Index)

1. In a large skillet, heat 3 tablespoons oil and saute eggplant, garlic, and onion until soft.

2. Grind soybeans using coarse blade of grinder.

3. Combine all ingredients in a 3-quart bowl.

4. Wash and dry skillet, then heat 3 tablespoons oil in it. Form mixture into patties about 2 inches in diameter and brown on both sides, adding more oil if necessary. Serve with tomato brown sauce.

Makes 24 fritters

Eggplant Garbanzo Parmesan 167

2	eggs, beaten
¼	cup milk
½	cup whole wheat flour
2	cups whole grain bread crumbs
4	teaspoons oregano
4	teaspoons basil
½	teaspoon black pepper
2	cups cooked garbanzo beans

1	medium-size eggplant (about 1¼ pounds), sliced into ¼-inch rounds
3	cups tomato sauce
½	cup grated Parmesan cheese
2	cups grated cheddar or mozzarella cheese

1. Combine eggs and milk in a 1-pint bowl, place flour in another 1-pint bowl, and combine bread crumbs and seasonings in a 2-quart bowl.

2. Place cooked garbanzo beans on the bottom of a 3-quart casserole.

3. Preheat oven to 350°F. Dip eggplant slices into the flour, then into the egg mixture, and finally into the seasoned crumbs. Arrange a layer of eggplant on top of the beans, overlapping slices slightly.

4. Pour half of the tomato sauce over eggplant. Combine the cheeses and sprinkle half of it over the tomato sauce. Make another layer of overlapping eggplant, top with the remaining tomato sauce, and sprinkle with remaining cheese.

5. Cover casserole and bake for 35 minutes. Remove cover and bake 10 minutes longer, until cheese on top has melted.

Serves 6

Eggplant Two–Bean Casserole

4½	cups peeled and diced eggplant
2	garlic cloves, minced
1	teaspoon oregano
2	teaspoons basil
½	teaspoon marjoram
2	cups cut green beans (1½-inch pieces)

4	cups tomato juice
4	cups cooked pinto beans
2	tablespoons brown rice flour
½	cup bread crumbs
3	tablespoons melted butter

1. Preheat oven to 350°F. Combine eggplant, garlic, herbs, and green beans with tomato juice in a 3-quart saucepan and simmer, covered, for 10 minutes.

2. Add pinto beans. Then stir in brown rice flour. Transfer to a 3-quart casserole.

3. Combine bread crumbs and melted butter, sprinkle over the top of the casserole, and bake 30 minutes or until bubbling.

Serves 6

in Cheese–Rice Crust

4½	cups cooked brown rice
3½	cups grated sharp cheddar cheese (about 10 ounces)
1	tablespoon butter
¼	cup coarsely chopped onions
1	garlic clove, minced
2	tablespoons rye flour or whole wheat flour
⅔	cup Yogurt (see Index)
3	packages frozen chopped spinach (10 ounces each), cooked and drained
6	eggs

1. Preheat oven to 350°F. Combine rice and 2 cups of the grated cheese. Press into an oiled 13 x 9 x 2-inch shallow baking pan or casserole. Build rice and cheese mixture up the sides of the pan as far as possible. Rice "crust" should be about ¾-inch thick.

2. Melt butter in a 2-quart, heavy-bottom saucepan. Add onions and garlic and saute over medium heat. Stir in flour and yogurt. Cook and stir until sauce has thickened.

3. Add spinach to yogurt sauce and mix well. Spread creamed spinach over the bottom of the rice and cheese crust.

4. With the back of a spoon, make six indentations in the spinach, each large enough to hold a raw egg.

5. Break an egg into a cup and gently slide it into an indentation. Repeat this process with each egg, taking care to avoid breaking the yolk.

6. Sprinkle remaining cheese evenly over the eggs. Bake for 5 minutes. Then cover casserole with aluminum foil, making a "tent" so that it does not touch the cheese. Continue baking for 15 to 20 minutes or until eggs are set but not hard-cooked. Remove cover and serve.

Serves 6

Fried Rice 169

3 to 5	tablespoons oil	½	cup Chicken Stock (see Index)
4	green onions, finely sliced	8	water chestnuts, finely sliced
1	cup finely chopped green peppers	1	cup coarsely chopped mung bean sprouts
1	cup finely chopped celery	6	eggs, beaten
1	cup finely chopped carrots	3	cups cooked brown rice
1	cup finely chopped mushrooms	2	tablespoons tamari soy sauce
¼	cup soy grits		

1. In a large skillet, heat 2 tablespoons oil and saute green onions, green peppers, celery, carrots, and mushrooms until tender. Turn vegetables out into a 2-quart bowl and keep warm.

2. Combine soy grits and stock in a 1-quart saucepan and cook, uncovered, over very low heat for 1 to 2 minutes, stirring occasionally. Add cooked soy grits to sauteed vegetables along with water chestnuts and bean sprouts. Toss gently to combine.

3. Heat 1½ tablespoons oil in a separate skillet and lightly scramble eggs over low heat. Remove skillet from heat while eggs are still loose and set aside.

4. In the same skillet used to saute the vegetables, add the cooked rice. Saute just until heated through, adding more oil if necessary. Then add vegetable mixture and sprinkle in tamari.

5. Break up the scrambled eggs with the serving spoon and add them to the fried rice. Serve immediately.

Serves 6

with Applesauce

6	tablespoons soy grits	1	teaspoon paprika
1	cup plus 2 tablespoons Beef	3	eggs
	Stock or Chicken Stock (see	3	tablespoons lemon juice
	Index)	¾	cup whole wheat pastry flour
6	cups grated potatoes	¾ to 1	cup oil
3	tablespoons grated onion	4½	cups Applesauce (see Index)
¼	teaspoon black pepper		

1. Combine soy grits and stock in a 1-quart saucepan and simmer, covered, over low heat for 3 minutes. Soy grits will absorb most of stock. Set aside to cool.

2. Combine potatoes, onion, spices, eggs, lemon juice, and flour in a 3-quart bowl. Add soy grits and mix well.

3. Heat oil in a large skillet. (Oil should be about ⅛-inch deep in skillet and hot so that the potatoes in the pancakes will be cooked by the time the pancakes have browned on both sides.) Drop batter into skillet by the rounded tablespoonful and flatten each cake to a thickness of ¼ inch. Brown pancakes on both sides, drain between paper towels, and keep in a warm oven until all the batter is used. Serve with warm applesauce.

Serves 6

═══════════Peanut Butter Tomato Soup ═══════════

2	tablespoons butter	½	cup peanut butter (preferably
1	cup finely chopped onions		with chopped peanuts in it)
1	cup finely chopped celery	1	cup tomato sauce
1	cup finely chopped green	3	cups Chicken Stock or Beef
	peppers		Stock (see Index)
2	cups finely chopped tomatoes	2	tablespoons lemon juice
¼	cup brown rice flour		

1. In a large skillet, melt butter and saute onions, celery, and green peppers until soft.

2. Add tomatoes and saute, while stirring, for another minute. Stir in flour.

3. Combine peanut butter and tomato sauce and stir into mixture. Add stock and simmer over low heat for 10 minutes. Stir in lemon juice before serving.

Yields 8 cups

Hominy Grits Souffle 171
with Garlic Cheese

2	cups milk	¼	teaspoon nutmeg
2	cups water	2	cups grated sharp cheddar
¾	cup stone-ground grits (do not use instant)		cheese (about ½ pound)
4	tablespoons melted butter	1½	teaspoons finely chopped garlic
½	teaspoon black pepper	6	egg yolks
¼	teaspoon hot pepper sauce	6	egg whites

1. In the top of a double-boiler, slowly bring milk and water to a boil. Then, without disturbing the boiling liquid, gradually add the grits. Stir, reduce heat, and cover. Cook 30 minutes or until grits are tender and thick, stirring occasionally.

2. While the grits are cooking, preheat the oven to 425°F and butter a 6-cup souffle dish with deep sides. To the grits add the butter, pepper, hot pepper sauce, nutmeg, half the cheese, and the garlic. Stir to blend and set aside to cool for 10 minutes. Then beat the egg yolks slightly and stir into the grits mixture.

3. In a small bowl, beat the egg whites until stiff. Fold half of the egg whites into the grits, then add the other half. Spoon into the souffle dish and sprinkle with the remaining cheese. Bake 25 to 30 minutes. Serve immediately.

Serves 4 to 5

9	tablespoons oil	1	tablespoon tamari soy sauce
3	cups sliced onions	6	eggs, beaten
1	tablespoon ground coriander	¾	cup raisins
1½	teaspoons ground cardamom	¾	cup roasted unsalted peanuts
½	teaspoon turmeric	4	large bananas, cut in half
6	cups cold cooked brown rice		lengthwise and then into thirds
4	tablespoons lemon juice		crosswise

1. In a large skillet, heat 3 tablespoons oil and saute half the onions and half the spices over medium heat until onions are soft. Add half the rice and saute, while stirring constantly, for 1 to 2 minutes. Lightly mix in half the lemon juice, then turn rice out of skillet onto large serving platter and place in a warm oven. Repeat process, using 3 additional tablespoons of oil and sauteing remaining onions, spices, and rice. Mix in remaining lemon juice. Transfer cooked rice to serving platter in oven.

2. Combine tamari with beaten eggs. Heat 1 tablespoon oil in another large skillet and lightly scramble the eggs over low heat until they are set but not completely dry. Cut cooked eggs into strips and distribute them over the platter of rice. Sprinkle with raisins and peanuts.

3. Then heat 2 tablespoons oil and saute banana pieces over low heat until soft and golden brown on both sides. Serve platter of rice topped with bananas.

Serves 6

Millet Cashew Souffle 173

3	cups water	½	teaspoon thyme
¾	cup millet meal (millet ground in blender)	½	teaspoon basil
		¼	teaspoon paprika
1	cup Beef Stock or Chicken Stock (see Index)	¼	teaspoon nutmeg
		1	cup coarsely chopped raw cashew nuts
2	tablespoons butter		
½	cup coarsely chopped onions	3	tablespoons lemon juice
2	cups finely chopped mushrooms	2	teaspoons tamari soy sauce
		5	egg whites
¼	teaspoon marjoram	5	egg yolks

1. In the top of a 2-quart double-boiler, bring water to a boil. Gradually stir in millet meal, using a wire whisk to avoid lumps. Then place the pan on the bottom portion of the double-boiler, cover, and cook over hot water for 20 minutes or until millet has absorbed liquid. Turn cooked millet meal out into a 3-quart bowl to cool. Add stock and mix well.

2. Preheat oven to 350°F. Melt butter in a medium-size skillet and saute onions and mushrooms until soft. Mix in herbs and spices and add to millet, along with cashew nuts, lemon juice, and tamari.

3. Beat egg whites until stiff but not dry. Then beat egg yolks until light. Stir beaten egg yolks into millet mixture. Then fold in beaten egg whites.

4. Empty contents into an ungreased 4-quart casserole and bake for 40 minutes. Serve at once.

Serves 6

4	eggs	3	tablespoons soy flour
5	tablespoons oil	¼	cup skim milk powder
½	cup diced celery	1	cup water
¾	pound mushrooms, sliced	¼	cup chopped parsley
3	tablespoons cornstarch		

1. Remove eggs from refrigerator and allow to remain at room temperature for at least ½ hour before using.

2. Separate eggs. Put whites in large bowl and yolks in medium-size bowl. Beat egg yolks well and set aside.

3. Preheat oven to 350°F. In a medium-size skillet, heat 2 tablespoons oil and saute celery until tender. Lift celery out and set aside. Saute mushrooms in the same pan about 5 minutes. Lift out and chop coarsely.

4. Put remaining 3 tablespoons oil in a heavy-bottom, medium-size saucepan. Stir in cornstarch and flour. In a small bowl, combine skim milk powder and water with a wire whisk and slowly add to saucepan, stirring constantly to keep mixture smooth and free from lumps. Place saucepan over medium heat and cook, stirring constantly, until the sauce thickens and bubbles. (It should be quite thick.) Reduce heat and add celery and mushrooms.

5. Remove from heat. Gradually pour into beaten egg yolks, stirring until well blended. Stir in chopped parsley. Set aside.

6. Beat egg whites until stiff. Gently fold mushroom mixture into beaten egg whites, blending thoroughly until no trace of whites shows. Turn mixture into ungreased, 1½-quart souffle dish or straight-sided baking dish.

7. Place souffle on middle rack of oven. Bake for 45 to 50 minutes or until souffle is puffed and golden and firm to the touch. Remove from oven and serve immediately.

Serves 5 to 6

Nancy's Layered Eggplant Casserole

1	egg, beaten	2	teaspoons honey
2	tablespoons water	⅛	teaspoon allspice
6	tablespoons fine whole grain bread crumbs	¼	teaspoon cinnamon
		¼	teaspoon ground coriander
2	eggplants, peeled (about ¾ pound each)	2¼	cups thinly sliced onions (about 2 large)
5	tablespoons oil	3	tablespoons butter
1¼	cups cooked brown rice	¼	cup rye flour
1¼	cups cottage cheese	1¾	cups Chicken Stock (see Index)
¾	cup chopped walnuts	¾	cup Yogurt (see Index)

1. Preheat oven to 400°F. Combine egg and water in a 2-quart bowl. Place bread crumbs in another 2-quart bowl. Cut eggplants into ¾-inch slices. Dip the slices into egg-water mixture, then dredge in the bread crumbs. Arrange them on a 15⅛ x 10½ x 1-inch jelly roll pan which has been coated with 3 tablespoons of the oil.

2. Bake eggplant slices 15 minutes. Turn slices over and bake 12 to 15 minutes longer or until browned and fork-tender.

3. Layer half of the sliced eggplant on the bottom of an oiled 3-quart casserole.

4. Combine rice, cottage cheese, walnuts, honey, and spices. Mix thoroughly with a fork. Set aside.

5. In a medium-size skillet, heat 2 remaining tablespoons oil and saute onions over medium heat until limp and golden brown.

6. Spread half of the cheese mixture over the layer of eggplant in the casserole. Then layer half the onions over this, then the remaining cheese mixture, and finally a layer of the remaining onions. Top with the remaining eggplant slices.

7. In the same skillet, melt butter over medium heat. Stir in flour. Then add stock and stir until thickened. Blend in yogurt with a wire whisk to avoid lumping. Pour sauce evenly over contents of casserole and bake 15 minutes or until sauce is bubbling.

Serves 6

Dough

2	tablespoons dry yeast	1	tablespoon nutritional yeast
1¼	cups lukewarm water	2	cups rye flour
1	teaspoon honey	¼	cup oil
1	cup soy flour, sifted		

Tomato Sauce

2	tablespoons olive oil	¾	cup tomato paste
2	tablespoons sesame or	1	tablespoon oregano
	safflower oil	1	tablespoon basil
1	cup chopped onions	2	teaspoons honey
3	garlic cloves, minced	2	cups grated mozzarella cheese
2	green peppers, diced		(about 1 pound)
4	cups cooked tomatoes	½	cup grated Parmesan cheese

1. Sprinkle dry yeast over surface of lukewarm water. Add honey. Let soak for 5 minutes.

2. Combine soy flour, nutritional yeast, and rye flour. Add along with oil to dissolved yeast mixture. Turn out onto lightly floured surface and knead until dough is smooth and elastic. Place in oiled bowl, cover with a damp cloth, and let rise 1 to 2 hours in a warm place until doubled in size.

3. Meanwhile, make the tomato sauce by heating both types of oil in a heavy-bottom pot and sauteing onions, garlic, and green peppers until tender. Add tomatoes, tomato paste, herbs, and honey and simmer over low heat for about ½ hour until flavors are well blended.

4. When dough has doubled in size, punch down and knead once more, briefly. Divide dough into 4 balls and roll each one out ⅛-inch thick on a cookie sheet or pizza pan which has been dusted with cornmeal. Make a rim around the pizza by pinching the crust into an edge.

5. Preheat oven to 450°F. Top each pizza with about 1 cup tomato sauce, then ½ cup mozzarella cheese and 2 tablespoons Parmesan cheese. Bake 15 minutes.

Makes 4 pizzas, 10 inches each

Potato and Carrot Kugel

Kugel

3½	cups grated potatoes (about 1¼ pounds)	2	egg yolks
2	cups grated carrots (about ¾ pound)	1	cup Yogurt (see Index)
		3	tablespoons brown rice flour
1	medium-size onion, grated	¾	cup grated medium-sharp cheddar cheese
2	cups water	2	egg whites

Topping

1	cup Yogurt (see Index)	2	tablespoons brown rice flour
¾	cup grated medium-sharp cheddar cheese	2	egg whites

1. Preheat oven to 375°F. Combine potatoes, carrots, and onions in a 2½-quart, heavy-bottom saucepan. Add water, cover, and cook over low heat for 5 minutes. Turn into a 3-quart bowl.

2. In a 1-quart bowl, combine egg yolks, yogurt, flour, and cheese. Add to potato mixture and blend thoroughly.

3. Beat egg whites until stiff but not dry, and gently fold into potato mixture. Turn out into a 3-quart casserole and bake for 20 minutes. Remove casserole from oven and set aside.

4. To make topping, combine yogurt, cheese, and flour in a 1-quart bowl. Beat egg whites until stiff but not dry, and fold into yogurt-cheese mixture.

5. Gently spread topping over the baked kugel and return the casserole to oven for 20 minutes until top is browned. Serve at once.

Serves 6

3	tablespoons butter	¼	teaspoon nutmeg
⅓	cup coarsely chopped onions	¼	teaspoon paprika
½	cup coarsely chopped celery	⅛	teaspoon black pepper
3	tablespoons rye flour or whole wheat flour	2¼	cups cooked soybeans
		4½	cups sliced cooked sweet potatoes
1¼	cups Chicken Stock (see Index)		
½	cup Yogurt (see Index)	¾	cup coarsely chopped pecans
2	teaspoons honey		

1. In a 2-quart saucepan, melt butter and saute onions and celery for 2 minutes over medium heat. Stir in flour. Then add stock and cook over medium heat, stirring constantly, until thickened. Blend in yogurt, honey, and spices until smooth.

2. Mix soybeans into the sauce.

3. Arrange a layer of sweet potato slices on the bottom of a 3-quart casserole, then a layer of the soybeans and sauce, another layer of sweet potatoes, ending with a layer of soybeans and sauce.

4. Top the casserole with the pecans, cover, and bake in a 350°F oven for 35 to 40 minutes or until bubbling. It is not necessary to preheat oven.

Serves 6

━━━━━ **Two–Bean Casserole** ━━━━━

5	tablespoons butter	¾	teaspoon dill weed
½	cup coarsely chopped onions	¾	teaspoon thyme
1	cup coarsely chopped celery	3	cups cooked baby lima beans
6	tablespoons soy flour	3	cups cooked kidney beans
1¼	cups Chicken Stock (see Index)	2	small tomatoes, sliced
½	cup sour cream	6	tablespoons fine whole grain bread crumbs
1	tablespoon honey		
3	tablespoons tomato sauce		

1. In a 2-quart saucepan, melt 3 tablespoons butter and saute onions and celery over medium heat for 2 minutes. Stir in flour. Add stock and stir constantly until thickened. Blend in sour cream, then honey, tomato sauce, and herbs.

2. Combine sauce with lima and kidney beans in a 3-quart casserole. Top with sliced tomatoes. Sprinkle bread crumbs over the tomatoes and then dot with remaining butter. Bake in a 350°F oven for 25 to 30 minutes or until bubbling. It is not necessary to preheat oven.

Serves 6

Spinach and Cottage Cheese ══ 179
Pancakes

2	packages frozen chopped spinach (10 ounces each)	1½	cups cottage cheese
1	teaspoon nutmeg	4	small garlic cloves
¾	teaspoon paprika	½	medium-size onion
¼	teaspoon ground white pepper	9	tablespoons whole wheat flour
1½	tablespoons lemon juice	3	egg whites
6	egg yolks	2 to 6	teaspoons oil

1. In a 2-quart saucepan, cook spinach, in as little water as possible, for 5 minutes. Drain well. Place spinach in a 1-quart bowl. Add spices and lemon juice and mix well.

2. Combine egg yolks, cottage cheese, garlic, and onion in container of a blender and process until smooth. Then add to spinach. Stir in flour and mix thoroughly.

3. Beat egg whites until stiff but not dry and carefully fold them into the spinach-cheese mixture.

4. Heat 2 teaspoons oil in a large skillet over medium-high heat. Drop spinach-cheese mixture by the teaspoonful into skillet, flattening each pancake with the spoon as much as possible, and brown on both sides. Continue this process, adding more oil as needed, until all of the mixture is used. Keep pancakes in a warm oven until ready to serve.

Serves 6

Remarks These pancakes may be served with butter, Applesauce (see Index), or Tomato Catsup (see Index).

2	packages frozen chopped spinach (10 ounces each)	2	eggs
2	garlic cloves, minced	1	cup Chicken Stock or Beef Stock (see Index)
¼	cup coarsely chopped onions	10	ounces tofu
4	teaspoons lemon juice	1	teaspoon tamari soy sauce
¼	cup brown rice flour	¼	cup grated Parmesan cheese
½	teaspoon nutmeg	2	tablespoons chopped parsley

1. Preheat oven to 325°F. Cook spinach, garlic, and onions together in a 2-quart saucepan, using as little water as possible. Drain well, pressing all liquid out of spinach. Add lemon juice, flour, and nutmeg to spinach and set aside.

2. Combine eggs, stock, tofu, and tamari in container of blender and process until smooth.

3. Add tofu-egg mixture to spinach mixture. Stir in Parmesan cheese. Then turn into an oiled 8½ x 4½ x 2½-inch loaf pan, set in 1 inch of hot water in a larger pan, and bake for 1 hour or until a knife inserted in center comes out clean.

4. To unmold loaf, loosen from pan by running a knife around it and carefully turn out onto a serving platter. Garnish with chopped parsley.

Serves 6

Remarks   Serve with Mushroom Sauce (see Index).

========= Sunflower Carrot Patties =========

2	carrots, grated (about 2 cups)	¾	cup sunflower seeds, finely ground in electric blender
2	small onions, grated	1	teaspoon dill weed
2	eggs, well beaten	1	tablespoon chopped parsley
2	tablespoons oil		oil for sauteing

1. Combine all ingredients except the oil for sauteing and mix well. Chill.

2. Shape mixture into patties and saute in oil until nicely browned on both sides. Serve hot or cold.

Serves 4 to 6

Remarks   May be served with Tomato Brown Sauce (see Index), if desired.

Tofu Stir-Fry 181

1½	pounds tofu (before pressing)		3	tablespoons tamari soy sauce
6	tablespoons oil		3	tablespoons honey
1	tablespoon minced ginger root		1½	teaspoons cider vinegar
1	tablespoon minced garlic		1½	teaspoons chili powder
9	green onions, finely sliced		2	tablespoons cornstarch
3¾	cups chopped mushrooms		¾	cup chopped water chestnuts
3	cups Beef Stock or Chicken Stock (see Index)		6	cups sliced Chinese cabbage
			3	cups mung bean sprouts

1. To press tofu, cut horizontally through each block to make thin rectangular pieces about ½ to ¾ inch in depth. Then place between folds of a clean towel. Lay a bread board and then a weight on top of the towel, and leave for 2 to 3 hours until tofu is fully pressed. It is important to retain the block shape of the tofu so that it may be cut into cubes after pressing. When the block of tofu can be held vertically without crumbling, it is fully pressed. Cut tofu into ½-inch cubes.

2. Heat 3 tablespoons oil in a large skillet. Add half the amount each of the ginger root, garlic, white ends of the onions, and tofu. Saute over medium heat for 2 to 3 minutes. Shake pan to stir (using a utensil would break the tofu).

3. Add half the mushrooms and saute 2 minutes longer, while shaking the pan. Gently turn contents of skillet out into a 3-quart container and set aside.

4. Repeat sauteing process, using remaining oil, ginger root, garlic, white ends of onions, tofu, and mushrooms.

5. Combine stock, tamari, honey, vinegar, chili powder, and cornstarch in a 2-quart bowl.

6. Place all sauteed ingredients in a 5-quart, heavy-bottom pot, add stock mixture, and heat slowly, shaking pan gently to mix.

7. Add water chestnuts, Chinese cabbage, sprouts, and green tops of onions, placing them on top of tofu mixture. Cover pot and steam over low heat for 3 to 5 minutes or until cabbage is tender but still firm. Serve immediately.

Serves 6

Remarks   Serve with cooked brown rice.

1	unbaked 9-inch Whole Wheat Pie Crust (see Index)	2	large tomatoes, skinned
4	tablespoons butter	2	tablespoons whole wheat flour
1	large onion, sliced	2	teaspoons basil
2	cups grated cheese, half Swiss and half cheddar (about 4 ounces total weight)	3	eggs, beaten
		½	cup half-and-half

1. Preheat oven to 400°F. Make pie shell and bake 8 minutes.

2. Meanwhile, melt butter in large skillet and saute onion slices until soft but not brown.

3. Put 1½ cups of the cheese in pie shell and top with the sauteed onion.

4. Cut tomatoes into slices ½-inch thick and drain juice. Sprinkle slices with flour and basil and saute them in the same skillet for 1 minute on each side. Arrange them on top of onion and cheese.

5. Combine eggs and half-and-half and pour over tomatoes. Sprinkle remaining ½ cup cheese over top of quiche. Bake 10 minutes, then reduce oven to 350°F and bake 15 to 20 minutes longer, or until set.

Serves 4 to 6

══════════════ Zucchini Soy Fritters ══════════════

1½	cups soy grits	½	teaspoon dry mustard
4	eggs	½	teaspoon oregano
½	cup warm Chicken Stock or Beef Stock (see Index)	½	teaspoon basil
1	cup creamed cottage cheese	½	teaspoon thyme
4	cups grated zucchini	½	teaspoon paprika
2	tablespoons grated onion	¼	cup brown rice flour
1	teaspoon tamari soy sauce	3 to 4	tablespoons oil

1. In a 3-quart bowl, combine soy grits, eggs, and stock. Set aside to soak for 5 minutes.

2. Add cottage cheese to soy grits mixture and blend well.

3. Add zucchini, onion, seasonings, and flour.

4. Heat oil in a large skillet and drop fritter mixture in by teaspoonfuls. Flatten top of each fritter and brown on both sides. Keep cooked fritters in a warm oven until ready to serve.

Makes about 20 fritters, 3 inches long

Remarks   Applesauce (see Index) goes well with the fritters.

Vegetable Pie, Mexican Style

Crust

1¼   cups cornmeal
3   tablespoons vegetable oil
½   cup hot water (approximately)

Filling

2   tablespoons oil
1   onion, coarsely chopped
1   green pepper, seeded and chopped
1   celery stalk, chopped
1   large tomato, chopped
1   teaspoon chili powder
½   teaspoon ground cumin
¼   teaspoon black pepper
2   teaspoons cornstarch

¼   cup cold water
1½   cups vegetables (any of the following, alone or in combination: green beans, corn, peas, zucchini, cooked kidney beans, cooked pinto beans, cooked chickpeas, spinach, or cooked carrots)
2   ounces Monterey Jack cheese, grated

1. In a medium-size bowl, mix cornmeal, oil, and enough hot water to make a pliable dough. Press the dough into a well-oiled 8-inch pie pan.

2. Preheat oven to 350°F. In a medium-size skillet, heat oil and saute onion, green pepper, and celery until soft. Add tomato, chili powder, cumin, and pepper. Cook 3 minutes longer.

3. Dissolve cornstarch in water and add mixture to skillet. Cook, stirring constantly, until thickened. Fold in vegetables. Spoon filling into pie shell, sprinkle with cheese, and bake for 35 minutes.

Serves 4

3	medium zucchini (1½ pounds)	¼	teaspoon black pepper
¼	cup oil	1	teaspoon oregano
1	teaspoon minced garlic	2	tablespoons chopped parsley
4	cups cooked tomatoes, drained	½	pound mozzarella cheese,
¼	cup tomato paste		coarsely grated

1. Cut zucchini lengthwise into strips ½-inch thick, then cut the strips in half. Set aside.

2. Preheat oven to 350°F. In a medium-size skillet, heat oil and saute garlic until transparent. Add tomatoes, tomato paste, pepper, oregano, and parsley. Simmer, uncovered, for 20 minutes or until thickened, stirring occasionally.

3. Pat zucchini strips dry, then lay them in an oiled jelly roll pan. Top with sauce and sprinkle with cheese. Bake for 30 minutes or until zucchini is just tender.

Serves 4

Accompaniments, Condiments, Sauces

Apple and Apricot Chutney

½	cup dried apricots	½	teaspoon ginger
2	tart apples, chopped	4	whole cloves
1	lime or ½ lemon, seeded and thinly sliced, including rind	½	teaspoon ground coriander
			chili powder to taste
1	garlic clove, minced	½	cup cashew nuts

1. In a saucepan, bring apricots to a boil in enough water to cover and simmer until soft. Add apples, cover pan, and simmer until apples are soft.

2. Add lime or lemon slices, garlic, and spices. Continue to cook for a minute or two. Add cashew nuts and cool. Serve at room temperature.

Yields about 2 cups

Applesauce

8	tart apples, peeled and sliced (about 7 cups)	½	teaspoon cinnamon
		1	tablespoon honey (optional)
2½	cups apple juice		

1. Combine apples and apple juice in a 3-quart pot. Bring to a boil, then reduce heat to medium and simmer, covered, for 5 to 10 minutes or until apples are soft.

2. Add cinnamon, and honey if used. Mix well.

3. Cool and refrigerate in a covered container.

Yields about 6 cups

2   tablespoons oil (optional)
1   oxtail or 2 to 3 pounds beef
      neck bones or beef short ribs
2   onions, cut into chunks
2   celery stalks with tops, cut into
      chunks

2   carrots, cut into chunks
2   quarts cold water
1   bay leaf
1   tablespoon peppercorns

1. Brown the meat and vegetables, using one of the following methods:

Oven Browning Method

Place bones and meat in a 13 x 9 x 2-inch baking pan. Add onions, celery, and carrots and brown about 30 minutes in a 400°F oven, turning occasionally to brown evenly.

Top-of-the-Stove Browning Method

Heat oil in a large skillet. Brown the soup bones and meat, then remove from the pan. In the same skillet, brown the vegetables.

2. Transfer the browned meat and vegetables to a 5-quart soup pot. Add water, bay leaf, and peppercorns and bring to a boil over medium-high heat. Reduce heat, skim any surface scum that accumulates, cover, and simmer over very low heat for 3 to 4 hours.

3. Remove meat and bones from the stock. Discard bones and store meat in the refrigerator for other uses, if you wish.

4. Strain the stock. Cool it and then place it in the refrigerator. When completely chilled, remove the fat that collects on the surface. Freeze stock in small amounts for future use.

Yields 1½ quarts

Chicken or Turkey Stock 187

3	pounds chicken backs, necks, or wings; or 2 turkey backs, necks, or wings; or the carcass from 2 roasted chickens or 1 turkey	2	celery stalks with tops, cut into chunks
		1	tablespoon thyme
		1	tablespoon marjoram
2	onions, cut into chunks	2	quarts cold water

1. Combine chicken or turkey parts and bones, vegetables, and herbs in a 5-quart soup pot. Add the water and bring to a boil over medium-high heat. Reduce heat, skim any surface scum that accumulates, cover, and simmer over very low heat for 2 to 3 hours. (If you wish to use the meat for soup, remove it from the bones after 1 hour of cooking. Return bones and skin to stock.)

2. Strain the stock. Cool it and then place it in the refrigerator. When completely chilled, remove the fat that collects on the surface. Freeze stock in small amounts for future use.

Yields 1½ quarts

Corn Relish

6	ears uncooked corn on cob	1⅓	tablespoons dry mustard
1	green pepper, diced	⅓	teaspoon turmeric
1	red pepper, diced	⅓	cup honey
2	medium-size onions, minced	½	cup vinegar

1. Remove corn from the cobs and combine with green and red peppers and onions in a medium-size bowl.

2. Combine remaining ingredients in a medium-size saucepan. Add corn mixture and simmer slowly 6 to 8 minutes.

3. Chill and serve.

Serves 6

1   cup dried soybeans
3   cups water

1. Wash soybeans and remove any foreign particles. Add water to soybeans and soak overnight in refrigerator.

2. Pour soybeans and liquid used for soaking in a large, heavy-bottom saucepan. Add more water to cover. Place over medium heat and bring to a boil; reduce heat, cover, and simmer 1 hour. (If desired, ½ teaspoon oil may be added to soybeans to keep mixture from boiling over.)

3. Preheat oven to 350°F. Remove saucepan from heat and drain soybeans thoroughly. Pour into a shallow pan and bake 45 minutes to 1 hour, or until soybeans are brown.

Yields 3 cups

══════════ Fresh Cranberry Relish ══════════

4	cups fresh cranberries (about 1 pound)	1	large or 2 medium-size oranges, quartered and seeded
2	medium-size red apples, cored	⅔	cup honey

1. Wash cranberries, drain, and remove stems. Alternately put cranberries, apples, and orange quarters through coarse blade of food chopper or grinder.

2. Blend in honey and combine thoroughly.

3. Cover and refrigerate for several hours or overnight before serving.

Yields 1 quart

tomatoes
lemon juice or vinegar or citric acid

Hot Pack Method

1. Dip tomatoes into boiling water until skins split. Peel, remove stem ends, and quarter the tomatoes.

2. Bring tomatoes to a boil in a heavy-bottom pot, stirring at the beginning to prevent sticking. Boil for 5 minutes.

3. Pack tomatoes into clean jars, leaving ½-inch head space. Add tomato juice or water if tomatoes have not made enough juice to be covered.

4. To every quart, add one of the following: 4 teaspoons lemon juice or 2 tablespoons vinegar or ½ teaspoon citric acid.
To every pint, add one of the following: 2 teaspoons lemon juice or 1 tablespoon vinegar or ¼ teaspoon citric acid.

5. Adjust caps and process jars in a boiling water bath: 10 minutes for pints and 15 minutes for quarts.

Raw Pack Method

1. Dip tomatoes into boiling water until skins split. Peel and remove stem ends. Leave tomatoes whole or cut into halves or quarters.

2. Pack tomatoes into clean jars, pressing gently to fill spaces. Cover with tomato juice or water to within ½ inch of the top.

3. To every quart, add one of the following: 4 teaspoons lemon juice or 2 tablespoons vinegar or ½ teaspoon citric acid.
To every pint, add one of the following: 2 teaspoons lemon juice or 1 tablespoon vinegar or ¼ teaspoon citric acid.

4. Adjust caps and process jars in a boiling water bath: 35 minutes for pints and 45 minutes for quarts.

Canning Tomatoes

In recent years there has been some question as to whether all tomatoes are acidic enough to be canned by the traditional boiling water bath method. It is known that the amount of acid in tomatoes can vary, depending on the soil and climate where they have been grown as well as the variety of tomato. Therefore, it is recommended that you add either lemon juice, vinegar, or citric acid to the tomatoes (as I do in these recipes) for adequate acidity.

15	tomatoes (about 3 pounds)	½	cup honey
½	cup water		lemon juice or vinegar or citric acid
3	cloves		

1. Wash tomatoes and remove stem ends. Chop coarsely.

2. Combine tomatoes, water, and cloves in a heavy-bottom, 4-quart pot. Cover and simmer over low heat for 25 minutes or until tomatoes are soft, stirring occasionally to prevent sticking. Cool slightly.

3. Puree mixture in a blender, then pass it through a coarse sieve. Add honey and mix well.

4. To every quart jar, add one of the following: 4 teaspoons lemon juice or 2 tablespoons vinegar or ½ teaspoon citric acid.
To every pint jar, add one of the following: 2 teaspoons lemon juice or 1 tablespoon vinegar or ¼ teaspoon citric acid.

5. Reheat juice just to the boiling point, but do not boil. Pour hot juice into clean jars, leaving ¼-inch head space. Adjust caps and process jars in a boiling water bath: 10 minutes for pints and 15 minutes for quarts.

Yields about 1½ quarts

══════ Home–Canned Tomato Paste ══════

1. Follow steps 1 and 2 of Home-Canned Tomato Sauce (next recipe).

2. Puree tomato sauce in a blender, then pour into a jelly sack or a cotton muslin cloth and hang over a bowl until all the liquid has dripped from the mixture. Discard the liquid (or save to use as flavoring for soups and other foods).

3. Scrape tomato paste from the cloth into the top of a double-boiler. Add the ¼ cup lemon juice and mix thoroughly. Heat over boiling water for 20 to 30 minutes or until very hot.

4. Pack into clean half-pint jars, leaving ¼-inch head space. Adjust caps and process half-pints for 45 minutes in a boiling water bath.

Home–Canned Tomato Sauce

5	pounds Italian plum tomatoes (about 25)	2	tablespoons chopped parsley
3	tablespoons olive oil	4	teaspoons basil
4	onions, coarsely chopped	4	teaspoons oregano
4	garlic cloves, minced	1	bay leaf
		¼	cup lemon juice

1. Dip tomatoes into boiling water until skins split. Peel and remove stem ends. Chop tomatoes coarsely.

2. Heat oil in a large, heavy-bottom pot and saute onions and garlic for 2 minutes. Stir in tomatoes and herbs. Simmer over low heat for 2 hours, stirring occasionally to prevent sticking. Cool slightly.

3. Puree mixture in a blender. Add lemon juice. Reheat sauce to boiling point, but do not boil. Pour into clean pint jars, leaving ¼-inch head space.

4. Adjust caps and process pints for 45 minutes in a boiling water bath.

Yields 4 to 6 pints

Hot Pepper Sauce

3	jalapeno peppers	1½	cups finely chopped celery
2	tablespoons oil	1½	cups tomato sauce
3	garlic cloves, minced	1½	cups Chicken Stock or Beef
1½	onions, finely chopped		Stock (see Index)

1. Cut jalapeno peppers in half, lengthwise, holding them under running cold water. Remove seeds and centers and discard. Cut into small pieces. (To avoid stinging, wash hands with cold water immediately after handling peppers.)

2. In a 2-quart, heavy-bottom saucepan, heat oil and saute peppers, garlic, onions, and celery until soft.

3. Add tomato sauce and stock and simmer 15 to 20 minutes over low heat. Cool and refrigerate in a covered container.

Yields about 3¾ cups

(Blender)

3 eggs at room temperature	3 tablespoons cider vinegar
1 teaspoon dry mustard	1 tablespoon honey
½ teaspoon paprika	3½ cups safflower oil
3 tablespoons lemon juice	

1. Combine eggs, mustard, paprika, lemon juice, vinegar, honey, and ¾ cup oil in blender. Process about 5 seconds or until well mixed.

2. Gradually add the remaining oil, a few drops at a time, until it is incorporated into the mixture. Stop the blender occasionally to scrape down the sides of the container.

3. Turn mayonnaise out into a clean quart jar and store, covered, in the refrigerator. It will thicken as it chills.

Yields 1 quart

Mushroom Sauce

2 tablespoons butter	2 tablespoons cold water
1½ cups thickly sliced mushrooms	¼ cup Yogurt (see Index)
¼ cup rye flour or whole wheat flour	2 teaspoons lemon juice
1 cup Chicken Stock or Beef Stock (see Index)	1 teaspoon tamari soy sauce
1 tablespoon cornstarch	⅛ teaspoon nutmeg
	¼ cup milk

1. In a 1½-quart, heavy-bottom saucepan, melt butter and saute mushrooms for about 2 minutes over medium heat, stirring constantly.

2. Stir in flour. Add stock, a little at a time, stirring to make a smooth sauce.

3. Dissolve cornstarch in the water and add it to the sauce, stirring until thickened. Reduce heat. Add yogurt and blend well. Then add lemon juice, tamari, nutmeg, and milk. Stir over very low heat until sauce is heated through. Serve warm.

Yields 1½ cups

Mustard

½	cup whole wheat flour	¼	cup vinegar
4 to 5	tablespoons dry mustard	⅓	cup water
1	teaspoon turmeric	4	teaspoons honey

1. Combine flour, 4 tablespoons dry mustard, and turmeric in a 1-pint bowl. Pass mixture through a strainer to remove any lumps.

2. Combine vinegar, water, and honey in another 1-pint bowl. Then stir this into the flour-mustard mixture with a wire whisk until smooth. Taste and add more dry mustard if desired.

3. Store in an airtight container in a cool place.

Yields about 1 cup

Oatmeal Crackers

1½	cups oatmeal flour (oats ground in electric blender)	½	cup water
		5	tablespoons oil
1	cup whole wheat flour	1	tablespoon honey

1. Preheat oven to 350°F. Combine dry ingredients.

2. In a small bowl, combine water, oil, and honey. Stir dry ingredients into wet ones to make a cohesive ball.

3. Butter a baking sheet and pat out dough in shape of pan. Roll to a thickness of ⅛ inch, using a rolling pin. Score with knife in desired shapes and bake 12 minutes. Cool 5 minutes before removing crackers from baking sheet.

Makes 4 dozen crackers, each 2 inches square

Potato Dumplings

3	quarts water	1	teaspoon poultry seasoning
3	cups loosely packed, riced, cooked potatoes	¼	teaspoon nutmeg
		1	egg, beaten
⅓	cup whole wheat pastry flour		

1. Bring water to a boil in a 4-quart pot.

2. Meanwhile, combine potatoes, flour, seasonings, and egg in a 2-quart bowl. Form the mixture into 1-inch balls and drop them into the simmering water. When all the dumplings rise to the surface, cover pot and simmer gently for 5 minutes. Remove dumplings with a slotted spoon and arrange them on a platter. Serve immediately.

Serves 6

Radish, Carrot, and Apricot Relish

¼ cup vinegar	¼ cup shredded carrots
1 tablespoon honey	3 dried apricots, cut in strips
⅔ cup shredded radishes, red or white	

1. Combine vinegar and honey, bring to a boil, and then pour over remaining ingredients.

2. Cover and let marinate in refrigerator for at least 30 minutes.

Yields about 1 cup

Red Beet Relish

2 cups cooked beets, grated (about 5 medium-size beets)	2 teaspoons honey
5 tablespoons horseradish	3 to 4 teaspoons cider vinegar

1. Combine all ingredients in a small bowl and mix thoroughly.

2. Cover and place mixture in refrigerator for several hours before serving.

Yields about 2⅓ cups

Savory Baked Rice 195

3	tablespoons butter	¼	cup chopped parsley
⅓	cup coarsely chopped onions	1	teaspoon basil
¼	cup coarsely chopped celery	1	teaspoon rosemary
3	cups cooked brown rice	1	teaspoon summer savory
2	eggs, beaten	½	teaspoon nutmeg
½	cup Chicken Stock or Beef Stock (see Index)	2	teaspoons lemon juice
			Mushroom Sauce (see Index)
⅓	cup chopped water chestnuts		

1. Preheat oven to 350°F. In medium-size skillet, melt butter and saute onions and celery over medium heat until soft but not brown.

2. Combine sauteed onions and celery with all remaining ingredients (except mushroom sauce) in a 2-quart bowl.

3. Turn mixture out into an oiled 1½-quart casserole. Set casserole in a 13 x 9 x 2-inch pan of hot water, and bake for 30 minutes.

4. Serve with mushroom sauce.

Serves 6

Spanish Tomato Relish

3	tomatoes, finely chopped	¾	teaspoon mustard seeds
½	cup finely chopped green peppers	1	tablespoon honey
		1	tablespoon chopped basil or ¼ teaspoon dried basil
½	cup finely chopped celery		
⅓	cup chopped parsley	¼	teaspoon dried, crushed red pepper (optional)
¼	cup finely chopped onions		
⅓	cup red wine vinegar		

1. In a medium-size bowl, combine tomatoes, green peppers, celery, parsley, and onions. Add wine vinegar, mustard seeds, honey, basil, and crushed red pepper. Mix together thoroughly.

2. Cover bowl and place in refrigerator. Chill thoroughly to blend flavors.

Yields about 3½ cups

½ cup coarsely chopped onions
¼ cup butter
6 tablespoons brown rice flour
2 cups Beef Stock or Chicken Stock (see Index)

1½ cups tomato juice
½ cup tomato sauce
1 teaspoon basil
1 teaspoon oregano

1. In a 2-quart, heavy-bottom saucepan, saute onions in butter until soft.

2. Stir in the flour. Gradually add stock and stir until smooth. Using a wire whisk to avoid lumping, stir in tomato juice, tomato sauce, and herbs.

3. Cook over low heat, stirring constantly, until thickened.

Yields 4½ cups

━━━━━━━ **Tomato Catsup** ━━━━━━━

2½ quarts sliced tomatoes (15 to 17, medium size)
1 cup coarsely chopped onions
1 garlic clove, minced
2 celery stalks with tops, coarsely chopped
3-inch piece cinnamon stick

1 teaspoon whole cloves
½ teaspoon whole allspice
¼ teaspoon cayenne pepper
1 tablespoon basil
1 tablespoon oregano
1 cup vinegar
1 cup honey

1. Combine tomatoes, onions, garlic, celery, and spices and herbs in a 5-quart, heavy-bottom pot. Simmer, covered, for 30 minutes. Press mixture through a sieve.

2. Add vinegar and honey to pureed mixture and simmer, uncovered, until mixture is reduced to one-half its volume. Stir frequently to prevent sticking.

3. Pour into clean, hot, sterilized jars, leaving a ¼-inch head space. Adjust seals and process jars for 5 minutes in a boiling water bath.

Yields 1 pint

Wheat Germ ══════ 197
Breading Mix

⅓ cup cornmeal
⅓ cup rye flour
⅓ cup wheat germ

1. Combine all ingredients in a small bowl and blend thoroughly.
2. Place in a tightly covered jar and store in the refrigerator for future use.

Yields 1 cup

Remarks   This makes a good coating for chicken, liver, fish, and chops.

Wheat Germ ══════
Giblet Stuffing

2 to 4	tablespoons butter	1	cup wheat germ
4	chicken livers	½	cup chopped parsley
1	onion, coarsely chopped	⅛	teaspoon black pepper
½	cup coarsely chopped celery	½ to ¾	cup Chicken Stock (see Index)
3	cups cooked brown rice		

1. In a large skillet, melt 2 tablespoons butter and saute chicken livers. Remove them from skillet and chop coarsely. Using the same skillet, saute onion and celery, using more butter as needed.
2. Combine cooked rice, chopped chicken livers, wheat germ, and sauteed mixture. Add parsley, pepper, and ½ cup stock. Mix well, adding more stock if needed.

Yields 3½ cups

| 1¼ | cups whole wheat pastry flour | 2 | tablespoons oil |
| ¼ | cup butter | 2 to 2½ | tablespoons ice water |

1. Place flour in a 1-quart bowl. Add butter and cut it into the flour, using a pastry blender or two knives, until the flour is completely moistened by the butter and the mixture resembles coarse crumbs.

2. Add oil and blend it into the mixture.

3. Add ice water, stirring it in lightly until the dough forms a ball. Allow pastry to rest a few minutes.

4. Flatten dough slightly and roll out between 2 sheets of wax paper, lightly floured, until it is about ⅛-inch thick. Remove top layer of wax paper and invert over a 9-inch pie plate. Remove the second piece of wax paper and press pastry into plate. Trim away excess dough and flute the edges. If you plan to bake the pie shell unfilled, prick pastry with a fork to allow steam to escape.

5. Bake in a preheated 425°F oven for 12 to 15 minutes or until pastry is lightly browned. Cool before filling.

Makes 1 9-inch pie shell

═══════════════════ Yogurt ═══════════════

1	quart milk
2	tablespoons unflavored yogurt
	(as starter)

1. Bring milk to a boil in a 2-quart, heavy-bottom saucepan. Remove from heat and cool to lukewarm (100°F to 110°F).

2. Place unflavored yogurt in a 1-pint bowl. Add a little of the milk to thin it. Stir until smooth. Add thinned yogurt to remaining milk, stirring with a whisk. Pour into an earthenware, glass, or stainless steel bowl, cover, and keep in a warm place 3 to 8 hours or overnight. (A gas oven with a pilot light is an ideal place.) The milk should be kept between 90°F and 105°F. If necessary, wrap the container with a tea towel to maintain the temperature.

3. When the yogurt has thickened, pour off any liquid that might have collected on the top. Cover and store in the refrigerator.

Thermos Method

1. To make yogurt in a thermos, simply stir the starter into the lukewarm milk and then pour into a wide-mouth thermos. Cover and let set for 4 to 6 hours. The well-insulated thermos will control the temperature.

2. When the yogurt has thickened, store it in the refrigerator.

Makes 1 quart

Appendix

Cholesterol Content of Some Animal Foods*

Food and description (100 grams, edible portion)	Cholesterol (milligrams)
Beef, raw	
With bone	70
Without bone	70
Brains, raw	2,000+
Butter	250
Cheese	
Cheddar	100
Cottage, creamed	15
Cream	120
Other (25% to 30% fat)	85
Cheese spread	65
Chicken, flesh only, raw	60
Egg, whole	550
Egg white	0
Egg yolk	
Dried	2,950
Fresh	1,500
Frozen	1,280
Heart, raw	150
Kidney, raw	375
Lamb, raw	
With bone	70
Without bone	70
Lard and other animal fat	95
Liver, raw	300
Milk	
Dried, whole	85
Fluid, skim	3
Fluid, whole	11
Mutton	
With bone	65
Without bone	65
Pork	
With bone	70
Without bone	70
Sweetbreads (thymus)	250
Veal	
With bone	90
Without bone	90

*Cholesterol content of cooked foods is slightly higher due to water loss during cooking.

SOURCE: *Composition of Foods, Raw, Processed, Prepared,* Agriculture Handbook No. 8, United States Department of Agriculture, 1963.

Percentage of Calories from Fat

Food	Percent
Butter	100
Mayonnaise	100
Vegetable oils	100
Cream cheese	95
Brazil nuts	92
Walnuts	89
Almonds	81
Bacon	79
Frankfurter	79
Pork, sausage	79
Pumpkin seeds	76
Sunflower seeds	76
Cashew nuts	75
Lamb chop	75
Peanuts	75
Pork, ham	75
Hamburger	74
Sirloin steak	74
Pork chop, lean	73
Porterhouse steak	71
Cheddar cheese	70
Turkey	69
Rib roast	68
Tongue, beef	65
Beef, chuck	64
Egg	64
Tuna, canned in oil	63
Brains	62
Lamb, leg roast	62
Chicken, roaster	57
Salmon, Atlantic	56
Kidney, beef	52
Roast beef	52

Percentage of Calories from Fat — *Continued*

Food	Percent
Round, beef	50
Yogurt, whole milk	45
Lamb, lean shoulder	42
Milk, 2% low-fat	38
Flank steak, lean	33
Liver, beef	33
Heart, beef	31
Liver, calf	31
Chicken, breast	29
Liver, chicken	26
Chicken, broiler-fryer	25
Yogurt, low-fat	25
Buttermilk	18
Cottage cheese, 2% low-fat	17
Rolled oats	14
Whole wheat bread	12
Skim milk	10
Apple	9
Noodles	8
Chestnuts	6
Macaroni	6
Tuna, canned in water	6
Brown rice	5
Mung beans, sprouted	5
Navy beans	5
Split peas	4
Banana	2
Haddock	2
Potato	0.8
Broccoli	trace
Cabbage	trace
Lentils	trace

Nutritional Values of Various Meats[1]

Food and description (100 grams, edible portion)	Water (percent)	Food energy (calories)	Protein (grams)	Fat (grams)	Carbohydrate Total (grams)	Fiber (grams)
Beef						
Chuck, braised or pot-roasted	59.7	214	30.0	9.5	0	0
Club steak, broiled (58% lean, 42% fat)	37.9	454	20.6	40.6	0	0
Flank steak, braised (100% lean)	61.4	196	30.5	7.3	0	0
Hamburger (ground beef)						
Lean, cooked	60.0	219	27.4	11.3	0	0
Regular ground, cooked	54.2	286	24.2	20.3	0	0
Porterhouse steak, broiled (57% lean, 43% fat)	37.2	465	19.7	42.2	0	0
Rib, roasted (64% lean, 36% fat)	40.0	440	19.9	39.4	0	0
Round, entire (round and heel of round), broiled (81% lean, 19% fat)	54.7	261	28.6	15.4	0	0
Rump, roasted (75% lean, 25% fat)	48.1	347	23.6	27.3	0	0
Sirloin steak, broiled (66% lean, 34% fat)	43.9	387	23.0	32.0	0	0
T-bone steak, broiled (56% lean, 44% fat)	36.4	473	19.5	43.2	0	0
Chicken						
Broilers, flesh only, broiled	71.0	136	23.8	3.8	0	0
Fryers (weight, ready to cook, with giblets, more than 1¾ pounds)						
Breast, fried	58.4	203	32.5	6.4	1.5	—
Drumstick, fried	55.0	235	32.6	10.2	1.0	—
Flesh, skin, and giblets, fried	53.3	249	30.7	11.8	2.9	—
Giblets, fried	51.7	252	30.8	11.2	4.7	—
Light meat with skin, fried	55.0	234	31.5	9.9	2.4	—
Dark meat with skin, fried	52.1	263	29.9	13.6	3.1	—
Light meat without skin, fried	59.5	197	32.1	6.1	1.1	—
Dark meat without skin, fried	57.5	220	30.4	9.3	1.5	—
Thigh, fried	55.8	237	29.1	11.4	2.5	—
Wing, fried	52.6	268	29.0	14.8	2.7	—
Roasters, roasted	53.5	290	25.2	20.2	0	0
Light meat without skin, roasted	61.3	182	32.3	4.9	0	0
Dark meat without skin, roasted	62.7	184	29.3	6.5	0	0
Heart						
Beef, lean, braised	61.3	188	31.3	5.7	0.7	0
Beef, lean with visible fat, braised	44.4	372	25.8	29.0	0.1	0
Calf, braised	60.3	208	27.8	9.1	1.8	0
Chicken, all classes, simmered	66.7	173	25.3	7.2	0.1	0
Hog, braised	61.0	195	30.8	6.9	0.3	0
Lamb, braised	54.1	260	29.5	14.4	1.0	0
Turkey, all classes, simmered	63.2	216	22.6	13.2	0.2	0
Kidneys						
Beef, braised	53.0	252	33.0	12.0	0.8	0
Lamb						
Leg, roasted (79% lean, 21% fat)	50.4	319	23.9	24.0	0	0
Loin, broiled chops (61% lean, 39% fat)	41.7	420	19.5	37.3	0	0
Rib, broiled chops (53% lean, 47% fat)	35.5	492	16.9	46.5	0	0
Shoulder, roasted (71% lean, 29% fat)	46.2	374	20.7	31.7	0	0
Liver						
Beef, fried	56.0	229	26.4	10.6	5.3	0
Calf, fried	51.4	261	29.5	13.2	4.0	0
Chicken, all classes, simmered	65.0	165	26.5	4.4	3.1	0
Hog, fried	54.0	241	29.9	11.5	2.5	0
Lamb, broiled	50.4	261	32.3	12.4	2.8	0
Turkey, all classes, simmered	63.3	174	27.9	4.8	3.1	0

Ash (grams)	Calcium (milligrams)	Phosphorus (milligrams)	Iron (milligrams)	Sodium (milligrams)	Potassium (milligrams)	Vitamin A (international units)	Thiamine (milligrams)	Riboflavin (milligrams)	Niacin (milligrams)	Ascorbic acid (milligrams)
0.8	13	160	3.8	2[2]	3[3]	20	0.05	0.23	4.6	—
0.9	9	175	2.7	2[2]	3[3]	70	0.06	0.17	4.3	—
0.8	14	150	3.8	2[2]	3[3]	10	0.06	0.23	4.6	—
1.3	12	230	3.5	48	558	20	0.09	0.23	6.0	—
1.3	11	194	3.2	47	450	40	0.09	0.21	5.4	—
0.9	9	168	2.6	2[2]	3[3]	70	0.06	0.16	4.2	—
0.7	9	186	2.6	2[2]	3[3]	80	0.05	0.15	3.6	—
1.3	12	250	3.5	2[2]	3[3]	30	0.08	0.22	5.6	—
1.0	10	197	3.1	2[2]	3[3]	50	0.06	0.18	4.3	—
1.1	10	191	2.9	2[2]	3[3]	50	0.06	0.18	4.7	—
0.9	8	166	2.6	2[2]	3[3]	80	0.06	0.16	4.1	—
1.1	9	201	1.7	66	274	90	0.05	0.19	8.8	—
1.2	12	276	1.7	—	—	90	0.05	0.22	14.7	—
1.2	15	236	2.3	—	—	140	0.07	0.40	7.1	—
1.3	13	254	2.3	—	—	820	0.07	0.57	9.1	—
1.6	18	336	6.5	—	—	5,760	0.17	2.18	8.0	—
1.2	11	260	1.5	—	—	130	0.05	0.27	11.9	—
1.3	12	228	2.0	—	—	210	0.07	0.45	6.7	—
1.2	12	280	1.3	68	434	50	0.05	0.25	12.9	—
1.3	14	235	1.8	88	330	130	0.07	0.45	6.8	—
1.2	13	236	2.3	—	—	200	0.06	0.48	6.8	—
0.9	10	236	2.0	—	—	250	0.05	0.26	6.8	—
1.1	10	220	1.9	—	—	960	0.07	0.22	7.4	—
1.5	11	272	1.3	66	422	110	0.08	0.10	11.8	—
1.4	14	235	1.8	88	330	160	0.12	0.19	5.3	—
1.1	6	181	5.9	104	232	30	0.25	1.22	7.6	—
0.8	—	169	—	—	—	—	—	—	—	—
1.0	4	148	4.4	113	250	40	0.29	1.44	8.1	—
0.8	4	107	3.6	69	140	(30)	0.06	0.92	5.3	—
1.0	4	121	4.9	65	128	40	0.20	1.72	6.7	—
0.9	14	231	—	—	—	100	0.21	1.03	6.4	—
0.8	—	—	—	61	211	(30)	0.25	0.98	5.7	—
1.2	18	244	13.1	253	324	1,150	0.51	4.82	10.7	—
1.7	10	195	1.6	4[4]	5[5]	—	0.14	0.25	5.2	—
1.4	8	150	1.1	4[4]	5[5]	—	0.11	0.21	4.5	—
1.0	7	128	0.8	4[4]	5[5]	—	0.10	0.18	4.0	—
1.4	9	163	1.2	4[4]	5[5]	—	0.12	0.22	4.6	—
1.7	11	476	8.8	184	380	53,400[6]	0.26	4.19	16.5	27
1.9	13	537	14.2	118	453	32,700[6]	0.24	4.17	16.5	37
1.0	11	159	8.5	61	151	12,300[6]	0.17	2.69	11.7	16
2.1	15	539	29.1	111	395	14,900[6]	0.34	4.36	22.3	22
2.1	16	572	17.9	85	331	74,500[6]	0.49	5.11	24.9	36
1.0	—	—	—	55	141	17,500[6]	0.16	2.09	14.3	—

[Continued on next page]

Nutritional Values of Various Meats — *Continued*

Food and description (100 grams, edible portion)	Water (percent)	Food energy (calories)	Protein (grams)	Fat (grams)	Carbohydrate Total (grams)	Fiber (grams)
Pork, fresh						
Boston butt, roasted (76% lean, 24% fat)	45.0	389	20.9	33.2	0	0
Ham, roasted (72% lean, 28% fat)	43.7	394	21.9	33.3	0	0
Loin						
roasted (76% lean, 24% fat)	43.7	387	23.5	31.8	0	0
broiled (68% lean, 32% fat)	40.2	418	23.5	35.2	0	0
Picnic, simmered (69% lean, 31% fat)	41.5	420	21.8	36.2	0	0
Spareribs, braised	37.2	467	19.7	42.5	0	0
Turkey						
Giblets, (some gizzard fat), simmered	61.0	233	20.6	15.4	1.6	0
Light meat, roasted	62.1	176	32.9	3.9	0	0
Dark meat, roasted	60.5	203	30.0	8.3	0	0

[1]Numbers in parentheses denote values imputed—usually from another form of the food or from a similar food. Zero in parentheses indicates that the amount of a constituent probably is none or is too small to measure. Dashes denote lack of reliable data for a constituent believed to be present in measurable amount.

[2]Average value per 100 grams of beef of all cuts is 60 milligrams for cooked meat.

[3]Average value per 100 grams of beef of all cuts is 370 milligrams for cooked meat.

[4]Average value per 100 grams of lamb of all cuts is 70 milligrams for cooked meat.

[5]Average value per 100 grams of lamb of all cuts is 290 milligrams for cooked meat.

[6]Values vary widely in all kinds of liver, ranging from about 100 international units to more than 100,000 international units per 100 grams.

[7]Average value per 100 grams of pork of all cuts is 65 milligrams for cooked meat.

[8]Average value per 100 grams of pork of all cuts is 390 milligrams for cooked meat.

SOURCE: *Composition of Foods, Raw, Processed, Prepared*, Agriculture Handbook No. 8, United States Department of Agriculture, 1963.

Ash (grams)	Calcium (milligrams)	Phosphorus (milligrams)	Iron (milligrams)	Sodium (milligrams)	Potassium (milligrams)	Vitamin A (international units)	Thiamine (milligrams)	Riboflavin (milligrams)	Niacin (milligrams)	Ascorbic acid (milligrams)
0.9	9	212	2.7	[7]	[8]	(0)	0.47	0.21	4.2	—
1.0	10	225	2.9	[7]	[8]	(0)	0.49	0.22	4.4	—
1.0	10	245	3.1	[7]	[8]	(0)	0.88	0.25	5.3	—
1.1	10	256	3.2	[7]	[8]	(0)	0.92	0.27	5.6	—
0.5	9	129	2.8	[7]	[8]	(0)	0.51	0.23	4.5	—
0.6	8	113	2.5	[7]	[8]	(0)	0.40	0.19	3.2	—
1.2	—	—	1.2	82	411	—	0.05	0.14	11.1	—
1.2	—	—	2.3	99	398	—	0.04	0.23	4.2	—
1.4	—	—	—	—	—	—	—	2.72	—	—

Soy Foods for Flavor and Economy

Soy flakes come from whole soybeans that have been toasted for about 30 seconds, then flaked in a roller mill. Flakes have all the qualities of whole soybeans yet have the advantage of being easier and faster to cook. They require soaking for only 5 to 10 minutes and cooking for 10 to 15 minutes. They can be used in a variety of ways, much the same as soybeans—with rice dishes, in casseroles, in baking.

Soy grits are coarsely ground soybeans. They differ from soy flakes in that they are neither cooked nor treated with heat, but simply mechanically ground. Grits can be cooked with rice pilaf or added to any grain dish.

Soy milk is a beverage prepared from soybeans. High in protein and easily digested, it's the base for many infant formulas. In liquid form, it can be substituted for whole cow's milk. In East Asia, where soy milk is bottled on a large scale and delivered daily to regular customers, children often start the day with a hot cup of sweetened soy milk.

Soy flour is a concentrated soy food with a high protein content (38 to 40 percent). Full-fat soy flour has 35 percent protein and 20 percent fat. Because of its fat content, it is not mixed with the dry ingredients in baking but is creamed with the shortening or blended with the liquids. Soy flour cannot completely replace regular flour because it has too low a gluten content. To modify a recipe with soy flour, substitute soy flour for 2 tablespoons of every cup of wheat flour. Products containing soy flour brown more quickly, so the baking temperature should be lowered by 25°F when substituting soy flour for wheat flour. Soy flour should be stored in a cool, dry place to keep it from turning rancid.

Soybean oil is rich in polyunsaturated fats. Unrefined soybean oil is dark brown, strong flavored, and aromatic. Though it can be used in the same way as other oils, it may unfavorably alter the taste of a dish. Be wary of this one. Before using it full strength, try blending it (in a one-to-one ratio) with another oil—peanut, sesame, or safflower.

Okara, or *soy mash*, is the solid material left after soy milk has been prepared. It has a bland flavor and coarse texture but retains some protein. When used in combination with other foods, okara adds nutritive value, and in ground meat dishes it serves well as an extender. Okara should be heated thoroughly before being used, to eliminate the beany flavor.

Tofu, bean curd, or *soy cheese* are the various names for the pulpy, custardlike product derived from the soy milk. The liquid should be mostly drained off before use, but some water should be left to cover the tofu before refrigerating in a tightly covered container. It will remain fresh that way for about a week. Tofu can be served sauteed or in soups, salads, and sandwiches, and appear as a main course or a side dish. It can even be whipped in the blender as a base for mayonnaise, dips, or salad dressings.

Tempeh is an Indonesian soy food made by inoculating cooked soybeans with a special culture and then incubating them for 24 hours. The result is a fragrant, firm, white cake with a chewy texture and a mild, meaty flavor. Tempeh can be fried, baked, broiled, or simmered. It works well as a burger or in tempura, a soup, or a casserole.

Nutritional Values of Tofu, Meat, and Cheese

Food and description (4 ounces or ½-cup serving)	Calories	Protein (grams)	Fat (grams)	Cholesterol (milligrams)
Tempeh (fresh)	179	22	9	0
Tofu (medium)	82	8.8	4.9	0
Tofu (firm)	100	12	6	0
Ground beef (lean, 10% fat)	202	23.4	11.3	106
Chicken (light meat, without skin)	168	35.6	3.9	90
Cottage cheese	120	15.6	4.8	22

SOURCES: William Shurtleff and Akiko Aoyagi, *The Book of Tempeh*, Harper & Row, 1979.
Shurtleff and Aoyagi, *The Book of Tofu*, Autumn Press, 1975.
Nutritive Value of American Foods in Common Units, Agriculture Handbook No. 456, United States Department of Agriculture, 1975.
"Cholesterol Content of Foods," *Journal of the American Dietetic Association.*

18 Common Seasonings and Their Uses

Seasoning	Breads	Meats
Allspice	Pumpkin bread	Beef
Basil	Herbed biscuits Yeast breads	Beef Lamb Meatballs Stews
Bay leaf		Beef Lamb Pot roast Stews
Celery seed	Cheese breads	Beef
Cinnamon	Biscuits Coffee cakes Fruit breads Muffins	Beef stew
Clove	Coffee cakes Fruit breads	Meatballs Pork Stews
Curry		Beef Fish Lamb Pork
Dill	Biscuits Dumplings Yeast breads	Beef Lamb

Poultry	Soups	Vegetables
	Fruit	Winter squash
Chicken Stuffing	Minestrone Pea Potato Spinach Tomato Vegetable	Asparagus Beets Broccoli Cabbage Carrots Celery Cucumbers Eggplant Peas Spinach Tomatoes Turnips Winter squash
Chicken stew	Chicken-rice Tomato Vegetable	
Chicken	Bisques Chicken-rice Chowders	Beets Cabbage Cucumbers
	Fruit	Beets Carrots Onions Pumpkin Sweet potatoes Tomatoes Winter squash
	Onion Stocks	Beets Carrots Onions Pumpkin Sweet potatoes Tomatoes Winter squash
Chicken Stuffing	Chicken Consomme Pea Tomato Vegetable	Beets Carrots Parsnips Sweet potatoes Turnips Winter squash
Chicken Turkey	Chicken and noodle Turkey	Beets Cucumbers Green beans Potatoes Tomatoes

[*Continued on next page*]

18 Common Seasonings and Their Uses — *Continued*

Seasoning	Breads	Meats
Marjoram	Herbed biscuits Herbed breads	Beef Meat loaf Pot roast Stews
Mustard	Cheese biscuits Cheese breads Herbed biscuits	Beef Pork
Nutmeg	Applesauce bread Banana bread Pumpkin bread	Meat loaf Swedish meatballs
Oregano		Beef Lamb Meatballs Meat loaf Roasts Stews
Paprika	Biscuits	Hungarian goulash
Parsley	Herbed biscuits Herbed breads	Beef Lamb Pies Pork Roasts Stews
Rosemary	Herbed biscuits Herbed breads	Beef Lamb Pork Roasts Stews
Sesame seed	Biscuits Coffee cakes Rolls Yeast breads	

Poultry	Soups	Vegetables
Chicken Stuffing Turkey	Creams Onion Potato	Beans Celery Collard greens Onions Peas Potatoes Turnip greens
	Bisques Chowders	Beets Cabbage Cucumbers
	Bean Split pea Tomato	Beans Pumpkin Tomatoes Winter squash
	Bean Minestrone Tomato	Broccoli Cabbage Eggplant Lentils Tomatoes
Chicken Paprikash Garnish	Bisques Chowders Creams Pea	Cauliflower Potatoes
Chicken Pot pies Stews Turkey	Chowders Stocks Vegetable	Beets Cabbage Carrots Cauliflower Celery Eggplant Onions Potatoes Turnips
Chicken Pot pies Stews Stuffing Turkey	Chicken Potato Tomato	Potatoes Turnips
Garnish Stuffing		Broccoli Corn Spinach Summer squash

[*Continued on next page*]

18 Common Seasonings and Their Uses — *Continued*

Seasoning	Breads	Meats
Tarragon		Lamb
Thyme	Cornbread Herbed biscuits Herbed breads	Beef Lamb Pork Roasts Stews

Poultry	Soups	Vegetables
Chicken	Chicken	Beans
Turkey	Pea	Cucumbers
	Tomato	Peas
		Potatoes
		Tomatoes
Chicken	Bisques	Onions
Pot pies	Chowders	Potatoes
Stews	Tomato	Summer squash
Stuffing	Vegetable	
Turkey		

Favorite Cheeses

Cheese[1]	Calories[2]	Fat (grams)
Blue	100	8.15
Brick	105	8.41
Cheddar	114	9.40
Colby	112	9.10
Cottage		
Creamed (4 ounces)	117	5.10
Creamed, 2% fat (4 ounces)	101	2.18
Dry curd (4 ounces)	96	0.48
Cream	99	9.89
Edam	101	7.88
Gouda	101	7.78
Gruyere	117	9.17
Monterey	101	8.58
Mozzarella		
Low moisture, part skim	79	4.85
Part skim	72	4.51
Muenster	104	8.58
Parmesan		
(1 tablespoon, grated)	23	1.50
Ricotta		
Part skim (½ cup)	171	9.81
Whole milk (½ cup)	216	16.10
Swiss	107	7.78

[1]All cheeses are 1 ounce unless otherwise noted.
[2]*Composition of Foods: Dairy and Egg Products; Raw, Processed, Prepared,* Agriculture Handbook No. 8-1, United States Department of Agriculture, 1976.

Description	Uses
Semisoft, crumbly, blue-veined, tangy	Salads, dips, dressings, appetizers
Semisoft, mild to sharp, white to yellow	Sandwiches, with fruit, appetizers, desserts, snacks
Hard, mild to sharp, smooth, yellow-orange	Sandwiches, casseroles, sauces, snacks, salads, soups
Hard, sweet to mellow, yellow-orange	Snacks, salads, sandwiches
Mild, slightly acid, soft, white, tender curds	Appetizers, salads, cheesecakes
Delicate, soft, smooth, white	Appetizers, icings, cakes, sandwiches, desserts, snacks
Firm-rubbery, gold, mellow, coated with red wax	Sandwiches, snacks, desserts, appetizers, sauces
Semisoft, mild but nutty, creamy yellow	Sandwiches, snacks, desserts, appetizers
Hard, nut-like, salty	Fondue, sandwiches, snacks
Semisoft, mild, creamy	Salads, sandwiches, snacks
Semisoft, mild, easy to melt	Lasagna, pizza, snacks
Semisoft, creamy white, mild	Sandwiches, with fruit, desserts, snacks
Very hard, granular, distinctive flavor	Grated on pizza, lasagna, spaghetti, soups, breads, salads, appetizers
Mild, sweet, nutty, soft and loose curds	Cheesecakes, salads, lasagna, ravioli
Large eyes, yellow, mild, nutty flavor	Fondues, sandwiches, snacks

Substitutes and Equivalents

Substitutes

1 cup	buttermilk	=	1 cup	plain yogurt
		=	1 cup	skim milk plus 1 tablespoon lemon juice or vinegar
1 cup	whole milk	=	1 cup	reconstituted non-fat dry milk plus 2½ teaspoons butter
1 teaspoon	lemon juice	=	½ teaspoon	vinegar
1 cup	tomatoes	=	½ cup	tomato sauce plus
			½ cup	water
1 cup	sour cream	=	1 cup	yogurt
½ cup	prunes, pitted and minced	=	½ cup	raisins

Equivalents

2 cups	brown rice, raw	=	8 cups	cooked
½ pound	cheddar cheese	=	2 cups	grated
1 slice	bread, fresh	=	1 cup	soft crumbs
1 slice	bread, dry	=	⅓ cup	fine crumbs
1 pound	almonds, unshelled	=	1¼ cups	nut meats
	shelled	=	4 to 4½ cups	nut meats
1 pound	Brazil nuts, unshelled	=	1½ cups	nut meats
	shelled	=	3 cups	nut meats
1 pound	peanuts, unshelled	=	2 cups	nut meats
	shelled	=	4 to 4½ cups	nut meats
1 pound	pecans, unshelled	=	2¼ cups	nut meats
	shelled	=	4 to 4½ cups	nut meats

Substitutes and Equivalents — *Continued*

Equivalents—*Continued*

1 pound	walnuts, unshelled	=	1¾ cups	nut meats
	shelled	=	4 to 4½ cups	nut meats
1 cup	bulgur, raw	=	4 cups	bulgur, cooked
1 cup	buckwheat groats, raw	=	4 cups	buckwheat groats, cooked
1 pound	macaroni	=	4 cups	raw
		=	8 cups	cooked
1 pound	noodles	=	6 cups	raw
		=	7 cups	cooked
1 pound	spaghetti	=	4 cups	raw
		=	7 to 8 cups	cooked
1 pound	cabbage	=	4½ cups	shredded
1 pound	kidney beans, dry	=	2½ cups	dry
		=	6 cups	cooked
1 pound	lima beans, dry	=	2½ cups	dry
		=	6 cups	cooked
½ pound	navy beans, dry	=	1 cup	dry
		=	2½ cups	cooked
1 pound	lentils, dry	=	2¼ cups	dry
		=	5 cups	cooked
1 pound	beef, cooked	=	3 cups	minced
		=	2 cups	ground
1 pound	raisins, seedless	=	2¾ cups	
1 pound	rolled oats	=	6¼ cups	raw
		=	8 cups	cooked
12 ounces	wheat germ	=	3 cups	wheat germ

Index